W9-CJP-172

SIR LOWRY COLE

GOVERNOR OF MAURITIUS 1823-1828
GOVERNOR OF THE CAPE OF GOOD HOPE 1828-1833

SIR LOWRY COLE

GOVERNOR OF MAURITIUS 1823-1828
GOVERNOR OF THE CAPE OF GOOD HOPE 1828-1833

A STUDY IN COLONIAL ADMINISTRATION

by

KEITH S. HUNT

DURBAN

BUTTERWORTHS

Standard Book Number 409 09790 X

SOUTH AFRICA:	BUTTERWORTH & CO. (S.A.) (PTY.) LTD.	
	DURBAN:	152-154 Gale Street
ENGLAND:	BUTTERWORTH & CO. (PUBLISHERS) LTD.	
	LONDON:	88 Kingsway, WC2B 6AB
AUSTRALIA:	BUTTERWORTHS PTY. LTD.	
	SYDNEY:	Chatswood, N.S.W., 586 Pacific Highway
	MELBOURNE:	343 Little Collins Street
	BRISBANE:	240 Queen Street
CANADA:	BUTTERWORTH & CO. (CANADA) LTD.	
	SCARBOROUGH, ONTORIO:	2265 Midland Avenue
NEW ZEALAND:	BUTTERWORTHS OF NEW ZEALAND LTD.	
	WELLINGTON:	26-28 Waring Taylor Street

Printed by Citadel Press, Lansdowne, Cape

LIST OF CONTENTS

ABBREVIATIONS USED IN FOOTNOTES

Apart from conventional technical words and phrases such as *ibid.* and Vol. etc., the following abbreviations has been used:

A.C. – Minutes of the Council of Advice of the Cape of Good Hope.

Adm. – Admiralty Papers in the Public Record Office.

B.F.S.P. – *British and Foreign State Papers* 1812- compiled by the Librarian and Keeper, Foreign Office, London 1832–.

B.M. – British Museum, Bloomsbury, London, W.C.1.

C.A. – Cape Archives, Queen Victoria Street, Cape Town.

C.H.B.E. – *Cambridge History of the British Empire.*

C.O. – Colonial Office Papers in the Public Record Office, except when it follows 'C.A.' in which case it refers to the Colonial Office Papers in the Cape Archives.

D.N.B. – *Dictionary of National Biography.*

ed. – Edited by.

G.H. – Government House Papers in the Cape Archives.

G.T.J. – *Graham's Town Journal.*

L.M.S. Papers – Papers of the *London Missionary Society* deposited at the Congregational Council for World Mission, Livingstone House, 11 Carteret Street, London, S.W.1.

M.A. – Mauritius Archives, Sir William Newton Street, Port Louis, Mauritius, except where it clearly refers to a university M.A. degree in which case the abbreviation is always given with the name of a university.

P.P. – Parliamentary Papers, except when it follows 'B.M.' in which case it refers to the reference given to the *Anti-slavery Reporter* in the catalogue of the British Museum.

P.R.O. 30/43 – The papers of Sir G. Lowry Cole deposited in the Public Record Office.

R.A. – Minutes of the Advisory Council in Mauritius and the governor's minutes in the Mauritius Archives.

S.A.C.A. – *South African Commercial Advertiser.*

Theal, *R.C.C.* – *Records of the Cape Colony* by G. McC. Theal.

Walker – *A History of Southern Africa*, 3rd edition, 1957, re-issued with corrections, 1959, new impression, 1965, London.

W.O. – War Office Papers in the Public Record Office.

Z.A. – *De Zuid-Afrikaan.*

DEFINITIONS

1. The term *colonies of conquest* has been used throughout this book to describe colonies acquired by Britain in battle, ceded to her in the subsequent peace treaty, and governed through the use of the Crown's prerogative. Sometimes these colonies are referred to in documents as *ceded colonies* or *Crown colonies* and it has been necessary to use these terms when quoting directly.

2. Racial nomenclature in southern Africa is constantly under revision. An attempt has been made to follow the most up-to-date usage except when quoting directly. Whenever a term appears in the text for the first time, an explanatory footnote has been given.

ACKNOWLEDGEMENTS

The financial assistance of the Human Sciences Research Council in connection with the publication of this work, is hereby acknowledged. Opinions expressed in this work or conclusions reached, are those of the author and must in no instance be regarded as a reflection of the opinions and conclusions of the Human Sciences Research Council.

I am also indebted to the British Council for the award of a scholarship to undertake research in the United Kingdom for a year, 1963–64, the generosity of the Council of Rhodes University, Grahamstown, who gave me leave to be absent on that occasion and again from 1967 to 1968, and my colleagues in the History Department of that university who shouldered my teaching responsibilities during my absence. The Council of Rhodes University also provided me with financial assistance to visit the Archives in Port Louis, Mauritius, and Cape Town in South Africa. The Central Research Fund of the University of London made a contribution towards the xeroxing of documents required for this study.

My gratitude is due to the encouragement, advice and learned assistance of many people. I am indebted to Professor Kenneth Robinson and Dr I. M. Cumpston of the University of London who supervised my researches into the colonial administration of Sir Lowry Cole for a doctoral thesis. I am also grateful to Dr A. F. Madden, Nuffield College, Oxford, and my colleagues at Rhodes University, in particular Professors H. J. Chapman, W. D. Hammond-Tooke, A. J. Kerr and W. A. Maxwell, and Dr T. R. H. Davenport with whom I discussed many problems, though they must in no way be held responsible for the conclusions I have drawn.

My thanks are also due to the staff of the Public Record Office and the Historical Manuscripts Commission in London, the Government Archives in Port Louis and Cape Town, and the Librarians and their staff at the Institute of Historical Research, the Institute of Commonwealth Studies, Birkbeck College and Senate House Library in the University of London, the British Museum in London, Rhodes House in Oxford, the South African Public Library in Cape Town, and the University Library and Cory Library at Rhodes University in Grahamstown. Thanks are also due to the South African Public Library for the use of the pictures used in this book and Dr J. Benyon who drew the maps.

I wish to acknowledge the services of the Institute of Social and Economic Research at Rhodes University who coped so well with typing the manuscript.

Finally, I owe a debt of gratitude to my wife who not only helped to check proofs but was a source of constant and cheerful encouragement without which this book would never have been finished.

PROLOGUE

Galbraith Lowry Cole was born on the 1st May 1772. He was the second son of William Willoughby Cole, the second baron Mount Florence, and Anne, daughter of Galbraith Lowry Corry and sister of the first earl of Belmore. The Cole family had been "planted" in Ireland in 1612 by James I who had given them a grant of land which included the town and castle of Enniskillen.[1] Through the seventeenth and eighteenth century they championed the protestants of northern Ireland and William Willoughby was recognised as a powerful Orange leader.[2] In 1776 William Willoughby Cole was created viscount Enniskillen, and three years later his peerage was raised to an earldom. But such were the principles of primogeniture that despite his father's elevated position Lowry and his younger brothers had to make their own careers: the family titles and the bulk of the fortune went to their eldest brother. Family influence and connections were used on their behalf, but to reach an office of distinction one had to have a fair measure of ability too.

A military career was chosen for Lowry, and he embarked upon his professional training when he was only thirteen years old – in 1785 he joined the army as a cornet in the 12th Light Dragoons. Five years later he went to the University of Stuttgart to continue his military studies because there was no military academy in Britain at that time. While he was at the university a lieutenancy was bought for him, and this was exchanged for a captaincy the following year. These crucial years in Lowry's education (1790-2) co-incided with the revolution in France. In 1793 when Lowry was just 21 years old Britain and France went to war. The war lasted until 1815 save for two brief periods of respite from 1802–5 and from 1814–15, and provided those interested in a military career a valuable opportunity for advancement. Lowry Cole was promoted to the rank of major in 1793, lieutenant-colonel in 1794, colonel in 1801, major general in 1808 and lieutenant general in 1813.

Lowry's active service gave him considerable experience. He was present at the conquest of the French West Indian Islands of Martinique and Guadeloupe in 1794 but the following year he returned to Ireland where he acted as deputy adjutant general and aide-de-camp to Lord Carhampton the commander-in-chief. He was wounded by Irish rebels in the battle of Vinegar Hill near Wexford. Soon after this he began a political career for he was returned to the Irish parliament as a member for County Fermanagh – a seat controlled by his family. The life of the Irish parliament was by then short-lived. Lowry Cole was amongst the majority who voted for its abolition and for union with England and Scotland.[3]

Having fulfilled his political duty, Lowry transferred to Egypt as military secretary to General Lord Hutchinson. Soon, however, he was appointed to command the 27th Inniskillings with whom he saw service in Malta and Sicily. He left Sicily during 1809 after a difference of opinion with Sir John Stuart, the commander-in-chief. Almost immediately he was posted to Spain where he took command of the 4th division which was regarded by the duke of Wellington as one of the three best he had under his command. The division contributed to the great victory at Salamanca in July 1812 and a series of battles known as the Battle of the Pyrenees in 1813. Lowry was rewarded with a knighthood of the

Order of the Bath, the Order of the Tower and Sword of Portugal and a gold cross with four clasps.[4]

Sir Lowry, as he was now called, was 42 years old when the war seemed to have ended and Napoleon exiled to the Island of Elba. He turned his mind to taking a wife and settling down. As a younger man he seems to have had only one serious flirtation – with Kitty Pakenham who rejected his suit and subsequently married the duke of Wellington.[5] He chose as his bride Lady Frances Harris, a daughter of the first earl of Malmesbury.

Arrangements for his marriage on the 15th June 1815 delayed Sir Lowry from answering the call of the duke of Wellington to join him in Belgium after Napoleon had escaped from Elba and war with France had been resumed. Three days after his wedding the battle of Waterloo was fought and won. Sir Lowry nevertheless joined the army of occupation in France and commanded the second division until the allies withdrew their forces in November 1818.

Retirement at 45 was no prospect for a man only four years married and possessed of a growing family. Sir Lowry's political career had been resumed in 1803 when he was returned to the Westminister parliament again representing County Fermanagh. Because of his military duties his attendance at debates was erratic until 1818. From 1818 to 1822 he sat and voted regularly, but his speeches were stilted and he showed no promise as a politician.[6] The qualities he displayed were courage, tact, loyalty and commonsense: it was precisely these which were required for the governor of a colony. He had refused the governorship of Corfu in 1815 and the governorship of Ceylon in 1816, but because he was concerned to make proper provision for his family he accepted the governorship of Mauritius in 1822. On the subject of his appointment as governor of Mauritius, Sir Lowry wrote to his brother, the second earl of Enniskillen, "It is nothing but a sense of duty towards my children that has inclined me to accept it". The annual salary of £10,000 in Mauritius attracted him. He was told that with prudence he could save half that sum, and with his private income he reckoned that in four or five years he could save £25 000 to £30 000 which would accrue to his children on his death.[7]

Sir Lowry Cole and his family sailed to Mauritius early in 1823. It was more than ten years before they returned to Britain. After five years in Mauritius he was transferred to the Cape of Good Hope. There is no record to show whether or not he attained his financial ambition. He complained on occasion that his expenses were greater than he had expected and, in any case, retrenchment in the colonial service reduced his salary by £1 000 soon after his arrival in Mauritius and at the Cape his salary was only £7 000 per annum.

The period, 1823–1833, when Cole served as a British colonial governor, covers a decade in which the British Government implemented changes in the economic structure of the empire and required colonies where there were slaves to ameliorate the condition of slaves preparatory to their emancipation. They also began to introduce judicial and limited constitutional procedures in colonies like Mauritius and the Cape of Good Hope which had been conquered in the Napoleonic Wars and ceded to Britain at the Peace of Paris in 1814. Policies framed in general terms had to be translated into practice in the colonies. Lofty though the intentions of the British Government might have been, their practical application was not accomplished without difficulty. Legislation did not always meet the peculiar conditions of a particular colony. Vested interests had to be placated. Governors could be placed in difficult circumstances. Sometimes they remonstrated with their superiors in London but in the final analysis they had to carry out the requirements of the British Government. This study of Sir Lowry Cole is an attempt to illustrate the complexities of colonial government through an official who was governor first in Mauritius and then at the Cape.

Sir Lowry Cole was typical of the kind of man chosen for governorships in the conquered colonies. Because of the peace after the Revolutionary and Napoleonic Wars there were too many generals. Hence the conquered colonies were a valuable avenue of employment for them. Their military background gave them experience in administration and command.

Sir Lowry Cole was not a man who was subject to flights of fancy. He was not very imaginative and his person stands strangely aloof from his official acts. He tried to carry out his instructions to the best of his ability even when, on occasion, he did not entirely agree with them. When there was conflict between the requirements of the British Government and the interests of the colony he used his commonsense. He stressed the need to win co-operation when administrative coercion was not possible. Sometimes the British Government censured him for what he had done. Their criticism hurt him for behind a facade of a highly disciplined individual lay the need for approval of one who had tried his best.

After his return to England in 1833, Sir Lowry and his family lived quietly at Highfield Park, near Hartford Bridge in Hampshire. He died suddenly on the 4th October, 1842 and was buried in the family vault at Enniskillen in Northern Ireland. On Fort Hill near Enniskillen a lofty column, with a spiral staircase inside, was built in his memory. A statue of Cole in full military uniform stands on top of the column. The monument, not unlike Nelson's column in Trafalgar Square, London, is a token of the esteem in which he was held by the Inniskilling Fusiliers whom he had commanded in Spain and of which regiment he was subsequently appointed Colonel. Sir Lowry Cole was a man of honour and a loyal servant of the Crown.

FOOTNOTES

1. M. L. Cole and S. Gwynn, *Memoirs of Sir Lowry Cole*, p. 1.
2. W. D. Jones, *Prosperity Robinson*, p. 14.
3. M. L. Cole and S. Gwynn, *Memoirs of Sir Lowry Cole*, p. 14.
4. *D.N.B.*
5. M. L. Cole and S. Gwynn, *Memoirs of Sir Lowry Cole*, pp. 27-28.
6. See Cobbett's *Parliamentary Debates*, Vols. I to XXII for period 22 November 1803 to 4 May 1812; *Parliamentary Debates*, printed by T. C. Hansard on behalf of several editors but a continuation of the former series, Vols. XXIII to XLI for period 5 May 1812 to 28 February 1820; *Parliamentary Debates*, published under the superintendence of T. C. Hansard, New Series, Vols. I to VII cover the period 21 April 1820 to 6 August 1822.
7. P.R.O. 30/43/84, Cole to Enniskillen, 28 July 1822.

CHAPTER I

THE FRAMEWORK OF EMPIRE

Traditionally historians have distinguished between the empire which terminated with the loss of thirteen American colonies in 1783 and a second empire which subsequently developed. The conceptual division between the two empires is artificial. The revolt of the thirteen colonies still left Great Britain with colonies in Canada and the West Indies, and the East India Company entrenched on the Indian sub-continent. Considerable though the impact of the American revolution must have been on Great Britain it did not immediately alter British colonial policy. The new approach which characterised British policy to colonies with substantial European communities in the mid-nineteenth century was not the product of an imperial blue-print designed in an atmosphere of post-revolutionary concern to prevent the disaffection of other colonies. It emerged out of a series of practical measures introduced to meet the altered circumstances of Britain's new world position after the Napoleonic Wars and her pre-eminence as a commercial and industrial power.

Although laissez faire policies were cloaked in the respectability of economic and political theory in the last quarter of the eighteenth century, the writers who propounded them were not supported by contemporary public opinion. Indeed immediately after the loss of the American colonies there was a dogged determination to hold on to the possession and to continue the exploitation of that part of the empire which remained. The desire was for tighter rather than looser control over the colonies.

It is not without significance that laissez faire policies only became practical after British industrial supremacy was underwritten by undoubted British control of the seas. Victory in the wars which engulfed the continent of Europe with little respite from 1793 to 1815 gave Britain that opportunity.

At the peace conferences in 1802, 1814 and 1815 Britain was in a position to keep all the colonies she had conquered from France, Spain, and the Netherlands, but in fact the majority were surrendered in the interests of "the right kind of Europe" and to avoid the charge of attempting to create a colonial monopoly.[1] However, in 1802 Trinidad was kept as a base for illicit trade with the Iberian colonies in South America, and in 1814 three provinces of Dutch Guiana were kept because they had already been anglicized by British planters who had migrated there even before 1793. Strategic interests principally motivated the retention, in the European zone, of Heligoland and Malta and control over the Ionian Islands; in the West Indies, of St Lucia and Tobago; and in the southern oceans of the Cape of Good Hope, Ceylon, and Mauritius with its dependencies.[2] By 1815, therefore, Britian was the hub of an empire in which colonies of conquest, deliberately captured in war and retained by treaty, constituted a major though not altogether novel problem. Retention carried with it the obligation to govern and, whatever the implied obligations to the governed, it would be normal for the views and interests of the imperial power to prevail.

Britain itself was a realm uniquely constituted, not only because it had no written constitution, but because of the strength of its legal traditions, the relative security of civil rights, and the fact that the politics of parliament, albeit the unreformed parliament, were subject to pressures by groups and interests which, though usually represented in parliament, derived much of their strength and influence outside it. Hence the problem was how to devise patterns of colonial government that would fulfil a plurality of conditions: they must to some extent be insulated against the vagaries of political and other pressures, yet they must in the last resort stand up to the scrutiny and challenge of parliament and, where possible, encourage the growth within the colonies of social and political patterns which roughly corresponded to ideas and practices in Britain.[3]

This was not an easy task in the colonies ceded to Britain by foreign powers because acquisition of new territories brought under the British Crown a host of alien subjects. Many of these were slaves. Others were free coloured. But the group which chiefly set the stamp upon the language, laws and traditions of the colony in which they lived were white people whose ties of kinship and culture lay with the nation from which the colony had been acquired. The task which confronted British administrators, therefore, was to find a system of government which would foster tranquillity and win the allegiance of the Crown's new subjects irrespective of colour or culture.[4]

The problem was not without precedent in 1815. The acquisition of "foreign" colonies stretched back to 1655 when Jamaica was taken from the Spanish. But it was only when Grenada and Canada were taken from the French in 1763 that British administrators gave special attention to the problem of governing people of non-British European descent. It had been the intention of the British Government to establish assemblies in both colonies on the same lines as those which existed in the older British colonies of settlement. In the island of Granada an assembly was introduced, but since an oath against transubstantiation was required most of the French Roman Catholic planters were excluded. Their exclusion meant that control passed into the hands of the protestant and British minority. The French planters found the position intolerable, sold their plantations, and left the colony.[5]

In Canada, a proclamation of the 7th October 1763 assumed the government of Quebec would comprise a governor, nominated council, and elected assembly in accordance with the usual pattern of British colonial government.[6] However, the governor's instructions allowed him some discretion and acknowledged it might be "impractical" to form an assembly immediately, in which case government by the council alone was authorized. The governor, believing that Roman Catholics could not hold office, chose the temporary expedient in order to shield the Catholic French Canadian community from precipitate anglicization.[7] Naturally enough, this policy incurred the displeasure of the small British mercantile community in Quebec who in the circumstances would have dominated an assembly. But so far as the British authorities were concerned, the French Canadians had to be placated if their allegiance was to be won for the British Crown.[8] Thus in 1774 the British Government decided to break with tradition and establish in Quebec, by act of parliament, "a nominated biracial legislature".[9]

The novel structure of government established in Quebec in 1774[10] was only intended to be temporary.[11] When the colony was sufficiently anglicized, it was to be brought into conformity with the rest of the Empire.[12] Meanwhile French civil law and social custom were restored with modifications and the privileges of the Roman Catholic Church formally recognized. English criminal law was maintained. Moreover, the legal code established in Quebec was made applicable to all who lived there. This seeming partiality for the King's "new" subjects irritated the small British minority: it became a major problem when Loyalists migrated to Canada after the American War of Independence. Revision of the Canadian constitution was imperative and major constitutional changes were made in 1791.[13]

The form of government and the recognition of local laws and customs first provided for in the Quebec Act of 1774, however, were favoured by Hobart[14] for introduction into the colonies conquered by Britain during the Napoleonic period. Hence when treaties of cession recognized existing forms of foreign colonial government these in no way invalidated the prerogative action of the Crown because no other European empire had developed powerful representative institutions like those that had evolved in the older British colonies. There was therefore no locally constituted opposition to government by the prerogative action of the Crown.

The right of the British Government to maintain "foreign" forms of government was supported by legal authority. In the case of *Campbell* v *Hall* in 1774, which was the decisive test case in Britain, Lord Mansfield[15] gave it as his decision that the laws of a foreign country continued in force until they were altered by the conqueror and were equally applicable to all who lived there. Moreover, he declared that the government of conquered colonies was vested in the free exercise of the Royal prerogative. The King's power could only be checked by his inability to function contrary to fundamental principles, exempt individuals from the laws of trade, or derogate from the authority of the British Parliament. Once the Crown had promised to create an assembly in a colony, Lord Mansfield held it exhausted its prerogative right to legislate for that colony without the consent of the local assembly or an act of the British Parliament.[16]

Mansfield's judgment was amplified by the law officers of the Crown in 1789 when they ruled that once a form of representative government was instituted the Crown automatically lost the prerogative power to amend that constitution.[17] This could only be done by act of parliament. Henceforward it became common practice for the Crown to reserve its prerogative powers in providing for the government of conquered colonies. The instruments of government devised by the Crown and its advisers for the government of colonies were based on feudal or mercantile origins in palatinate or corporation.[18] Prerogative action proved invaluable when the supervision of colonial administration was transferred from the Home Office to the War Office in 1801. It was obviously undesirable for the King to weaken or undermine the policy of direct rule when his country was involved in the conduct of a major war in which the colonies were vital strategically and as sources of supply.[19]

The evolutionary constitutional process in Britain had reached a point in the early nineteenth century where effectively the monarch's prerogative powers were the tools of the ministry who advised him and, in colonial matters, of the secretary of state for War and the Colonial Department in particular. Ministers tried to keep discussion on colonial affairs out of parliament and sometimes even out of the cabinet, though the secretary of state might discuss his problems with his colleagues individually. Professor Manning says that William Huskisson in ten months' office as secretary of state for War and the Colonial Department "seems to have consulted his colleagues very little, even in his most important decisions".[20] On the other hand Sir George Murray's correspondence shows that the cabinet "criticized and revised sentence after sentence in the drafts drawn up at the Colonial Office, whether for Acts of Parliament . . . or for orders in council dealing with the regulations of slavery in the crown colonies, or even for dispatches where such documents might have to be laid before the House of Commons".[21]

Meanwhile Parliament began to assert over the executive a control much more systematic than that afforded by its legislative sovereignty and its power to grant and appropriate supply.[22] Thus increasingly the formulation of colonial policy reflected the opinion ofParliament. By and large though, Parliament was content to prescribe general principles and leave the details of colonial administration to the secretary of state for War and the Colonial Department. Colonial business normally emptied either House[23] but on occasion debates could become very heated – especially if the topic affected any one of the numerous "interests" represented in Parliament.

These "interests" were broad, nebulous groups which were difficult to define but which would draw together on a particular issue or set of issues.[24] Of particular importance in colonial matters were those associated with commerce, humanitarianism, or both. The "commercial interests" was naturally more interested in investment and profit. In colonial affairs, the "humanitarians" almost entirely concerned themselves, in the early years of the nineteenth century, with the protection of free people of colour and the question of slavery. They took their stand on ethical and religious grounds but often made common cause with the secular approach of the Benthamite radicals. They were helped on occasion also by divisions within the commercial interest, notably the division between the East India interest and the West India interest. Both sections held a substantial number of seats in the House of Commons: out of a total membership of 658, the East Indian interest held 57 seats in 1802 and increased its numbers to reach a peak of 68 in 1830;[25] the West India interest held an average of 24 seats from 1796 to 1812 and 34 seats from 1818 to 1831.[26] The increase in both cases reflects a general increase in the commercial interest in the House of Commons during these years.[27] Directly as well as indirectly the commercial interests therefore played an important role in the shaping of colonial policy.

In the immediate post-war years the Tory administration had concerned itself mainly with the defence of property,[28] but Lord Liverpool's cabinet reconstruction after the suicide of Castlereagh in 1822[29] ushered in a new era of reform. The regulation of trade was strongly influenced by Huskisson[30] as president of the Board of Trade, and to some extent by F. J. Robinson as chancellor of the exchequer. There was considerable support in the country for the removal of some at least of the restrictions on trade as a remedy for commercial depression[31] and Huskisson was in close contact with business interests. It fell to Huskisson's lot, therefore, to carry forward the relaxation of the trade laws commenced in 1822 by Robinson and Wallace as president and vice-president of the Board of Trade. Important duties on a wide variety of commodities were substantially reduced. Restrictions on colonial trade were modified by reciprocity treaties with foreign powers and the trade laws were relaxed in the interest of the British re-export trade.[32]

To some, the expansion of trade by relaxation of controls was the answer to Britain's difficulties; to others, the obvious remedy was the old Whig cry of "economical reform". With regard to the latter there were two interlocking processes at work. The one was the simple emphasis on economy especially in military expenditure. The heavy war debt and the dislocation of the economy which followed the conclusion of the war in 1815 made members of parliament anxious to keep down overheard expenses. Whig politicians in particular called for greater economy in imperial defence.[33]

Garrisons stationed in the colonies cost the British Treasury more than three million pounds in 1816. The colonies contributed only one-tenth of that figure towards the military defence of the Empire. Attempts were made to get them to shoulder more of the cost but generally they met with little success. By 1829 the British Government's costs had been cut by half a million pounds a year and the colonial contribution increased by a meagre £35 000. There were still 30 000 British troops stationed in the colonies and the Whigs, who came to power in 1830, attempted further reductions. In 1834, however, a parliamentary select committee claimed that this could only be done at a risk to security. Additional savings, they thought, could be made only on staff appointments, stores and administrative charges.[34]

The second interlocking process in the drive for economy, was part of an older and broader process of administrative reform.[35] A determined attempt was made to use the Treasury as an effective co-ordinator of departmental expenditure.[36] The Colonial Audit Department was created by act of parliament in 1814[37] to scrutinize the revenue accounts of Ceylon, Mauritius, Malta, Trinidad and the Cape, and the expenditure of any sums granted by parliament in aid of those revenues, as well as the accounts of other colonies especially referred to them by the Treasury.[38] Governors had to prune expenditure so that it balanced income. The necessity to spend money on capital development as a boost to the economy was not always appreciated. Indeed governors who embarked on development programmes when their colonial account showed a deficit could find themselves personally liable for the expenditure incurred.[39]

Meanwhile the British Government attempted to promote economic cohesion by the introduction of British currency as a standard throughout the Empire. British silver and copper coins were brought into circulation through the commissariat and the payment of salaries to British troops. The measure was sound in itself but caused crises in some colonies where it drew attention to the reduced value of colonial currency.[40] Moreover, lack of technical knowledge in the vast undertaking of currency conversion and a short supply of silver coins added to the difficulties of colonial authorities.[41]

The humanitarians, led in the House of Commons by T. F. Buxton,[42] were less concerned about economy than social reform. They were disappointed that the Slave Trade Abolition Act of 1807[43] had not led to the mitigation and gradual extinction of slavery in British colonies.[44] They gathered their forces, therefore, for an attack on slavery itself. In 1823 Buxton proposed a motion in the House of Commons calling for a gradual abolition of slavery.[45] The motion was withdrawn when Canning proposed a series of resolutions from the government benches. Abolition of slavery was stated to be the goal of British policy; meanwhile preliminary measures would be taken to ameliorate the condition of slaves throughout the Empire.[46] Such a policy would clearly clash with vested interests in the colonies. In the older West Indian colonies colonial legislatures frequently obstructed measures to ameliorate the condition of slaves. In the conquered colonies without legislatures but where there were slaves there was resistance, on occasion to the point of violence.[47]

An act[48] to abolish slavery was signed by the King on the 28th August 1833 and came into operation on the 31st July the following year. It provided for the immediate emancipation of slave children under the age of six years and stipulated periods of apprenticeship for older slaves. Predial slaves were to serve their masters without payment for six years on the basis of a forty-five hour week. Non-predial slaves were to serve four years but no limitation was placed on the hours they could be expected to work. All apprentices were placed entirely under the jurisdiction of stipendary magistrates who were paid and controlled by the British Government. Compensation of £20 000 000 was to be paid to slave-owners in terms of a prescribed formula to determine individual values.

Apprenticeship proved unpopular with slave-owners hence the terminal date was moved forward to the 1st August, 1838, for all slaves.[49] Thus was removed a problem which was a source of serious friction between Great Britain and her slave-owning colonies. The attempt to make uniform regulations work irrespective of local conditions had not only provoked the muster of opposition and criticism in the slave-owning colonies, but it had also demonstrated the impracticability, even the illogicality, of improving the conditions of slavery when the status of slavery itself was condemned by lawyers, humanitarians and utilitarians.

The Colonial Department in London was responsible for the execution of British colonial policy. The Department was firmly established in the framework of British administration by 1821.[50] A subsequent increase in colonial business and improved economic conditions in Great Britain, however, explain a considerable increase in personnel from 1823 to 1825.[51] By the latter date the permanent establishment included an under-secretary and a full-time legal counsellor shared with the Board of Trade, but decisions rested with the secretary of state for War and the Colonial Department and his parliamentary under-secretary. Five secretaries of state – one of whom, Lord Goderich, administered the Colonial Department on two separate occasions – and six under-secretaries held office in the decade of Cole's two governorships.[52]

Earl Bathurst was secretary of state when Cole took up office in Mauritius in 1823. Bathurst, who had been secretary of state since 1812, did not enjoy popularity in the contemporary press. When he resigned the seals of the Colonial Department in 1827, *The Times* commented "that there never was tolerated a worse colonial minister than that unrespected Lord".[53] This can, perhaps, be explained by the absence of any flamboyance in an age of colourful personalities like the duke of Wellington, and statesmen of the calibre of Castlereagh, Canning and Peel. Young, who has made a detailed study of the Colonial Department in the early nineteenth century, contends that it was because Bathurst was self-effacing to a fault that he made so little impression on his contemporaries.[54] But Young has found that "discretion, loyalty, an excellent memory, a well informed mind, an ability to express himself clearly and an aptitude for compromise made him (Bathurst) a valued man in the cabinet".[55] He was by nature conservative but his despatches to Cole show that he was not blind to progress. Indeed it was under Bathurst's supervision that the social and economic changes planned by the British Government for the colonies were initiated. His despatches reveal him as patient, but persistent, in his endeavour to fulfill the spirit as well as the letter of the policies prescribed by Parliament.

Viscount Goderich briefly succeeded Bathurst in 1827, but his second period of office (1830-1833) was of greater significance. His biographer describes him as a member of the liberal movement.[56] In colonial affairs his liberalism amounted only to a cautious implementation of policies already devised. He supported emigration as a means of providing a fresh start in life "redundant" British citizens and relieving the poor rate.[57] He was also concerned for "the protection of primitive people against exploitation,"[58] and whenever possible "to promote the growth of self government in the colonies".[59] It was he, moreover, who finally committed the British Government to the abolition of slavery[60] though it was his successor Lord Stanley who in 1833 moved the bill to abolish slavery in the British colonies.[61]

Perhaps the most dynamic of the secretaries of state was William Huskisson. However, his tenure of office was so short – only nine months – that Young concludes that "if his reputation as an imperial statesman rested on his work as secretary of state, it would be based on promise and intention rather than performance".[62] Huskisson's approach to colonial problems resembled that of Bathurst and Goderich. This was most evident in his approach to slavery. Brady says, "He looked forward to the eventual emancipation of the negro population, but considered it could not with expediency be hurried".[63] But if Huskisson's tenure of office at the Colonial Department was short, it was off-set by the profound effect he had on the Empire through the economic policies he initiated while president of the Board of Trade.

Huskisson resigned from Wellington's cabinet in May 1828 and was succeeded by Lieutenant-General Sir George Murray, the duke's former quartermaster general and chief of staff. Murray was well-known to Sir Lowry and Lady Frances Cole and a letter from Lady Frances to her mother, the countess of Malmesbury, reveals their surprise at his selection as secretary of state. "However," she conceded, "he has excellent talents and what the French call 'une bonne tête' and therefore, though I am not at all surprised at the feeling his appointment has excited, I have little doubt he will do well."[64]

Despite the prognostication of Lady Frances, Murray was the least distinguished secretary of state under whom Cole served. Young says, "He proved totally incapable of grasping the details of the mass of business that confronted him."[65] Yet the minutes of the Anti-Slavery Society record that he shared with others who held the seals of the Colonial Department from 1823 to 1833 a personal abhorrence of slavery.[66] He initiated plans, subsequently concluded by Goderich, to consolidate in a single Order in Council all the measures to ameliorate the condition of slavery in the conquered colonies. He hoped the chartered colonies would use the order as a model for legislation of their own, but he made it clear to a deputation from the Anti-Slavery Society that the British Government was not prepared to interfere with their legislatures. Indeed the deputation came away from their interview with Murray with the distinct impression "that whatever may be Sir George Murray's personal feelings and opinions on the subject (of slavery) the determination of the ministry at the present is *to do nothing;* and that if left to the government and the colonial legislatures, West Indian Slavery may exist, with little mitigation, for ages yet to come."[67]

The parliamentary under-secretaries generally shared the views of their superiors. Many of them were destined for high office in later life,[68] but on the whole they seem to have been less influential in the Colonial Department than the senior permanent officials.

The permanent under-secretary from 1825 till 1836 was R. W. Hay. Young says that his correspondence indicates he had "a greater concern for personalities than for ideas".[69] He conceived that his rôle only called upon him to give advice when it was asked of him, and he seems to have been content merely to supervise the internal administration of the

Colonial Department, prepare routine reports and circulate despatches, and prepare all papers relating to secret service money.[70]

James Stephen, who was legal counsellor to the Colonial Department from 1813 to 1834 and assistant under-secretary from 1834 until he succeeded Hay in 1836, frequently had more influence on colonial policy than Hay. Initially he had been a part-time consultant of the Department but official business increasingly occupied his time so that in 1823 he was added to the permanent establishment. Lord Bathurst preferred Stephen's opinion to that of any other person,[71] thus no doubt he was occasionally called to comment on matters of policy as well as interpretation of law. The duke of Wellington, on the other hand, objected to the way Stephen introduced what Wellington described as Stephen's partisan view in favour of the abolition of slavery in the slave legislation he drafted.[72] His influence in the Department therefore was variable in these early years and depended in part on the attitude of the ministers.

A major factor which emerges from a study of colonial policy from 1823 to 1833 is its consistency despite the numerous changes in the political leadership. The degree of pressure with which policy was pursued altered but the principles of policy remained unchanged. Economically it was motivated by the principles of freer trade associated with the name of Huskisson, and socially by the House of Commons resolutions to ameliorate the condition of slaves in preparation for their emancipation. In the colonies of conquest where the British Government was free to apply these policies it nevertheless moved with caution. The advice of men on the spot was heard and given formal encouragement by the creation of councils to advise the governor, and judicial practice was reformed in an effort to create in these colonies a society which reflected British principles of legal equality and individual liberty.

Policy decisions taken in Britain had to be executed in the conquered colonies by the governor. Within the colony a governor's power was considerable because it depended constitutionally upon the delegation of the prerogative powers of the Crown which acted politically on the advice of a responsible minister. A governor was the servant of the Crown and apart from formal instructions issued on his appointment he received further directions in the form of additional instructions, letters patent, orders of the Privy Council, or through the secretary of state for War and the Colonial Department. The governor for his part was bound to report all his activities to the secretary of state, seek instructions if he was in any doubt and confirmation on some issues if specifically instructed to do so.

Officials of the Colonial Department in London did not rely entirely upon the governor for local information. Reports were sometimes made to them by private individuals or public bodies acting as pressure groups, but official information seems to have been preferred. After 1814, the Colonial Audit Department kept a close check on the accounts of several colonies, including Mauritius and the Cape.[73] In 1819, instructions were given for colonial almanacs to be sent regularly to the Colonial Department and in 1822 a system of regular annual reports was instituted. Known as "Blue Books" these reports supplied detailed statistics and general information.[74] But perhaps more valuable to the Colonial Department were inquiries occasionally undertaken by formally appointed commissioners. They were used to establish facts and recommend improvements. This method of obtaining information about the colonies was not a nineteenth century invention: as early as 1664 a royal commission was sent to make investigations in some American colonies.[75] But in the second and third decades of the nineteenth century there were three important commissions. One was a commission to inquire into the state of New South Wales,[76] another in the West Indies,[77] and yet another, the Commission of Eastern Inquiry to inquire into the affairs of the Cape of Good Hope, Mauritius and Ceylon.[78] It is the latter which is of particular interest to the present study.

The terms of reference of the commissioners of eastern inquiry were very broad. They had to inquire into the whole state of each colony. The commissioners' instructions drew their special attention to general problems as well as specific ones in the individual colonies. These included, amongst other things, an investigation into the general administration of government, the governor's control over the civil and military establishment, local institutions – particularly those charged with justice and finance – the state of the laws and the practice and administration of justice, the possibilities of reducing government expenditure and measures to augment government revenue, and, in Mauritius and the Cape, the condition of slaves. They were asked to suggest remedies for abuses they might find and recommend improvements they thought would be practicable.[79]

Two commissioners were appointed in 1823 – J. T. Bigge[80] and W. M. G. Colebrooke.[81] A third commissioner, W. Blair,[82] was added in 1826 because of the pressure of business. The commissioners visited the Cape first, Mauritius second, and Ceylon third. With respect to the first two colonies, they reversed the movements of Sir Lowry Cole who was governor of both Mauritius and the Cape. He was governor of the former from 1823 to 1828 and of the latter from 1828 to 1833. The commissioners' inquiry at the Cape occupied them from 1823 to 1826. They arrived in Mauritius in 1826 and stayed until 1829. Cole's personal contact with them extended over two years. But much that he accomplished in Mauritius was done before they came. On the other hand, some of their reports on the Cape had been received and acted upon by the Colonial Department in London before Cole arrived in that colony. Other reports reached London while Cole was in office at the Cape. His work at the Cape, therefore, must be seen in the wake of their investigation.

The role of a governor was a difficult one: within the colony he governed he was the most important person because he represented the Crown, but within the framework of a vast empire he was simply the servant of the Crown whose government in a small part of the Empire he was expected to manage. A governor had to be allowed some initiative, but he was reckoned best who most accurately interpreted the general policy of the Colonial Department in London.

Within a conquered colony the paramountcy of the governor in both civil and military affairs was undisputed. Initially he legislated by proclamation. But it became usual practice to constitute a formal body of official advisors as a council. Even after the institution of a council the governor retained the sole power to initiate legislation and, as in India after 1786,[83] he could legislate without the concurrence of the council provided he justified his actions to the secretary of state. Legislative measures by the governor with the advice of the council were termed "ordinances". Legislation in either form – proclamation or ordinance – had to be submitted to the King for his approval. Ideally, this should have been done prior to publication; in practice this would have occasioned too great a delay. Frequently, therefore, colonial legislation was published in the colony, then submitted for approval. In cases of doubt as to the legality of colonial legislation the legal adviser to the Colonial Department was consulted. If a proclamation or ordinance met with disapproval the governor would be told that the King could not be advised to approve it and the governor was commanded to withdraw it.

In addition to administrative control by the officials of the Colonial Department, a governor was circumscribed in the exercise of his powers by the limited resources of colonial revenue and the increasing insistence by the British Government on colonial solvency. Most colonies raised some revenue by direct taxes on land and internal commerce. But indirect taxation was the staple of colonial finance and the greater part of this was raised from import and export duties. Governors therefore sought to improve the local economy and the volume of colonial trade. But here too innovation had to accord with the general trade policy of Britain: changes in Britian's fiscal policy on occasion hit back harshly on the economic interests of particular colonies. Reform at the centre then, often caused dislocation at the periphery.

A colony was a unit – economically, socially and politically. Changes required by Britain upset the status quo in the colony and caused dissatisfaction, especially in those social groups whose privileges were threatened thereby. Governors had to move cautiously if open confrontation was to be avoided. They had to be more pragmatic than theoretical in their approach to problems: the same governor might seek abolition of a tariff in one circumstance and yet appeal for it in another. Indeed a governor was the arbiter of the particular problems of the community he governed. His success or failure depended upon his ability to adapt the decisions of the British Government into practical politics in the colony he governed, or alternatively persuade the British Government to amend its policy to meet the special circumstances of that colony.

The place of a conquered colony in the framework of the British Empire in the post-Napoleonic period is much more complicated than would at first appear. In theory the government of the colony rested simply on the prerogative power of the monarch, some of which was delegated to his governor; in practice government in a conquered colony was influenced by a number of groups or individuals covering a broad spectrum of interests. The Crown instructed the governor on the advice of the secretary of state for War and the Colonial Department. This political official was responsible to the British Parliament for the advice he tendered to the monarch and therefore had to take account of political pressure groups in the shaping of colonial policy. He also had the advice of specialists: in the first place, there were permanent officials in the Colonial Department who even helped to prepare despatches; and in the second place, commissioners who could be sent to a colony or colonies to investigate and report. Yet for all the weight of power and influence behind the directives given to the governor by the secretary of state, his instructions could not be applied without consideration for local circumstances. Sometimes in conquered colonies the governor alone was responsible for the execution of policy but often he had some body whose opinion he had to consult, for example, the councils of officials created to advise the governors of Mauritius and the Cape in 1825. The members of these councils did not hesitate to express their opinion and although the governor did not have to take their advice he had to explain his action to the secretary of state when he declined it. Admittedly a nominated council was independent of local public opinion, but no government can govern without the assent of the governed unless by force of arms. In neither Mauritius nor the Cape were there sufficient troops to cope with widespread insurrection, and reinforcements from Britain would have taken several months to arrive. The execution of policy therefore had to depend less upon force than upon the ability of the governor to win the confidence of the colonists and gain their support for government measures. Obviously there were occasions when there was a clash of interests. The measure of a governor's success lay in his resolution of the conflict.

FOOTNOTES

1. C. K. Webster, *The Foreign Policy of Castlereagh, 1812–1822*, Vol. I, p. 491.
2. These included Rodrigues, the Seychelles, the Amirante Islands, St. Paul and Amsterdam Islands, Tromelin Island, and two islands – Roquepiz and St. George – now known to have existed only in the imagination of cartographers. See R. Scott, *Limuria*, p. 3.
3. *C.H.B.E.*, Vol. II, p. 158.
4. H. T. Manning, *British Colonial Government after the American Revolution 1782–1820*, p. 293.
5. V. T. Harlow, *The Founding of the Second British Empire 1763–1793*, Vol. II, p. 773-774.
6. H. Neatby, *Quebec, the Revolutionary Age, 1760–1791*, p. 33.
7. *Ibid.*
8. D. K. Fieldhouse, *The Colonial Empires*, p. 79.
9. Harlow, Vol. II, p. 713.
10. 14 Geo. III, c. 83.
11. Harlow, Vol. II, p. 713, fn. 96 quotes Lord North in the debate in the House of Commons on the Quebec Act: "That this establishment is not to be considered perpetual, is admitted in the Bill itself . . . As soon as the Canadians shall be in a Condition to receive an Assembly, it will be right they should have one." (Cavendish Debates, p. 290).
12. Harlow, Vol. II, p. 713.
13. Neatby, pp. 258–261. For details of the Canadian constitution of 1791, 31 Geo. III, c. 31, see A. F. Madden *Imperial Constitutional Documents, 1795–1965: a Supplement*, pp. 12–18.
14. The secretary of state for War and the Colonial Department, 17 March 1801 to 12 May 1804.
15. William Murray, first earl of Mansfield (1705–1793) was lord chief justice of the Court of King's Bench, 1756–1788. See *D.N.B.* Vol. XXXIX.
16. A. Berriedale Keith (ed.), *Selected Speeches and Documents on British Colonial Policy 1763–1917*, pp. 35–52. Extracts of the judgment are also published in V. Harlow and A. F. Madden, *British Colonial Developments, 1774–1834*, pp. 78–79.
17. Harlow, Vol. II, p. 774.
18. A. F. Madden and K. Robinson (ed.), *Essays in Imperial Government presented to Margery Perham*, Chapter 1, p. 20.
19. *C.H.B.E.*, Vol. II, p. 145.
20. H. T. Manning, "Colonial Crises before the Cabinet, 1829–1835", *Bulletin of the Institute of Historical Research*, Vol. XXX (1957), pp. 41–61.
21. *Ibid.*, p.46.
22. D. L. Keir, *The Constitutional History of Modern Britain since 1485*, (9th edition), p. 373.
23. Fieldhouse, p. 244.
24. G. P. Judd, *Members of Parliament 1734–1832*, p. 66.
25. *Ibid.*, p. 66.
26. *Ibid.*, p. 69.
27. *Ibid.*, p. 56.
28. L. Woodward, *The Age of Reform 1815–1870* (2nd edition), p. 58.

29. G. Canning succeeded Castlereagh as foreign secretary in September 1822; F. J. Robinson (later viscount Goderich, then earl of Ripon) was brought into the cabinet as chancellor of the exchequer in January 1823; and W. Huskisson entered the cabinet as president of the Board of Trade in October 1823. R. Peel had already gone into the cabinet as home secretary in January 1822.
30. Huskisson's control over tariff policy has been challenged by W. D. Jones, *Prosperity Robinson.* He asserts that Robinson as chancellor of the exchequer was primarily responsible for the formulation of policy, but I. R. Christie, *History*, February 1968, pp. 139–140, considers that the evidence led by Jones is not conclusive.
31. Woodward, p. 70.
32. A. Brady, *William Huskisson and Liberal Reform*, Chapter V.
33. *C.H.B.E.*, Vol. II, p. 808. See also H. T. Manning, "The Colonial Policy of the Whig Ministers 1830–7", Part I, *Canadian Historical Review*, Vol. XXXIII (1952), p. 205.
34. *C.H.B.E.*, Vol. II, p. 809.
35. E. W. Cohen, *The Growth of the British Civil Service, 1780–1939*, Chapter IV.
36. D. M. Young, *The Colonial Office in the Early Nineteenth Century*, pp. 184–196. See also J. E. D. Binney, *British Public Finance and Administration, 1774–92.*
37. 54 Geo. III, c. 184.
38. H. T. Manning, *British Colonial Government after the American Revolution*, p. 516.
39. For example, see Chapter VIII, pp. 127–128.
40. In Mauritius the paper dollar had depreciated 37% below its nominal silver equivalent by July 1820. At the Cape, the rixdollar had depreciated from 4s to 1s 6d by 1825. M. H. de Kock, *Economic History of South Africa*, p. 360, asserts that depreciation of the colonial currency was in part due to the appreciation of English sterling through the resumption of specie payments in Britain in 1821.
41. R. Chalmers, *A History of Currency in the British Colonies*, pp. 23–24, 417–425.
42. T. F. Buxton (1786–1845), Member of Parliament for Weymouth 1818–37, philanthropist and foundation member of the Committee of the Anti-Slavery Society. He succeeded Wilberforce as leader of the anti-slavery group in the House of Commons in 1824.
43. 47 Geo. III, sess. 1, c. 36.
44. Rhodes House, Oxford, E2/1, Minutes of a meeting of the Committee of the Anti-Slavery Society, 31 January 1823.
45. R. Coupland, *The British Anti-Slavery Movement*, p. 124. See also W. L. Mathieson, *British Slavery and its Abolition 1823–1838*, pp. 119–120.
46. Mathieson, pp. 121–122.
47. *C.H.B.E.*, Vol. II, p. 318.
48. 3 and 4 Will. IV, c. 73.
49. R. Coupland, *The British Anti-Slavery Movement*, pp. 144–145.
50. D. M. Young, *The Colonial Office in the Early Nineteenth Century*, p. 46.
51. *Ibid.*, p. 83.
52. See Appendix A, p. 177.
53. H. F. G. Tucker, *The Press and the Colonies*, unpublished M.A. Thesis, Bristol University, 1936, pp. 39–40.
54. Young, p. 18.
55. *Ibid.*
56. W. D. Jones, *Prosperity Robinson*, p. 217.
57. *Ibid.*
58. *Ibid.*, p. 221.
59. *Ibid*, p. 219. Jones quotes Goderich to Grant, 25 May 1831, in Harlow and Madden, *Colonial Developments*, p. 97: "The benefits resulting from the election by the proprietary body, in every country, of the members of the popular branch of the legislature, are too familiar to require notice, and are so universally admitted as to preclude all controversy on the abstract principle."
60. *Ibid.*, p. 224.
61. 3 and 4 Will. IV, c. 73.
62. Young, p. 105.
63. Brady, p. 152.

64. P.R.O. 30/43/34, Lady Frances Cole to the countess of Malmesbury, 13 October 1828.
65. Young, p. 111.
66. Rhodes House, Oxford, E2/3, Minutes of the Anti-Slavery Society, 9 February 1830.
67. *Ibid.*
68. *R. Wilmot Horton* became governor of Ceylon, 1831–1837; *E. G. Stanley* later viscount Stanley, then fourth earl of Derby, was paymaster-general and secretary for Ireland, 1831–1833, secretary of state for War and the Colonial Department, 1833–1834 and 1841–1845, first lord of the Treasury, 1852, 1858, and 1866–1868; *Lord Francis Leveson Gower* became chief secretary to the lord lieutenant of Ireland, 1828–1830, and secretary at War, 1830; *Viscount Howick*, later third earl Grey, became under-secretary for Home Affairs, 1834, secretary at War with a seat in the cabinet, 1835, secretary of state for War and the Colonial Department, 1846–1852; *Sir J. G. Shaw-Lefevre* served on numerous commissions and in 1855 became clerk of parliament – he was annually elected vice-chancellor of London University, 1842–1862.
69. Young, p. 88.
70. *Ibid.*, pp. 86–87.
71. *Ibid.*, p. 92.
72. *Ibid.*, p. 113.
73. *Ibid.*, pp. 185–186.
74. *Ibid.*, pp. 34–35.
75. A. Berriedale Keith, *Constitutional History of the First British Empire*, pp. 102–103.
76. C.O. 201/114–142.
77. C.O. 318/57–80, C.O. 137/174–6, and C.O. 320/4.
78. Records may be found for
    (a) the Cape, C.O. 414/1–15, and C.O. 48/90–1, 100–5, 118, 120–1, 123, 128–9, 134 and 160;
    (b) Mauritius, C.O. 415/1–19, and C.O. 167/117–146;
    (c) Ceylon, C.O. 416/1–32, and C.O. 54/110–1, 116, 131–2, 139 and 145.
    In the case of the Cape some of the commissioners' records have been published in Theal, *R.C.C.* see index in Vol. XXXV, pp. 402–403, and in the case of Ceylon a selection of their records is published in G. C. Mendis (ed.), *The Colebrook-Cameron Papers; documents on British Colonial Policy in Ceylon, 1796–1833.*
79. Theal, *R.C.C.*, Vol. XV, pp. 237–242, instructions given to the commissioners of inquiry proceeding to the Cape of Good Hope, Mauritius and Ceylon, by Bathurst, 18 January 1823.
80. *J. T. Bigge* (1780–1843) was called to the Bar at the Inner Temple in 1806. He subsequently studied Spanish law at Madeira which probably explains his appointment as chief justice of Trinidad in 1814. In 1819 he was appointed a commissioner of inquiry in New South Wales. Bigge remained at the Cape when the other commissioners went on to Mauritius in order to complete the work there. He only visited Mauritius to finalise the commissioners' reports on the Cape after which he retired from the commission. For further biographical detail see *Dictionary of Australian Biography.*
81. *W. M. G. Colebrooke* (1787–1870) was appointed to the commission of inquiry after several years' military service in the Far East. Subsequently he became governor of the Bahamas (1834), the Leeward Islands (1837), and New Brunswick (1841). For further biographical detail see *Dictionary of Mauritian Biography* and *D.N.B.*, a Supplement, Vol. II.
82. *W. Blair* (1799–1873), was admitted to the Faculty of Advocates in Scotland in 1820 and practised as an advocate until he was appointed to the commission of inquiry. He later served for many years as a member of the Supreme Court of Justice, Ionian Isles. For further biographical detail see F. J. Grant (ed.), *The Faculty of Advocates in Scotland, 1532–1943.*
83. *Cambirdge History of India*, Vol.V., p. 203; A. Aspinall, *Cornwallis in Bengal*, p. 7; and R. C. Majumdar, H. C. Raychaudhuri and K. Datta, *Advanced History of India*, pp. 787–788. The decision to strengthen the power of the governor-general sprang directly from the difficulties Hastings had experienced with his council.

CHAPTER II

THE ACQUISITION AND GOVERNMENT OF MAURITIUS

The British conquest of Mauritius[1] in December 1810 was the direct result of the difficulties in which the East India Company had been placed by the war with France. Together with the Cape of Good Hope,[2] Mauritius was captured and kept because its port was one of a chain which, in the possession of foreign powers, had threatened the safety of the sea route to Britain's possessions in the east in time of war. The importance of this sea route had grown in direct proportion to the increase in the volume and value of trade with India and China. In the days of sailing ships, when the 11 000 mile journey from the English Channel to the Bay of Bengal might take six months or more, it was vital to have harbours where ships could call for supplies and repairs. All the principal ports on the journey to the orient, save St. Helena which was British, were in the hands of the Portuguese, Dutch or French. The British were thus dependent on foreign powers for harbours. Once the French were ensconced in the Netherlands with the support of the Dutch republican party (January 1795), the British were clearly at a disadvantage. With the authority of the Prince of Orange who was living in exile in Britain, British forces occupied the Cape (June 1795) and Ceylon (August 1795). The Cape was restored to the Batavian Republic (1803)[3] by the Peace of Amiens, only to be retaken finally in 1806 after war had been resumed. The value of Cape Town had been enhanced by improved sailing techniques which shaped a more direct course from Cape Verde to the southern tip of Africa.[4] But the occupation of the Cape and Ceylon was insufficient in itself to check French aggression in the Indian Ocean.

The East India Company suffered considerable financial loss from 1807 to 1809 when French cruisers based on Mauritius captured fourteen of their ships.[5] The authorities in India therefore decided to take firm action to remove an expensive enemy. An expedition was prepared in India under the command of Abercromby.[6] Assisted by ships of the Royal Navy stationed at the Cape these troops occupied Rodrigues in 1809, and, in the following year, the islands of Bourbon and Ile de France. Apart from the military arrangements, the terms of capitulation were generous. All private property was respected and the conquerors guaranteed to preserve the religion, laws and customs of the colony. Provision was made for those colonists who so desired to quit the colony with their private property within two years.[7] At the peace in 1814, Bourbon which had no natural harbour was returned to France as it posed no threat to British Indiamen. Mauritius and its dependencies, which included the Seychelles and Rodrigues, were retained in the interests of security.[8]

At first there was administrative confusion concerning the government of the conquered islands. Lord Minto, the governor-general of Bengal, made an ad hoc arrangement whereby Robert Farquhar, an experienced administrator,[9] was made governor of the islands with his headquarters in Mauritius. He was instructed to model the administration on company government in India.[10] Almost at once there was difficulty. Abercromby complained that the garrison at Port Louis, the principal town, was under his command, yet he could not exercise control over them. For, in accordance with Indian forms, Farquhar considered the military government sub-ordinated to the civil government; consequently the military commander could "barely . . . issue an Order" without the governor's previous sanction, and his consent was necessary before a single soldier could be moved.[11]

A month earlier, in November 1810, Lord Liverpool, then secretary of state for War and the Colonial Department, had taken, in London, a contrary decision to that of Minto's for the government of Mauritius. Company rule in Ceylon between 1795 and 1802 had not been successful because of the difficulty of governing a complex racial community of Dutch, Eurasians and non-Europeans.[12] Lord Liverpool's instructions, which arrived in Mauritius in April 1811, placed the government of the newly conquered islands under military control.[13] The government of Mauritius was put in the hands of the commander of the land forces, Major General Warde,[14] who had taken over the command of the troops in Mauritius when Abercromby returned to his headquarters in India. Farquhar was given a subordinate post in charge of the civil government of Bourbon. He was naturally very disappointed. He sailed for Bourbon where he took the oath as provisional governor on 26th April 1811.

Within three months Farquhar was back in Mauritius. A copy of the *London Gazette* of 2nd March 1811,[15] had come into his hands. From it, he learned of his own appointment to the governorship of Mauritius. He immediately returned to Mauritius and persuaded Warde to hand over the government on the authority of the notice in the *Gazette*.[16]

This somewhat unorthodox procedure for the tranfer of authority in Mauritius was overlooked in London where Farquhar's commission as governor had been signed on the 9th April 1811, and his formal instructions the following day.[17] By the Treaty of Paris, 30th May 1814, France formally ceded Mauritius and its dependencies to Britain but recovered Bourbon.[18] Farquhar's commission and instructions were not altered after the formal cession of the colony. Moreover, pencil alterations on the copy kept in the Colonial Department show that these documents were used as the model for Sir Lowry Cole's commission and instructions in 1822. Apart from minor alterations, Cole's commission and instructions were substantially those of his predecessor.

Farquhar's commission and instructions followed a conventional pattern. The power of the Royal prerogative was reserved in its entirety, so that the Crown was free to revoke, amend or add to the powers conferred on the governor whenever it desired.[19] The governor was given full executive authority and put in charge of the administration. He was authorised to raise troops and call out militia for the maintenance of peace, order, and good government in the colony; but he was forbidden to declare war without the King's authority except as a preventive measure or in an emergency. He had to administer the civil government in the colony so far as was possible in conformity with the laws and institutions which existed at the time of the capture.

Christians of all denominations were to enjoy full civil rights but the special place hitherto accorded to the Roman Catholic Church by the French administration was recognized. The governor was directed to consult the superior official in Maritius of the Roman Catholic Church in all matters which concerned the Catholic clergy, the education of youth, instruction of negroes, and acts of charity. He was, however, specially warned to take care that the Roman Catholic clergy did not assume any authority over Christians of a different communion or use the cloak of religion to foster political discontent. The instructions, moreover, ordered the governor to keep an indirect check on the Roman

Catholic Church through superintendence of its revenue. All religious houses and estates had to transmit to the government an account of their revenue every year. From this revenue the governor was required to deduct a suitable allowance for the comfortable maintenance of the religious establishment. All sums formerly used for public or charitable purposes had to be paid into the public treasury of the colony for the benefit of the public service.

Provision was made in the governor's instructions to continue French judicial procedures and law in the form in which the British found them. Farquhar was told "that the . . . Courts of Judicature which were subsisting in the Island at the time of your arrival therein shall for the present be continued in the Exercise of all Judicial Powers belonging to them in all Criminal and Civil Causes and that they shall proceed according to the Laws by which the said Island are now governed." At that point the civil and commercial law of the colony was "the new French code"[20] but the criminal law was still based on the Ancient Ordinance of 1670 except for some modifications made by a decree of the National Assembly of the 12th November 1789.[21] The transfer of sovereignty from France to Britain, however, clearly necessitated revised procedure for appeals from the local courts. The King in Privy Council replaced the Court of Cassation in France as the court of final appeal. Appeals were allowed in civil cases involving sums in excess of £500 provided they were made within fourteen days of the decision and sufficient security was given by the appellant to cover costs. Appeals were likewise allowed in all cases which involved duty payable to the Crown, or any fees of office, annual rent, or other subject likely to create a precedent. Once an appeal was allowed the execution of the decision of the local courts was suspended until the result of the appeal was known.

The governor's instructions also embraced trade matters. Mauritius, like the other conquered colonies, was arbitrarily pulled into the British mercantilist pattern. Duties hitherto weighted to favour France were now weighted to favour Britain. The governor was required to see that external trade conformed in every particular with the British laws of trade and navigation. His special attention was drawn to two acts: one to encourage British shipping and navigation,[22] and the other to prevent "certain instruments" from being required from ships of the United States, and giving the King temporary powers to regulate the trade of the British dominions with that country.[23] Every three months the governor had to send to the secretary of state a comprehensive account of the foreign trade of the colony. He had to submit details of merchant ships that came to the colony, a schedule of goods traded, and a list of bonds taken in terms of British legislation. To facilitate the application of the trade regulations, the governor had to see that the collector of customs lived in close proximity to the naval officers and, if the Customs House had not already been sited, he had to fix a place for it in consultation with the collector of customs.

Offenders against the trade acts had to be brought before the local courts and the governor was especially charged to see that only British subjects served on juries in cases which involved duties on ships or goods liable to forfeiture if their import or export was proven illegal. If officials offended, the governor had to report fully to the commissioner of customs in London so that he could take action. If the governor himself was found guilty of an offence, he was warned that he would be immediately removed from office and fined £1 000 in addition to the penalties imposed by the courts.[24]

Finally, the governor had to make a comprehensive annual report to the secretary of state on conditions in the colony and the attitude of the colonists, and propose reforms he thought were necessary.

This was the legal basis of government in 1823 when Cole succeeded Farquhar as governor of Mauritius.

Before Cole sailed for Mauritius he had paid frequent visits to the Colonial Department in London to examine their papers on Mauritius. He thus gained first-hand knowledge of the administrative inefficiency of his predecessor. Despite instructions sent to Mauritius in 1818, enclosures to despatches had not been marked either with reference to their contents, or to the order in which they were intended to be read, or to the communication to which they belonged. Since the enclosures were usually sent loose, they were liable to be mislaid. Binding was made difficult too because, despite the remonstrance of Bathurst,[25] enclosures sent by Farquhar seldom had a margin and when they did it was on the wrong side of the paper. Cole, by contrast, was to be meticulous in his attention to administrative details. He acknowledged that he lacked experience in dealing with detail and office routine, yet his despatches were clear and conformed to the requirements of the officials in London. Sometimes he was slow to learn a new procedure as, for example, the form in which ordinances had to be drafted after the formation of a council in Mauritius in 1825.[26] But once the error was pointed out to him, he did not err again.

Cole was both conscientious and honest. In his second despatch to Bathurst, he admitted frankly that the governorship of Mauritius "must be arduous and laborious to any person, however qualified".[27] He was bound in fact to serve two masters. On the one hand he must conform to the financial and administrative requirements of the Colonial Department in London for Bathurst required in the colonies the same pattern of retrenchment and reform which the Treasury sought in British administration. On the other hand, he must study the logic of the situation in Mauritius.

The colonial expenditure in Mauritius was vastly in excess of its revenue.[28] The total deficit for the period 1811–1823 amounted to £1 645 652. In an effort to cut costs, Bathurst had instructed Farquhar, while he was in England on leave,[29] to reduce the colonial establishment, when he returned to Mauritius. This he had not done to Bathurst's satisfaction.[30] Thus, both Cole and the commissioners of inquiry who were appointed in 1823 were asked to inquire into and report on the revenue and expenditure of the colony. Pending the outcome of this inquiry, Bathurst refrained from giving Cole detailed instructions for a reform of the establishment. However, he thought "much retrenchment" was necessary and, where practicable, should be immediately effected. He hoped that the civil servants in Mauritius would assist the governor in carrying through this policy. If they proved intractable, Cole was told that the King, in view of his confidence in Cole's "zeal and discretion", would sanction any action Cole was prepared to adopt to carry through what must inevitably be unpopular measures.[31]

It was necessary to strengthen the governor's hand in this way because the integrity of many civil servants in Mauritius was doubtful. Henry Goulburn, a former under-secretary for War and the Colonial Department,[32] asked Cole's aunt, Lady Grantham, to warn her nephew of conditions in Mauritius. ". . . There are not any official servants of the government there, in whom he can place any confidence with the exception of Mr. Hart Davis", he wrote. Goulburn asserted that the colonial civil servants had "a common interest in deceiving the Governor, and though many of them, men of ability, have yet a paramount desire to promote their own interest and to continue under a new Governor that system of irregularity and confusion which has hitherto prevailed. Their object will therefore be to endeavour to draw the new Governor into measures which will afterwards embarrass him considerably".

Goulburn counselled that Cole should depend upon his own judgments, or in a case of particular difficulty postpone taking action until he was quite sure of his ground. The situation was so serious that it was Goulburn's private opinion that as a result of the commissioners' inquiry many of the officials would be removed from office.[33]

There were grounds for Goulburn's concern. Theodore Hook, the colonial treasurer, had been removed from office in 1818 because of a deficiency in the chest estimated at more than £12 000.[34] Subsequent inquiry over several years by the commissioners of colonial audit revealed that other civil servants were also implicated. The commissioners of inquiry were delayed at the Cape by pressure of work and did not reach Mauritius until 1st October 1826. As a result Cole was instructed in 1826, in advance of the arrival of the commissioners of inquiry, to undertake what amounted to a purge of the administration. Barry, the chief secretary, George Dick, the auditor general, and Chaillet, the assistant treasurer, were suspended from office. Death saved Andrew Dick, the assistant auditor general, from a similar fate. Bradshaw, who had been a most inefficient registrar of slaves, was transferred to the post of auditor general,[35] but he chose to leave the colony for personal reasons.[36] Later, Madge, the government agent in the Seychelles, was also removed on the recommendation of the commissioners of inquiry for complicity in illegal transactions.[37] Barry and George Dick, however, were able to prove their innocence. Both returned to their post in June 1828,[38] and Dick succeeded Barry as chief secretary when the latter retired in 1831.[39]

Cole had already tackled the problem of retrenchment before the commissioners arrived and in 1823 reported an annual saving of £4 400.[40] There is no evidence to suggest that the civil servants proved other than co-operative.

Among the smallest of Britain's newly conquered territories, Mauritius seemed to include within its compass all the problems which could confront a colonial governor at the time. Its culture was French, and its economy was dislocated by the transfer to British control. Formerly it had been an entrepôt for the French possessions in the Indian ocean, but its cession to Britain had severed its association with them because of the controls placed on foreign trade by the British trade acts.[41] A large labour force of slaves, moreover, increased the racial and social complexity of the population. The compactness and relative isolation of the island emphasised the interdependence of the population and created the mirage rather than the actuality of a close-knit community.

Population statistics were not very reliable and made more difficult to interpret because different commentators used different kinds of classification. There were, for example, three accounts published in the first forty years of British occupation. The first published was M. J. Milbert's *Voyage pittoresque a L'Ile de France* in 1812. This was followed in 1825 by D'Unienville's *Statistique de L'Ile Maurice*. The author wanted a post as government archivist in Mauritius and sent the manuscript to the Colonial Department where it was filed and subsequently tranferred to the Public Record Office in London.[42] It was published in 1838. Although it was revised and brought up to date before publication, the editor was very careless and it is doubtful whether the revised figures are more correct than the original ones.[43] Finally, in 1846, C. Pridham published a work entitled *England's Colonial Empire: An Historical, Political and Statistical Account of the Empire, its Colonies, and Dependencies*. Volume 1 covered Mauritius and its dependencies.

Writing in 1948, Kuczinski attempted a thorough investigation of the available data.[44] He detected that "different figures appear in different documents" and that "none of the figures are all inclusive".[45] Kuczinski divides the population into eight groups but for administrative purposes in Cole's time there were three broad groups: white, free coloured, and slave.

When Cole arrived in Mauritius in 1823 the white population numbered approximately 8 000 of which some 1 300 were troops.[46] The greater proportion of the civilian population was French-speaking: some were immigrants who had been born in France and others were descended from colonists who had settled in Mauritius during the French occupation of the island, 1721-1810. There is no count of the British merchants in the colony but there could not have been more than a handful judging by a petition signed by British merchants in Mauritius in 1826.[47] There were only twenty-five signatories to the document.

About one-third of the whites, including the British officials, lived in Port Louis, the capital. Several French civil administrators who had been kept in their posts, professional men and a considerable group of businessmen made up the majority of the population of the town. The rest of the white population, mainly owners of landed estates, were scattered through the remaining eight cantons into which Mauritius was divided[48] and the island dependencies of the colony.[49] They were chiefly occupied in growing cash crops like cotton, coffee, cloves, ebony and sugar. The white farmers were largely dependent on a population of coloured peoples some of whom were free while others were slaves who worked as labourers on the plantations, as artisans, or domestic servants.

The free coloured people increased steadily during the early years of the British occupation. In 1811 they numbered some 8 000, but by 1823 they were reckoned to number about 14 000. The rise in the number is partly explained by natural increase, partly by the manumission of slaves by purchase, bequest, or marriage, and partly by the number rescued from slavery by the Royal Navy. From 1813 to 1826, 2 986 people were freed from slavery through cases brought before the Vice-Admiralty Court in Mauritius. Of these, only 10 were repatriated, 291 died before they could either be apprenticed to a proprietor or enlisted in the army or navy, and 52 were reported missing. Of the remainder, 224 were taken into the military and naval service, and 2 409 were apprenticed.[50]

Indians first came to Mauritius in the French period. In 1806 there were 6 162 Indian slaves on the island, that is, about 10% of the slave population. Farquhar brought in some Indian convicts in 1815 to rear silkworms. Subsequently Indians were employed building roads, but there was no considerable Indian immigration before 1829.[51]

Statistical returns of the slave population are more difficult to evaluate. Tax evasion, smuggling and administrative inefficiency account for the confusion.[52] In 1823 the returns made by the slave-owners for the purpose of internal revenue gave an estimate of 61 833 slaves, but the number of slaves calculated on the collector's tax rolls in the same year was 64 709.[53] In addition there were 1 466 slaves belonging to the government.[54] No exact count of slaves was available until 1828 when the total figure for Mauritius and the dependencies was given as 76 308.[55]

The place of origin of these slaves is difficult to determine because this was not recorded when they were brought into Mauritius. According to Milbert, in 1806 28% of the slave population was born in Mauritius, 44% in Mozambique, 18% in Madagascar, and 10% in India. Later demographers give the same sources, though in varying percentages. D'Unienville, for example, estimated in 1825 that $33\frac{1}{3}\%$ were born in Mauritius, 45% in Mozambique, 15% in Madagascar, and $6\frac{2}{3}\%$ in India. But, according to Kuczinski, D'Unienville's estimate was wide off the mark because of the slaves registered between 16th October 1826 and 16th January 1827 50% were born in Mauritius, 28% in Mozambique, 18% in Madagascar, and only 4% were Indians (including Malays).[56] Those born in Mauritius could be descended from any one or more of the above-mentioned groups and could even have European blood in them. The diverse culture of the slaves probably explains why no African language persisted in Mauritius. Instead a French patois became the lingua franca.[57]

The community in Mauritius was undoubtedly complex. Although the terms of the capitulation recognized local practice and traditions, once Mauritius had become a permanent acquisition of the British Crown a major problem was to discover ways and means to win the allegiance of the new subjects. Acculturation seems to have been favoured more by administrators on the spot than by officials in the Colonial Department in London. There were practical reasons for this: the administration, for example, was English. But there seems also to have been more than a trace of confidence in the cultural, and not merely the economic and political, superiority of English. In India, for example, the price of pax Britannica was to be mores Britanniae.[58]

A policy which in effect amounted to one of anglicization had to begin with the education of the young: it would have to provide for all sections of the population. Even in England there was no state system of education: the education of the working classes was left to the voluntary action of the churches, and no subsidy was provided until 1833.[59] By most contemporary standards Mauritius was fairly well provided with schools. Cole was particularly interested in education, probably as a means to anglicization.

The school which surpassed all others on the island in influence and status was the Royal College in Port Louis.[60] It had been started by the French Government to provide education for the sons of French colonists. The College drew its pupils not only from Mauritius but also from Bourbon and other neighbouring islands.[61] It was a fee-paying school, and its funds came almost entirely from this source of revenue. Grants of money from the colonial government were rare and given only to meet some extraordinary expenditure as, for example, that occasioned by hurricane damage.[62]

Even before Cole left Great Britain he queried whether or not the College should be placed under an English headmaster, adopt English educational methods, and use the English language as the medium of instruction. But Wilmot, the under-secretary in the Colonial Department, reasoned that while it was desirable to encourage the study of the English language the existing system was adapted to "the religion, wants and usages of the Colony". Any change of policy might involve the colonial government in expense, and possibly prove impolitic. If the school became an English institution the number of pupils would probably decrease because the French population would send their children elsewhere and the colonial government would be obliged to make up any resulting financial loss.[63] In the financial circumstances of the colonial government this was undesirable.

In February 1824, however, the Commission of the Royal College, the governing body, reported to the governor that they had set aside funds to procure from Britain two "professors" of the English language. Cole considered the decision so much in the British interest that he suggested to Bathurst that the government should consider authorizing some small addition to the College funds. He thought that if two or three teachers were engaged at moderate salaries they would easily be able to augment their income through private tuition. He suggested to Bathurst that clergymen of the Established Church would be the best men for the job. Dr. Slater, the Roman Catholic bishop, disagreed with Cole on his choice of type, but Cole was content to leave the decision in the hands of the secretary of state.[64]

Bathurst was not prepared to supplement the funds of the College from the public chest. He contended that the College could only afford one teacher, and that this would be sufficient provided the appointee had an adequate command of Greek. He did not think the salary offered sufficient to attract a university graduate, let alone a clergyman of the Established Church.[65] An English Roman Catholic was appointed to the position.

Though Bathurst was reluctant to spend public money on education, he was obliged to approve support given by Cole to the Royal College after it was severely damaged in a hurricane in February 1824. Cole was so convinced of the importance of the College to Mauritius that he considered that repairs had to be undertaken immediately. Without waiting for instructions from Britain, he asked the officer commanding the Royal Engineers in Mauritius to survey the damaged buildings and advise on repairs.

Reconstruction of the building was estimated at 50 000 Spanish dollars, of which the College could only contribute 6-7 000 Spanish dollars, leaving a residue of about 44 000 Spanish dollars to be paid by the government. Cole was not perturbed by this expense. He explained to Bathurst that in the fifty years of its existence the College had become an institution in the colony and delay or refusal to reconstruct the building would have been a severe blow to all classes of inhabitants.[66] Building operations were expected to take eighteen months, though it was hoped that part of the building would be available before then. Meanwhile inadequate temporary accommodation was provided in a house.[67]

This expense was balanced by reduced expenditure on another front. In 1824 the British Government decided to discontinue a scholarship which each year took to Britain, for higher education, the most oustanding pupil in the final year of study at the Royal College. Cole appealed to Bathurst to reverse his decision and at least permit the colonial government to pay half, or a portion, of the expense of sending young men to Britain for further training. Such a concession, he argued, would not only help the parties immediately concerned, but would benefit the colony as a whole.[68] Bathurst told Cole to put the subject before the commissioners of inquiry. Meanwhile, Cole said, in the absence of financial support, colonists sent their sons to France to be educated instead of Britain and they returned "very anti-English".[69]

The education of the coloured community, both free and slave, also lacked any positive direction by the government though official encouragement was given to those who were prepared to provide it. In 1811 le Brun, a missionary of the London Missionary Society, had opened a school for the education of the poor with Governor Farquhar's approval.[70] By 1822 le Brun was able to report to Society officials in London that there were three schools in Port Louis for the education of poor people: one school in the centre of the town was attended by 112 boys, another on the Chausée was attended by 50 girls, and a third in Malabar town was attended by 30 children whose sex was not specified.[71] The first was visited in 1823 by Telfair, a prominent English slave-owner in the colony. He reported to the headquarters of the London Missionary Society that he was agreeably surprised by the children's progress. Not only were they proficient in reading, writing and accounts, but also in French and English grammar, composition and translation of both languages. Scholars capable of learning trades were bound as apprentices and attended the school for half the day only, but at that age they were usually "very far advanced in general, being able to read well and write legibly in both languages". Telfair thought that the school was "admirably conducted" and complimented le Brun's assistant, "a man of color, that appears to be perfectly master of his business, and most assiduous in attending to it". Indeed he thought the school did more "for extending the use of the English language in this island than any institution he knew of".[72]

The colonial government also sponsored a free school in Port Louis for boys and girls under the direction of the senior civil chaplain in Mauritius, the Rev. and Hon. Edward Finch. This school opened in January 1823 shortly before Cole's arrival. It was accommodated in a small badly ventilated house. During the summer months the boys were not allowed to attend classes regularly to avoid over-crowding. The girls suffered too: even during the cooler months they found their schoolroom so confined that the women teachers were unable to attend their classes regularly. Yet the school survived the handicap and seemed to thrive.

In August 1825 Finch reported to Cole that there were 129 boys registered as pupils. He did not record the number of girls who attended the school, but stated that in the last two years 141 boys and 117 girls had left the school to get jobs. Among the 117 girls were 35 who had reached the highest class. As larger premises had become available Finch sought permission of the governor to incur further expense of 30 Spanish dollars a month for rent making a total of 80 Spanish dollars a month. The alternative was to restrict the educational facilities for the poor.

Finch urged that the larger premises should also be used to give some instruction to slave children. Cole himself was disturbed that there was no fixed place where slaves could be regularly assembled for religious instruction. He had encouraged Finch to develop a school for slave children at the governor's country estate, Réduit. It met with considerable success. Finch thought that many slave-owners would follow the governor's example if facilities were provided.[73] Cole approved the grant of a small sum of money for this purpose subject to the confirmation of the secretary of state.[74] Bathurst agreed and expressed general satisfaction on behalf of the British Government with the benefits expected to accrue from the schools.[75] The authorities were optimistic, but the French slave-owners opposed all attempts to instruct slaves whether by catholics or protestants. Le Brun told one official of the London Missionary Society that parents of coloured children kept their children away from school because "the French inhabitants tell them that it is to make soldiers and sailors of their children".[76] It was unlikely, therefore, that the French slave-owners would encourage the slaves to send their children to school.

The proportion of free coloured children who received any education was very small. A report found among the papers of the London Missionary Society indicates that for a population of nearly 100 000 there were but four free protestant schools which together provided education for 300 pupils most of whom were free people of colour.[77] Apparently the Roman Catholics did not run any free schools. Education in the country districts was especially neglected. Six districts with a total population of 60 000 had no school at all.[78] But even where there were schools in the country districts they did not have many pupils. A school opened at Rivière du Rempart in 1825, for example, was attended by only 22 pupils although there were enough places for 60 to 80 children.[79]

If it be accepted as axiomatic that there is a relationship between school attendance and anglicization in Mauritius, then the examination of the school structure suggests that so few went to school that anglicization through education was so small as to be insignificant. This was serious. Though some of the French officials and some of the English were bilingual, the degree of rapprochement between the old and the new would depend to a great extent on the language question. In both Mauritius and the Cape a substantial number of administrative officials appointed respectively by the French and Dutch Governments had continued to serve the British. Clearly in time these men had to be replaced. In India, Munro and Elphinston had shown the value of increased participation of Indians in the more junior ranks of the administration.[80] A locally recruited civil service was necessary.

As government, especially in a small community, extended its range of bureaucratic supervision, points of possible friction would tend to multiply. Non co-operation based on a claim of ignorance or misunderstanding is the oldest of all forms of passive resistance. In Mauritius the Conseil de Commune established by Farquhar in 1816 and representative of the white élite had had to be abolished in 1818 because of the vigour of its opposition to the colonial government.[81] During the period of Cole's governorship, though the pace of change was slow, there were changes which heightened the awareness of difficulty both for the governor and those he governed.

The conciliar pattern of government was not a novelty in the nineteenth century. When the government of India was re-shaped (1784-6)[82] authority on the spot was placed in the hands of a governor-general and a council of three. Cornwallis, however, only agreed to become governor-general if he was empowered to override the majority of his council in special cases and also to hold the office of commander-in-chief in emergencies.[83] Parliament accepted the condition and an act was passed to give it effect.[84] This constitutional arrangement strengthened the governor-general by spreading responsibility, yet left him power and initiative to act in a crisis.

The principle of combining shared responsibility while retaining strong gubernatorial power was obviously convenient to apply in colonies of conquest. It was, for example, introduced in Ceylon in 1801[85] and at Mauritius and the Cape in 1825.[86] In the two latter instances, additional instructions to introduce a council were forwarded to the respective governors under cover of a despatch from the secretary of state on the same day – the 9th February 1825.[87] Both councils were similar in composition, as indeed were the powers granted to them.

Cole's military training had accustomed him to unrestricted use of his authority. Thus he was at first perturbed[88] when unexpectedly he received the additional instructions from the Crown creating a council of senior officials to advise him in the government of the colony.

The governor himself was appointed president of the council, and the other members in order of precedence were the chief justice, the chief secretary to the government, the officer next in command of the forces to the governor, and A. W. Blane, the collector of customs who was specially named in the instruction.[89] Cole had to assemble these officials, administer the oath of allegiance to them, and communicate his additional instructions to them and all other such instructions as he might from time to time find convenient to impart to them for the good of the King's service. Meetings of the council had to be fully minuted by a clerk whom the governor was empowered to appoint. Copies of these minutes had to be forwarded to the Crown every six months through the secretary of state.

The governor's authority although modified by the creation of a council nevertheless remained very considerable. He alone or, in his absence, the officer administering the government could summon the council and initiate discussion. But he had to consult and take the advice of the Council "in all things" and he was restrained from exercising the powers and authority of his commission other than with the concurrence and advice of the Council except in matters of urgency. In the latter case, he had to submit to them the action he had taken for their revision or sanction. In a covering despatch Bathurst explained to Cole that it was not intended to impose on him the need to resort to the Council for advice on all the less important details of public business. It was in the governor's discretion to apply the general rules of the instructions in particular cases as they arose.[90] Moreover, the governor was not bound by the advice of the Council. He could act in opposition to it provided he made a full and satisfactory explanation to the Crown. Council members, however, could record their opinion in the minutes. If a member desired to bring a subject before the Council, he could submit his proposal in writing to the governor who was not thereby bound formally to bring it before the Council. But the member concerned could have his letter and the governor's reply recorded in the minutes.

The governor had to preside over all council meetings except in special circumstances such as his illness or unavoidable absence when the most senior member of the Council present took the chair. A quorum was fixed at two members in addition to the presiding officer but if, on the occasions when only the bare minimum attended the meeting, there was a difference of opinion the question in dispute had to be adjourned to another meeting attended by a greater number of members. If there were not enough available councillors to form a quorum the governor was authorized as an emergency measure to appoint a maximum of four "fit and proper persons" members. When a vacancy occurred in the normal course of events the governor had to notify the Crown immediately giving the reason for it and submit the name of a successor for the King's confirmation or disallowance. Until this was known, the person whom the governor appointed was entitled to all the powers and privileges of a councillor.

The governor could suspend members from sitting, voting, or assisting in the work of the Council provided he recorded in the minutes his reasons for doing so and the reply of the member suspended. If the governor felt it necessary to suspend a member and withhold from the Council the reasons for this action, then he was required to make an immediate and adequate explanation to the Crown: but Bathurst advised Cole to abstain from the exercise of this power if it was possible.[91]

Cole did not think that the time chosen to introduce a council in Mauritius was politic.[92] He said he had no personal objection to consultation with the Council, because hitherto before taking action he had always sought the opinions of those best qualified to give them. But, he pointed out to Wilmot Horton with some perspicacity, whilst it is a compliment to ask a person his opinion other feelings may sometimes be excited when advice is given as a matter of right. One further interesting point he raised was whether or not debates in council were to be kept secret and confidential. No reply to this pertinent question was given. In the case of the Cape the public were not admitted to what was really an executive committee meeting,[93] nor were they admitted in Mauritius while Cole was governor.

The Council met for the first time on the 17th August, 1825.[94] There were, however, no regularly appointed meetings. The most junior member of the Council, A. W. Blane, then the collector of customs, decided in March 1826 to challenge Cole's position. Blane argued that the additional instructions required the governor to consult the Council on all matters relating to his executive powers except in emergencies. With two minor exceptions,[95] the governor had only called the Council when some legislative enactment was required. Blane thought that his duty as a council member was an uninterrupted participation in the administration. He argued that if he were only summoned in isolated cases to vote upon the expediency of a particular ordinance already drawn up, without any previous knowledge of the matter out of which it might have arisen, he would be imperfectly qualified to give an opinion without asking for information. This might create delay, or even suggest opposition, or an indelicate scrutiny into acts previously done under the governor's immediate authority and direction when no such motive was intended. Blane therefore asked the governor to allow the Council to discuss the point he raised, or record his letter and the governor's reply in the minutes.[96] Cole chose the latter alternative.

In his reply to Blane, Cole observed that Bathurst's despatch of 9th February 1825 had clearly interpreted the instructions so as to reserve the governor's initiative in routine matters as well as in emergencies.[97] This meant logically that the Council met ad hoc when there was important business to discuss. Blane, however, regarded the governor as having a duty to arrange regular meetings of the Council which, he considered, had a quasi-constitutional right to be summoned.[98]

Although the additional instructions to the governors of Mauritius and the Cape and the covering despatches from the secretary of state were almost identical, the procedure at the Cape seems to support Blane's theory as to the intention. This council met regularly twice a month and did discuss administrative minutiae. But the position at the Cape was different from that in Mauritius when the Council was inaugurated there in that the commissioners of inquiry were on the spot and active discontent at the Cape was among the reasons for its creation.[99]

In Mauritius, Cole was not content merely to leave the constitutional issue raised by Blane recorded in the minutes of the Council. He promptly sent the full correspondence to the secretary of state. In a covering despatch he told him that Barry, the chief secretary to government, shared Blane's views and impressions. Cole said he had worked well with Barry and Blane and the other heads of department until the formation of the Council. It was only after the Council was created that he had reason to suppose they were not satisfied with his decisions and procedures.[100]

Cole was clearly distressed by criticism though his letter to Wilmot Horton in August 1825[101] had anticipated the situation. He was suspicious of Blane's motives and sceptical about his arguments. He insisted that as governor he had followed the letter of Bathurst's despatch in the matter of ordinances. If, however, Bathurst ruled that Cole had erred and that the British Government intended that the general administration and public business of the colony should be conducted in the Council, then that raised other issues. The members of council were heads of departments each with important responsibilities. It followed, he argued, that if the chief administrative officials were also required to attend councils, and councils were to meet frequently and regularly, then the day to day business of their respective departments would suffer.[102]

Cole had put his finger on an interesting point. Whereas in Britain at the time a clear line was drawn between the minister holding executive office from the Crown on the one hand, and the non-political administration on the other, this distinction was elided in the advisory council pattern. The closest analogy to an advisory council in British constitutional practice would have been the Privy Council of the Crown in the early Tudor period. Cole seems in fact to have been arguing from his rather limited political experience as a member of parliament. He pointed out quite shrewdly that regular meetings of the Council might lead to the introduction of a party feeling not only in the Council, but in the colony generally.[103]

By "party feeling" Cole probably meant in the first place, the expression of anti-British feeling in Mauritius, understandably present since 1810, though dormant since the dissolution of the Conseil de Commune in 1818. In the second place, like many of his contemporaries in Britain, he probably tended to equate party with faction and even disloyalty. Though his idea that party meant faction was fast becoming obsolete in Britain,[104] he had grounds for concern about possible disloyalty. In addition to the record of the Conseil de Commune, Cole was very well aware that measures dealing with trade and the whole question of amelioration of the conditions of slaves had already begun to challenge traditional outlook and vested interests by 1826.

Bathurst's reply endorsed not the view of Blane, but that of Cole. He regretted that the Council had not been the help to the governor that had been anticipated. It was created, he wrote, to relieve the governor of some responsibility. Its sole purpose was to assist him with advice. Blane's interpretation of the instructions, he said, would take the executive government out of the governor's hands and virtually vest it in the Council. "It must be superfluous to acquaint you", wrote Bathurst, "that such never could be the meaning, or intent of His Majesty's Instructions". He admitted that it was difficult to decide exactly what should be put before the Council, but recommended that "all questions presenting any real difficulty in their solution or involving any of the prominent interests of the colony, together with all acts of Government or Ordinances, should be so submitted". Bathurst reaffirmed the governor's right to use his discretion though he reminded Cole that if he by-passed the Council he incurred the risk of sole responsibility for any decision. The duty of councillors was to give their advice to the governor when they were summoned to the Council. They had a right to exercise the duties of their office until formally excluded from that body. But, Bathurst stated emphatically, no member of the Council had any right to call the governor to account for the way in which he exercised his discretion to assemble the Council.[105]

Bathurst's despatch was followed by additional instructions from the Crown which set the matter at rest. They stated,

> "That nothing in the . . . Additional Instructions of the 9th February, 1825, . . . shall prevent your exercising the several powers and authorities granted and committed to you by your Commission and General Instructions . . . or any of

such powers and authorities without the advice and concurrence of Our said Council in any case, or upon any occasion, which may appear to you not to be sufficiently important to require their assistance, or which may be of such a nature that in your Judgment Our Service would sustain material prejudice by consulting Our Said Council thereupon."[106]

Bathurst's reply to Cole is of considerable interest. If the position in Mauritius be considered in isolation, then Bathurst's clear approval of the stand taken by Cole is easy to explain. He had always respected Cole and trusted his judgment. Yet, while Bathurst clearly endorsed Cole's autocratic interpretation of his position vis à vis the Council in Mauritius, he tacitly approved the very different practices which were developing at the Cape. Although Bathurst publicly supported the Cape governor, Lord Charles Somerset, the outcry against Somerset's government both in Britain and at the Cape[107] must have given him moments of doubt. Moreover, Bourke who acted as governor from March 1826 until Cole's arrival at the Cape in September 1828 would necessarily have depended more upon the Council because of the temporary nature of his appointment. Thus the Council at the Cape developed into a more powerful body and exerted a stronger influence on the government of that colony[108] than did the corresponding body in Mauritius. It is possible that Barry, Blane and other members of the Council in Mauritius were aware of developments in the neighbouring colony, though the writer has seen no evidence to this effect. The different lines of development within the framework of similar constitutions seems to support the view that British policy at this point and under Bathurst's direction was pragmatic, not systematic, in the field of political experiment.[109]

Cole was gratified by Bathurst's support. He hoped that he would not have to refer the question of the Council to the secretary of state again. He admitted to Bathurst that the problem had worried him because he thought Bathurst might get the impression that he was indisposed to consult the Council. He confessed that whilst he would have been better pleased if the Council had never been established, it was his duty to act according to his instructions. Ruminating on his acts since the Council was formed, he remarked that he was unaware of any action he had taken independently of it where it might have been advisable for him first to have taken its advice. He assured Bathurst that for some time "everything had gone smoothly" and he hoped this would continue to be the case.[110] Certainly no member of the Council ever questioned Cole's authority again. Furthermore, it is probable that he appreciated the shield provided by the Council as, for example, in negotiations between the colonial government and Roman Catholic bishop. There was obviously a clash of personalities between the governor and the bishop with the result that contact between the two broke down over trivialities.[111] Cole was content on these occasions to leave the matter in the hands of the Council. He always withdrew from discussions about these negotiations and the chief justice presided.

Blane meanwhile was appointed to act as chief secretary because of the suspension of Barry.[112] Duties of office brought him into daily contact with the governor. Cole appreciated Blane's ability as a public officer and, though he admitted he was "not quite as cordial" in his manner towards him as formerly, he felt Blane had "no reason to complain of any want of attention to his opinion".[113] Whilst Cole obviously nursed a private grievance, his official attitude was one of forget and forgive. The public service was more important to Cole than personalities.

The governorship of Mauritius was clearly no sinecure. The problems of supervising the transition of sovereignty from one country to another necessitated change and were bound to arouse the hostility of formerly alien colonists, especially those with vested interests in the status quo. In Mauritius, the governor's position was made even more difficult because the integrity of some of the civil servants was suspect. Moreover, the British Government failed to take full advantage of the schools to anglicize the youth of the colony. Nevertheless the governor was in a strong position. He was given considerable power and the erection of a council, so far from detracting from his authority, assisted and advised him in its exercise. Although Cole himself did not like the Council, it was better that problems of the colony should be considered by several minds rather than only one. This was particularly important in view of the changes required by the British Government in the regulation of the trade of the Empire and the policy to ameliorate the condition of the slaves. Ultimately, however, the successful introduction of these changes and policy depended largely on the personality of the governor.

FOOTNOTES

1. Mauritius was named in honour of Prince Maurice of Nassau in 1638 when it was first occupied by the Dutch. It was renamed Ile de France by the French after their occupation of the island in 1721. The British restored the original name after the conquest in 1810.
2. Traditionally the name was given to the Cape by King John II of Portugal when he learned that Diaz had rounded the most southerly point of Africa in his quest for a sea-route to India, 1487. Walker, p. 14, suggests that it may have been Diaz himself who thus named the Cape.
3. The name Batavian Republic was the name by which the Netherlands was known from 1795 to 1806.
4. H. L. Hoskins, *British Routes to India*, pp. 84–85.
5. *C.H.B.E.*, Vol. II, pp. 110 and 565–566.
6. Sir John Abercromby (1772–1817) was commander-in-chief at Bombay from 1809 till 1812.
7. C.O. 167/4, Articles of capitulation, 3 December 1810. R. R. Kuczinski, *Demographic Survey of the British Colonial Empire*, Vol. II, p. 761, quotes a figure of 7 194 for the white civilian population of Mauritius in 1808, and, p. 762, a figure of 6 864 in 1811. This suggests that approximately 250 left the colony. B. Benedict, *Mauritius, the Problems of a Plural Society*, p. 13, says that several French settlers returned to France in the early years of British rule, but their place was taken by refugees from post-Napoleonic France.
8. D. K. Fieldhouse, *The Colonial Empires*, p. 77.
9. Robert Townshend Farquhar (1776–1830) was appointed commercial resident at Amboyna in 1797, and was subsequently named lieutenant-governor of Pulo Penang. At the Peace of Amiens in 1802 he was appointed commissioner for adjusting the British claims in the Moluccas, and for the transfer of those islands to the Batavian Republic. See *D.N.B.*, Vol. XVIII.
10. C.O. 168/1, Abercromby to Liverpool, 7 December 1810, and Farquhar to Liverpool, 17 December 1810.
11. C.O. 167/5, Abercromby to Liverpool, 1 January 1811.
12. *C.H.B.E.*, Vol. II, pp. 76–7. See also *Cambridge History of India*, Vol. V, p. 403.
13. C.O. 167/4, Liverpool to the Officer Commanding His Majesty's Land Forces in the Isles of Mauritius and Bourbon, November 1810.
14. Sir Henry Warde (1766–1834) served under Abercromby at the capture of Mauritius. From 1821 to 1827 he was governor of Barbados. See *D.N.B.*, Vol. LIX.
15. *London Gazette*, 1811, p. 381.
16. C.O. 167/7, Warde to Liverpool, 15 July 1811, and enclosures.
17. C.O. 168/2 for the copy of the documents kept by the Colonial Department.

18. *B.F.S.P.*, 1812–14, Vol. I, Part 1. Definitive Treaty of Peace and Amity between His Britannic Majesty and His Most Christian Majesty – signed at Paris, 30 May 1814. Article VIII.
19. J. C. Beaglehole, "The royal instructions to colonial governors, 1783–1854: a study in British colonial policy" – a summary of a Ph.D. thesis, *Bulletin of the Institute of Historical Research*, Vol. VII, number 21, February 1930.
20. See *Cambridge Modern History*, Vol. IX, (1st edition), Chapter VI by H. A. L. Fisher.
21. C. O. 168/1, Farquhar to Liverpool, 15 February 1811.
22. 26 Geo. III, c. 60.
23. 23 Geo. III, c. 39.
24. C.O. 168/2, Trade instructions to Farquhar, 10 April 1811.
25. C.O. 168/6, Bathurst to Farquhar, 30 October 1822.
26. See pp. 39–40.
27. C.O. 167/67, Cole to Bathurst, 28 June 1823.
28. C. Pridham, *England's Colonial Empire:* Vol. I, Mauritius and its Dependencies, p. 391.
29. 19 November 1817 to 5 July 1820.
30. C.O. 168/6, Bathurst to Farquhar, 14 March 1822; and Bathurst to Cole, 24 March 1823.
31. C.O. 168/6, Bathurst to Cole, 24 March 1823.
32. He held the office from 5 August 1812 to 11 December 1821.
33. P.R.O. 30/43/95, Goulburn to Lady Grantham, 19 March 1823.
34. C.O. 167/80, Treasury Minute.
35. C.O. 168/8, Bathurst to Cole, 18 January 1826.
36. C.O. 167/104, Bradshaw to secretary of state, February 1828, and 14 June 1828.
37. See Chapter IV, p. 70.
38. C.O. 167/104, Barry to Hay, 26 February 1828.
39. *Dictionary of Mauritian Biography.*
40. C.O. 167/67, Cole to Bathurst, 28 June 1823.
41. See Chapter III.
42. C.O. 172, Vols. 39 to 42 inclusive.
43. Kuczinski, Vol. II, 759.
44. *Ibid.*
45. *Ibid.* p. 762.
46. Kuczinski, Vol. II, pp. 764–765. Official returns estimate 1 381 troops (including the Colonial Corps); Major Tulloch, *Statistical Reports on the Sickness, Mortality and Invaliding among the troops in Western Africa etc.* (1840) pp. 27c–29c estimates 1 243; other figures suggest 1 212.
47. C.O. 167/86, Enclosed in Cole to Bathurst, 10 December 1826. The petition begged the governor to persuade, the chief justice to open the Vice-Admiralty Court to them. The petitioners claimed that they suffered many inconveniences because they had no recourse to an English court to seek justice and the enforcement of contracts relating to English mercantile affairs.
48. Pamplemousse, Rivière du Rempart, Flacq, Grand Port, Savanne, Rivière Noir, Plaines Wilhems, and Moka.
49. Mainly in the Seychelles and Rodrigues.
50. Kuczinski, Vol. II, p. 766.
51. B. Benedict, *Indians in a Plural Society*, p. 17.
52. D'Unienville, *Statistique de l'Ile Maurice*, p. 25 says, "It has been realised that several causes, particularly the carelessness of a number of owners and the desire to escape taxes and the provision of labour have at all times led to many inaccuracies in the slave censuses, particularly since 1790. The omissions were estimated at one-quarter by several administrators, but this was an exaggeration." Revenue was raised in Mauritius by a capitation tax on slaves, and a corvée was imposed when labour was required for public works.
53. Kuczinski, Vol. II, p. 768, Table II.
54. *Ibid.*, p. 766.
55. See Chapter IV, p. 69.
56. Kuczinski, Vol. II, p. 764.

57. Benedict, p. 17.
58. A minute on education by T. B. Macaulay, 2 February 1835, persuaded the British government in India to make English the chief medium of instruction and western science and literature the chief subject of study in the State system of education in India. For extracts from the minute, see R. Muir, *The Making of British India 1756–1858*, pp. 298–301.
59. L. Woodward, *The Age of Reform 1815–1870*, (2nd edition), p. 478.
60. Sometimes called the Colonial College.
61. C.O. 167/67, Cole to Wilmot, 20 February 1823.
62. See pp. 37 and 52.
63. C.O. 167/67, Wilmot to Cole, 20 February 1823.
64. C.O. 167/72, Cole to Bathurst, 9 February 1824.
65. C.O. 168/8, Bathurst to Cole, 14 July 1825.
66. In the 1850's it was described as the only place in the colony where whites and coloureds could meet on an equal footing. See B. Benedict, *Mauritius, the Problems of a Plural Society*, p. 14. It would seem that when Cole was governor it was open to all.
67. C.O. 167/73, Cole to Bathurst, 14 August 1824.
68. C.O. 167/83, Cole to Bathurst, 2 June 1826.
69. P.R.O. 30/43/87, Cole to Smith, 12 March 1827.
70. L.M.S. Papers, Mauritius; Box 1, Folder 1, Jacket A, Farquhar to Rev. G. Burder, 20 June 1814.
71. L.M.S. Papers, Mauritius; Box 1, Folder 2, Jacket B, le Brun to Burder, 7 January 1822.
72. L.M.S. Papers, Mauritius; Box 1, Folder 2, Jacket C, C. Telfair to "My dear Sir".
73. C.O. 167/78, Finch to Barry, 15 August 1825, enclosed in Cole to Bathurst, 30 August 1825.
74. C.O. 167/78, Cole to Bathurst, 30 August 1825.
75. C.O. 168/8, Bathurst to Cole, 25 December 1825.
76. L.M.S. Papers, Mauritius; Box 1, Folder 3, Jacket B, le Brun to Burder, 28 November 1826.
77. L.M.S. Papers, Mauritius; Box 1, Folder 4, Jacket C, undated and unsigned memorandum entitled "Suggestion for Establishing a permanent system of moral and religious instruction among the free and apprentice population of Mauritius". Date thought by the author to be *circa* 1835.
78. *Ibid.*
79. L.M.S. Papers, Mauritius; Box 1, Folder 3, Jacket B, le Brun to Cole, 20 September 1826.
80. G. D. Bearce, *British Attitudes towards India 1784–1858*, pp. 135–139.
81. See P. J. Barnwell and A. Toussaint, *A Short History of Mauritius*, pp. 130–131, and A. G. Field, *The expedition to Mauritius in 1810 and the establishment of British control*, unpublished M.A. thesis of the University of London, pp. 110–112.
82. *Cambridge History of India*, Vol. V, pp. 200–204.
83. *Ibid.*, p. 203.
84. 26 Geo. III, c. 16. Articles 7 and 8.
85. *C.H.B.E.*, Vol. II, p. 169.
86. A similar constitutional arrangement was made for New South Wales by act of parliament in 1823, (4 Geo. IV, c. 96. Article 24). However, in this case the governor had to have the support of at least one member of the council to legislate in opposition to the majority of the council. See A .C. V. Melbourne, *Early Constitutional Development in Australia; New South Wales, 1788–1856*, Part I, Chapter XI.
87. See C.O. 168/8, Additional instructions to Cole, 9 February 1825, enclosed in Bathurst to Cole, 9 February 1825; and C.O. 49/16, Additional instructions to Lord Charles Somerset, 9 February 1825, enclosed in Bathurst to Somerset, 9 February 1825. The latter document is printed in Theal, *R.C.C.*, Vol. XX, pp. 7–11, and V. Harlow and A. Madden, *British Constitutional Developments 1774–1834*, pp. 111–114.
88. C.O. 167/78, Cole to Wilmot Horton, 19 August 1825.
89. It would seem that he was the next most senior official on the island after those who were appointed in terms of their office.
90. C.O. 168/8, Bathurst to Cole, 9 February 1825.
91. *Ibid.*
92. C.O. 167/82, Cole to Bathurst, 23 March 1826.

93. A. K. Fryer, "The Government of the Cape of Good Hope, 1825–54; The Age of Imperial Reform", *Archives Year Book for South African History*, Vol. I, 1964, p. 26.
94. C.O. 167/78, Cole to Wilmot Horton, 19 August 1825.
95. Negotiations between the colonial government and the bank over the use of Bengal gold mohurs, and matters concerning the construction of an aquaduct called the Bathurst Canal.
96. C.O. 167/82, Blane to Cole, 18 March 1826, enclosed in Cole to Bathurst, 23 March 1826.
97. C.O. 167/82, Cole to Blane, 19 March 1826, enclosed in Cole to Bathurst, 23 March 1826.
98. C.O. 167/82, Blane to Cole, 23 March 1826, enclosed in Cole to Bathurst, 23 March 1826.
99. See Chapter V, pp 84–85. The position at the Cape will be compared with that in Mauritius later in this chapter.
100. C.O. 167/82, Cole to Bathurst, 23 March 1826.
101. C.O. 167/78, Cole to Wilmot Horton, 19 August 1826.
102. C.O. 167/82, Cole to Bathurst, 23 March 1826.
103. *Ibid.*
104. See A. S. Foord. *His Majesty's Opposition 1714–1830* especially pp. 1–29 and 439–445. The term *His Majesty's Opposition* was used for the first time in a debate on the Civil List Act in 1826.
105. C.O. 168/11, Bathurst to Cole, 11 August 1826.
106. C.O. 168/11, Additional instructions to Cole, 15 August 1826, enclosed in Bathurst to Cole, 15 August 1826.
107. See Walker, pp. 160–162. See also M. Roberts, "Lord Charles Somerset and the 'Beaufort Influence'", *Archives Year Book for South African History*, 1951, Vol. II, pp. 3–34.
108. See Chapter IX.
109. For example, see Beaglehole, pp. 184–187.
110. C.O. 167/91, Cole to Bathurst, 3 February 1827.
111. C.O. 167/88 is solely concerned with the bishop's controversy with Cole. The dispute feature among the despatches too.
112. See p. 34.
113. C.O. 167/91, Cole to Bathurst, 3 February 1827.

CHAPTER III

THE CHANGING PATTERN OF TRADE IN MAURITIUS

The peace settlements of 1814–15 provided a solid foundation for orderly international relations that enabled Britain to develop her economic and commercial potentialities. It was possible within a decade of peace for Britain to resume the process of sloughing off the protective and monopolistic legislation framed in different circumstances by statesmen in the seventeenth century. A new generation of merchants was impatient of artificial restraints, and sought, through Parliament, to promote economic development at home and abroad by a moderation of trade regulations and tariffs and the abolition of restrictions on the export of capital and machinery.[1] Leading statesmen slowly came round to this point of view. As early as 1812 Lord Liverpool had noted that "the less commerce and manufacturers were meddled with, the more they were likely to prosper".[2] Seen from the advantage of hindsight, the revision of the East India Company's Charter in 1813 marks a positive step in the decline of protectionist economics, but in 1815 trade was still regulated by a network of 2 000 acts of parliament of which 1 500 were effective.[3] The task of revision would clearly be formidable.

In 1820, a Select Committee of the House of Commons declared that the statutes regulating trade cramped the operations of wealth through foreign trade. It was appreciated that the immediate destruction of the "intricate mosaic structure"[4] of trade acts would lead to serious administrative, economic, and fiscal consequences. The Committee made no proposals to resolve problems which would be created by a change of policy, or state clear principles to guide the future. It was content merely to indicate the necessity for change in vague terms and advocated "a gradual and prospective approximation to a sounder system as the standard of all future commercial regulations, no less with a view to the interests of this country than to the situation of surrounding nations".[5]

The task of revision began under Frederick Robinson,[6] Thomas Wallace,[7] and William Huskisson.[8] The first move was taken in 1822. In that year preferential duties on timber from Canada were reduced. This was followed by five acts[9] which repealed 300 obsolete statutes dating from the reign of Edward III to 1660, repealed some and consolidated others passed in the reign of Charles II, and substituted other regulations to encourage navigation and commerce through the regulation of imports. The carrying trade from continental to British ports was partially opened to foreign ships. British vessels were allowed to load Asian, African, and American produce in the ports of any European country for trans-shipment to Britain provided the goods were for re-export. Direct trade was legalized with Spanish colonies as well as with independent territories previously part of the Spanish Empire. Other legislation removed restrictions on trade between the British West Indian colonies and the United States.Direct trade between British colonies and certain ports in Europe was permitted, provided the articles traded were carried in British ships.

After Huskisson became president of the Board of Trade in 1823 the modifications and relaxations were extended. In Huskisson's view the reduction of restrictions was not only good in itself, but would also go far to produce goodwill and fair treatment abroad.[10] He did not have a free hand because the abandonment of income tax in 1816 made the pressure on tariff revenue even greater, so that even as late as 1840 taxes on imports still comprised some 46% of the revenue. Moreover, tariff reductions were resisted by vested interests, both agriculturalists and industrialists among them.[11] However, an examination of the measures for which Huskisson was responsible indicates the degree to which the British Government were prepared to set aside out-moded ideas and re-cast British economic policy to meet the challenges of changed circumstances.

A new Warehousing Act[12] aimed at developing Britain as an entrepôt for world trade: foreigners were entitled to deposit goods in British warehouses for re-export free of duty. But, more important, Huskisson's reciprocity acts[13] gave the British Government power to offer either by treaty or Order in Council equal treatment for all goods brought in or taken out legally in foreign ships, provided the foreign country concerned levied no discriminating duties on British ships, or on the goods imported in them. Prussia, Denmark, Sweden, the Hansa towns, Mecklenburgh, Hanover, the United States, France, Austria, and nearly all the South American Republics struck some bargain with Britain in terms of the acts. Not all the states were prepared to offer equality, but the measure of their concession was equated, and more, by Britain.[14]

New ideas were cautiously applied. The Navigation Act of 1825[15] loosened up the former structure, but did not destroy it .It took into account not merely the interests of Britain, but also the interests of individual colonies and the charter rights of the East India Company. British ships continued to have the sole right to carry British internal trade and British inter-colonial trade. Restrictions were maintained on the import of several articles of European produce[16] unless they were carried in British ships or the ships of the country from which the goods were imported. Likewise commodities imported from Asia, Africa or America for consumption in Britain were discriminated against unless carried either in British ships or the ships of the country of origin. A complementary act for the registration of British vessels[17] defined the term *British* ship even more closely than seventeenth century legislation had done. Either it had to be built in Britain or the Empire, or condemned in the Court of Admiralty as a prize of war, or acquired by forfeiture for breach of the laws made to prevent the slave trade. Moreover, it had to be legally owned by a British subject or subjects, and the master of the ship and three-quarters of the crew had to be British subjects.

The Colonial Trade Act of 1825[18] reflected the same policy: new ideas were incorporated without entirely breaking with past practice. A "Table of Prohibitions and Restrictions" either excluded or elaborately regulated the importation of several enumerated articles into the British possessions in America or Mauritius. For example, beef and pork could be imported into Newfoundland from a foreign country but not into the other colonies in America or in Mauritius. Coffee, coconuts, sugar, molasses and rum if produced in non-British territories or, with the exception of Mauritius, within the charter area of the East India Company,[19] were excluded from British possessions in South America and the West Indies except the Bermuda and Bahama Islands. Minimum duties were prescribed for the import of several articles of foreign production. The revenue derived therefrom was credited to the account of the colony where it was collected. Meanwhile this act gave an impetus to trade through the extension of the principle of free ports. Port Louis was not proclaimed a free port in the act but it seems that so far as Mauritius was concerned the intention was not so much to limit its imports as to encourage the export of its own produce and partially to extricate it from its accidental entanglement with the East India Company.

The first free port act had been passed in 1766. Armytage[20] has shown that the intention of that act was not only to establish new channels of trade, but also to revive a trade which had formerly existed with the Spanish Indies. In the post-Napoleonic era when the former Spanish American colonies had established their independence the free ports of the West Indies declined because of the creation of a direct link between Britain and the Latin American states. It would seem, though, that the extension of the principle of free ports by Huskisson to areas outside the West Indies, and the power given by Parliament to the King in Council to proclaim free ports as and when it saw fit, was the means to an extension of freer trade by an old device applied in new zones. It was the key to the translation into practical economics of Huskisson's conviction that the commercial interests of every country were "most effectually consulted by leaving (sic) to every part of the world to raise those productions for which soil and climate are best adapted".[21]

In Britain the reforms associated with the name of Huskisson reflected a gradual reconstruction tempered by tradition. In Mauritius, however, they created something like a commercial revolution albeit complicated by administrative difficulties. After the suspension of the privileges of the French East India Company in 1769, Mauritius had become an entrepôt for French trade in the east.[22] In 1787, one year after the Eden treaty had revised the pattern of Anglo-French trade,[23] Mauritius, then a French colony, had been given free trade. The outbreak of war between France and England in 1793 had repercussions in India and the Indian Ocean and it was only after the cession of Mauritius to Britain by the Treaty of Paris, 30th May, 1814, that new norms could be established. Five months later, on the 31st October 1814, Farquhar issued a proclamation which showed his intention to bolster the position of Mauritius as an entrepôt. With the exception of enumerated items which remained excluded, only a nominal duty ($1\frac{1}{2}\%$) was levied on imports into Port Louis provided they were to be re-exported within eighteen months and carried in any vessel regularly cleared from any port covered by the East India Company's Charter. Such goods were placed in bond and a minimum surety of 5 000 Sicca Rupees required as security against illegal resale in Mauritius. Exception was made for coffee, cotton, cocoa and cloves produced in the dependencies on production of evidence that export duty had been paid at the port of exit. Goods imported for consumption in Mauritius and its dependencies had to pay a duty of 6% if brought in a British vessel, or 8% if brought in a foreign one.

Although the external trade of Mauritius was subsequently regulated by British Orders in Council[24] they did not negate the terms of Farquhar's proclamation. Indeed to prevent any misconception on this score, Farquhar issued a declaratory proclamation to this effect when he published an Order in Council of the 12th July 1820.[25] This Order in Council, which was in operation when Cole arrived in Mauritius, though purely local in its application, anticipated in some ways the later reciprocity treaties. British vessels were authorised to bring to Mauritius or its dependencies, cargoes of goods grown, produced, or made in any country in amity with Great Britain except articles made of cotton, iron, steel or wool. The only duty payable was that levied by the colonial government. These vessels could then load a cargo of Mauritian produce, or a cargo of goods legally imported into the colony, for the return voyage. Foreign goods could be imported into Mauritius on the same terms as British goods provided they were carried in the ships of the country of origin and that country admitted British vessels to their carrying trade on equal terms. If, however, a foreign state charged a higher export duty when the goods were carried in a British vessel, then a countervailling duty of equal amount was charged on goods off-loaded from vessels of that state in Mauritius. If, moreover, British ships were discriminated against by a foreign state, the cargoes carried by the ships of that state had to pay a duty of 8% ad valorem above the duties charged when those goods were exported in British vessels. Conversely, if it could be proved that exports from Mauritius would be admitted into a foreign state on equal terms whether carried in a British ship or a vessel of the foreign state concerned, then no differential export duty was levied in Mauritius.

The majority of ships that called at Mauritius were British vessels, but French, American, Danish, Portuguese, Dutch and Arab vessels also called. The total value of imports and exports in 1823 was made up as follows:

Imports Spanish dollars	*Exports* Spanish dollars	*Carried in ships of*
2 215 072,85	1 889 866,21	Britain
493 049,15	305 993,87	France
10 864,74	18 910,08	America
46 373,67	68 282,00	Other
2 765 360,41	2 283 052,16	

The most ominous fact which emerges from these figures was the size of the unfavourable balance of trade in 1823. It amounted to 482 308,25 Spanish dollars. Articles imported consisted chiefly of manufactures and food and wine. The principal items of export were cloves, coffee, cotton, nutmeg and sugar.[26]

The island was not an ideal entrepôt centre. It was too near the markets of the east and merchants engaged in trade with Asia could get a better bargain in a more direct trade.[27] Mauritius, moreover, fell within the geographical area covered by the Charter of the East India Company. Hence sugar grown in Mauritius, like all sugar imported into Britain from the east, paid duty of ten shillings per hundredweight in excess of the duty payable on West Indian sugar. The higher duty, together with the higher cost of freight because of the longer distance to market, amounted to a prohibition on the sale of Mauritian-grown sugar on the London market. Since foreign powers raised protective tariff barriers on sugar in favour of their own colonies, Mauritius could find no alternative market. A further shrinkage of exports was the result of unforeseen consequences of the Treaty of Paris (1814) which left Bourbon in French hands. French ships brought cargoes to Mauritius in terms of the 1820 Order in Council, but instead of loading a cargo of Mauritian exports they sailed to Bourbon in ballast and there loaded their cargoes for the return voyage to France. Such practice not only effectively deprived Mauritius of a market for her goods, but drained the colony of specie as well.[28]

Clearly if a favourable balance of trade was to be struck, new impetus had to be given to the Mauritian economy. Mauritian merchants repeatedly petitioned the Crown for a reduction of the duties on sugar.[29] Officials in the Colonial Department were sympathetic, and even supported a petition which proposed that if the duty on Mauritian-grown sugar could not be reduced to the same level as that on West Indian sugar by executive action, then perhaps some relief could be afforded by taking bonds. These were to be met after relief had been secured by legislative action.[30] This was a doubtful proposition. There was no guarantee that Liverpool's cabinet would propose legislation to make the duty on East India sugar equal to that from the West Indies. To the contrary, West Indian sugar interests, already sensitive to pressure to ameliorate the conditions of slaves, were sure to muster in opposition along with others anxious to preserve privilege.

Meanwhile in Mauritius conditions deteriorated as a result of two severe hurricanes which swept the island in 1824. In February, the first hurricane destroyed several houses in Port Louis and other houses were burnt in a fire following the storm. Public buildings were damaged and the Royal College was rendered unfit for use.[31] The gale wrought havoc in the country districts too: coffee plants, spice and clove trees which had promised an abundant harvest were so battered that it was reckoned that it would take five or six years before they would again produce a payable crop; fields of maize and manioc, the staple diet of the labourers, were flattened. Sugar cane suffered to a less degree.[32] The colony hardly had time to recover when, in April, it was dealt the staggering blow of another hurricane. Crops only partially injured by the previous storm, as well as newly planted crops, were entirely destroyed. It was then too late in the growing season to sow more crops.[33] Remedial measures were essential. Cole imported rice from India in order to keep a basic supply of food. This increased the foreign exchange deficit, but the rice itself was sold by the colonial government on a credit of four to six months at a price which covered costs.

They were worrying days for a governor anxious to balance the accounts of his colony. Cole looked to the future and studied the general position. He thought sugar would have to develop into the chief staple. In the first place it withstood gales better than other crops did; in the second place, it matured more quickly than the other cash crops of the island. This meant a quicker return for capital invested. Hence Cole strongly supported a further petition of 246 sugar planters and merchants of Mauritius who begged to be relieved of the burdensome additional ten shillings duty on their sugar sold in Britain. "I feel deeply impressed with the justice of their appeal to the equity of government", Cole wrote to Bathurst. The governor thought that a positive gesture from the British Government could not come at a better moment to incline the colonists to his policy of anglicization.[35] The British Government now acknowledged that something had to be done for the colony. The cabinet submitted a series of resolutions to the House of Commons as the possible basis of legislation. These were designed to effect the admission into Britain of sugar, coffee and other articles grown in Mauritius on payment of the same duties charged on similar articles imported from the West Indian colonies.[36]

The proposed measure met with the expected opposition of the West India interests who were anxious to preserve the tax privilege long enjoyed by sugar grown in the West Indies when imported into Britain. The Standing Committee of the West India Planters set down the reasons which entitled them to protection in the form of a resolution which they submitted to senior ministers of the Crown.[37] They pointed out that the West Indian colonies were the first established sugar colonies, and that Englishmen had been encouraged by the

Crown and Parliament to invest capital in the West Indies for the advantage of the maritime and commercial policy of Great Britain. They had had no objection to the extension of the privilege enjoyed by the older West Indian colonies to the conquered colonies in the West Indies because the latter were intimately connected with British commercial interests, and considerable sums of British capital had been invested there. But, they reckoned, the extension of these privileges to an island where there was little or no investment of British capital, and which, moreover, was part of the eastern possessions of the Empire would afford an alarming precedent. They submitted that a further source of supply of sugar could only depress prices on an already saturated market. Moreover, they claimed that while the West Indies had "faithfully obeyed the laws for the abolition of the slave trade, by reason of which the cultivation of those colonies has been checked, it is notorious that (in Mauritius) an illicit and secret importation of slaves has taken place to a great amount".[38] They noted that the treaty signed when Mauritius capitulated in 1810 did not acknowledge any right of that colony to equal privileges with the West Indies, but equal privileges of participation in the trade and commerce enjoyed by British subjects in the East Indies. What is more, they pointed out, Mauritius had been opened by Britain to foreign trade in 1814 "a privilege always refused to the West Indies".[39]

It may be inferred from the statement of the Standing Committee that they saw in the move to admit Mauritian-grown sugar to the British market on equal terms with their own sugar, a wedge which in due course would ultimately lead to the extension of the privilege to all sugar grown in the British possessions in the eastern hemisphere. Their reference to the trade privileges of Mauritius was hardly justifiable in the light of the decline of the entrepôt trade in Mauritius, and, even though it was itself declining, the long established free port system in the West Indies.[40] Indeed the decline of the West Indian free ports must in part explain West Indian resentment of Mauritian intrusion into the British sugar market. The allusion of the West India sugar planters to an illicit trade in slaves to Mauritius was a clever tactical move. The Slave Registry in Mauritius was known to be faulty, and there were rumours that the slave trade to Mauritius had persisted, but until there was a proper register of slaves it was impossible to prove or disprove the point.[41]

The case of the West Indies was taken up by the agents of the several West Indian colonies. Their tactic was to play for time. Because it was late in the parliamentary session they begged that a subject so important as extending to Mauritius every privilege enjoyed in the British market by the British West Indian colonies might be held over until the next session of parliament. They emphasised that the measure might excite "feelings of disappointment and alarm" in the West Indies, which might "check that spirit of cordial co-operation in the measure contemplated".[42]

The opposition of the West Indian interests certainly carried some weight. The legislation proposed was held over because the lords of the Committee of the Privy Council for Trade and Plantations decided that if justice was to be done to both parties, Mauritians had to choose between an equalization of the sugar duties and the freedom of trade they had hitherto been allowed.[43] This proposition was submitted to the colonial government[44] and was published and debated in the Mauritian *Government Gazette*.[45] Then Cole convened a meeting of 36 local merchants and planters to consider the alternative proposals. The meeting was held in the theatre in Port Louis on the 22nd November 1824, under the chairmanship of Barry, the chief secretary to government. Sir Robert Barclay, the collector of revenue, and Blane, the collector of customs, were also required to attend. These officials were instructed to give to the meeting information relevant to their departments, but they were not to vote on either side of the question. Because it was known that there were considerable differences of opinion, Cole took the precaution to recommend to Barry that the meeting should take place behind closed doors and be conducted "with that temper and moderation so necessary in the discussion of questions of such importance to the community at large".[46]

Instead of the stormy meeting the governor anticipated, deliberation was "calm and patient".[47] On one point there was consensus. The meeting declined to make a choice between the alternatives, and suggested that the status quo be maintained for a further year. Meanwhile they sought information on the precise nature of the restrictions imposed on the commerce of the West Indies and particulars of regulations which would control trade between Mauritius and America and countries to the eastward of the Cape of Good Hope if they were to elect parity with the West Indian colonies. But the meeting also pointed out that Mauritius had enjoyed the advantages of free trade since 1787,[48] not 1814, and that the articles of capitulation signed in 1810 had agreed to maintain the customs and privileges of the island.[49]

Cole was more positive in his opinion. He was convinced that it would not only be just, but wise to equalize the sugar duty and keep Port Louis open subject to limitations decided on by the British Government. He could not see in what way the free trade of Mauritius could be injurious to the interests of the West Indian islands. Indeed he thought it was to their advantage. "By permitting the Mauritius to send any portion of its sugars to a foreign market, certainly there would be a less quantity to compete with the West India produce at home", he wrote. He pointed out that the abolition of Mauritian trade privileges would throw some people out of employment and reduce the customs revenue – a factor he thought important in view of the low state of the finances of the colonial government. Thus he thought it would be wise to equalize the sugar duties and open the port. It would help "to secure the affections of the colonists and . . . wean them from France".[50] If forced to choose between the alternatives confronting him, Cole had no doubt that it was the open port that should go. He thought that the equalization of the sugar duty was absolutely necessary for the welfare of the colony.[51] He stated that the foreign trade of Mauritius was inconsiderable except with France – and in that particular case, the balance was against Mauritius because of the high duty levied in France on foreign-grown sugar and the additional ad valorem duty levied in Mauritius on exports to foreign countries.[52]

The British Government were obviously not disposed to permit Mauritius to have both generous trade privileges and equality with the West Indies with respect to duty on sugar imported into Great Britain. They determined upon the latter. Despite discreet lobbying, careful propaganda, and firm opposition in parliament, the West Indian stand was broken. In 1825 an act of parliament[53] put Mauritius on an equal footing with the West Indian colonies with respect to its external trade and the duties levied thereon. Effectively this meant that the rate of duty on Mauritian-grown sugar imported into Britain was made the same as that on sugar from the West Indies; but it also obliged Mauritius to accept the same restrictions on her foreign trade as were placed on the West Indian colonies. The privilege of trade through free ports as in the West Indies seems to have been overlooked with respect to Mauritius, and continued to be so in the Colonial Trade Act of 1825[54] as well. Although the King in Council was empowered by the latter measure to add to the list of free ports, Port Louis was not given that status until 1832.[55]

Meanwhile a curious situation arose in Mauritius. The new regulations made by the British Government for the trade of Mauritius could not be immediately known in the colony because of its distance from Britain. In the interim the Order in Council of the 12th July 1820, by which the trade had been regulated, expired. Merchants and planters in Mauritius requested the governor to permit trade to continue as if the Order were still effective.[56] Cole agreed – and in doing so anticipated an instruction sent by the secretary of state in March 1825.[57] Bathurst told Cole that the British Government was undecided whether or not to introduce amendments in a new Order in Council and until he received further instructions he was to continue to act under the old Order. The British Government's indecision, however, was resolved in 1825 by the Colonial Trade Act and the act to extend to Mauritius the duties and regulations which related to the British West Indian colonies. But Cole was not officially informed of this legislation. He therefore considered himself bound by the last official communication he had received from the secretary of state on the subject, and thus obliged to continue to regulate the trade of Mauritius in terms of the Order in Council of the 12th July 1820. He sought the co-operation of the senior naval officer stationed in Port Louis. This official agreed to permit foreign vessels to enter Port Louis to trade provided they had the governor's "direct licence or permission", but told Cole that the navy was bound "to enforce the execution of all Acts of Parliament without considering local or individual convenience".[58] Thus a crisis was unavoidable when the naval officers had received copies of the revised legislation while the governor had not. In a despatch to Bathurst explaining the action he had taken, Cole remarked that he felt justified in doing so because he had received news from the Cape of the "very liberal views" entertained by the British Government with respect to colonial trade.[59]

All went well until the arrival in Mauritius on the 29th April 1826, of H. H. Christian, commodore of the Cape station. The commodore enjoyed the hospitality of the governor and no evidence has been found that he objected to the policy the governor considered himself obliged to pursue. On the 10th June Christian took his ship out of the harbour of Port Louis, anchored off the entrance, and wrote to Cole expressing his thanks for civilities he had received during his stay in Mauritius and stated he would immediately proceed to sea. Instead, however, he reappeared just as the Portugese vessel *Gratidao* was about to sail and seized her as a smuggler.[60] This vessel had been admitted to Port Louis, at the risk of the parties concerned, by the governor with the advice of the Council. The special attention of the consignees had been drawn to the fact that the governor had no authority over the officers of the Royal Navy.[61]

The commodore claimed that a cargo of tea brought from Macao by the *Gratidao* and unloaded in Mauritius was contrary to the Colonial Trade Act of 1825,[62] and asked the collector of customs in Mauritius to seize the vessel and bring its papers to him so that it could be libelled in the Vice-Admiralty Court.[63] The governor gave the collector of customs authority to decline the commodore's request,[64] and wrote to Christian explaining that the trade of the colony was still regulated by the Order in Council of the 12th July 1820 and Farquhar's proclamation of the 31st October 1814. He also told the commodore that similar action on the part of the senior naval officer some years previously had incurred the disapprobation of the lords of the Treasury.[65] But Christian was not impressed. He told the governor that the Admiralty would not suffer his conduct to be commented upon by the Treasury. His duty was to apply the laws of the British Parliament, and no colonial legislation could bind or alter the duties of a captain of the navy. Christian informed Cole that until the colonial government received a new Order in Council he intended to prevent foreign ships entering Port Louis "contrary to law, and to the manifest injury of British and native merchants".[66]

A long and tedious correspondence ensued between the commodore and the governor, marked by the arrogance of the former and courtesy of the latter. After some delay the *Gratidao* was libelled in the Vice-Admiralty Court. The trial was presided over by Judge Blackburn, the chief justice of Mauritius, and was notable for the appearance of the governor in the witness box.[67]

In his judgement Blackburn reasoned that the secretary of state's instructions to continue the trade of the colony in terms of the Order in Council of 12th July 1820 amounted to no more than that the Order should serve as a rule for the governor's guidance with respect to imports, the collection of duties, the regulation of the coasting trade and commerce with Madagascar[68] and the dependencies, and all internal municipal interests which the local government had the power to regulate provisionally. He did not believe it was the intention of the instructions to confer upon foreigners a privilege which they did not derive from the Order in Council itself and contrary to the principles of the navigation laws. In Blackburn's opinion, Farquhar's proclamation of the 31st October 1814 was no longer valid. Although Christian objected to the judge's detailed verdict, he had won the material point.[69]

The commodore was determined that there should be no breach of the law and maintained a vigil off Port Louis. All ships that approached the outer anchorage were searched. Several were seized. Many of the cases the judge dismissed because he reckoned that the importation had not been completed. The vessels had neither entered the port nor was the intent to land the cargo established. The judge held that intent to land cargo could be either expressed or implied – either from the fact that the vessel had no destination beyond Port Louis or from some overt act of disembarkation by the master. In one case the judge found that the importation was complete in law and ruled the goods liable to confiscation. Christian claimed that since all the vessels were detained by him at the same place the judge was being inconsistent. In these circumstances, he reasoned, no seizure could be successfully prosecuted by the Naval Department unless the goods were taken in transit between the ship and the shore.[70]

An intolerable situation had developed. The governor continued to await the promised new Order in Council. Privately he wrote to Hay, " . . . if this severity is permitted to be continued on the part of the navy, the trade of this Colony under Foreign Flags will be materially injured, if not destroyed".[71]

Meanwhile the colonists who supported the local government in the controversy with the navy also wanted to take advantage of the duties prescribed in the Colonial Trade Act of 1825. These were lower than required by the legislation of the colony.[72] But duties on imports and exports provided the main source of revenue for the colonial government. Cole, concerned to balance his budget, told Bathurst, "If these Export and Import duties should cease, and be not replaced by others, the Revenue will be most materially diminished and the demands on the Treasury at home, to meet the colonial expenditure, must increase in proportion".[73] The problem was passed to James Stephen. He ruled that it was not the intention of Parliament to discontinue colonial laws which imposed duties but to fix the minimum duty payable. The colonies were entitled to charge higher duties if they wanted to, and when the colonial duty exceeded the parliamentary duty, then the colonial duty was payable.[74] This opinion was conveyed to the collector of customs in Mauritius[75] and the matter was set at rest.

The acts passed by Parliament in the summer of 1825[76] were officially received in Mauritius in January 1827, and were published in the *Government Gazette*.[77] This resolved the question of the trade laws applicable to the colony, but now raised two other issues of local concern. One turned on the restriction of ownership and mastership of British vessels to British citizens,[78] and the other was caused by the absence of any statutory recognition of Port Louis as a free port.[79]

Since the occupation of Mauritius by the British in 1810, several foreigners, mainly Frenchmen, had become permanently domiciled there. Some of them had invested money in ships registered in Port Louis; others earned their living as masters of the vessels. These people were placed in difficult circumstances by the requirements of the law:[80] those who owned ships, even though British built, found their investment in jeopardy; those who were masters were obliged to abandon that occupation.[81] Naturalization was only obtainable by Letters Patent under the Great Seal or by act of parliament. Both these methods were expensive. A suggestion to delegate the King's prerogative of naturalization to the governor of Mauritius was scotched by Stephen. He argued that it was inconceivable for the governor of a small colony to have power of imperial dimensions: equally it was impossible for the governor to be empowered to proclaim a man a British citizen within the colony under his jurisdiction while the same man would be a foreigner in all other parts of the British Empire. In Stephen's opinion the grant of British citizenship to aliens had to be jealously guarded, and the machinery established for naturalization was adequate. If expense was a well founded objection, he recommended that the proper remedy lay in a reduction of the costs involved and in the introduction of a more economical procedure to acquire citizenship. He pointed out that the benefit of British citizenship was mostly sought by persons of considerable capital. "The expense of the grant is not a tax on the poor," he said, "but a price paid for a valuable privilege by the rich."[82]

On the subject of a free port, Cooper, the standing English counsel in Mauritius, argued that the publicly declared intent of Parliament when the legislation was under discussion was to give the West Indian colonies and Mauritius the same rights and privileges in their trade and commerce. This suggested to Cooper that the omission to name Port Louis in the Colonial Trade Act[83] was accidental or that the Act confirmed the privileges Mauritius had hitherto enjoyed. In support of his argument, Cooper pointed to the form of words used in section 44 of the Act:

> "... all ships and vessels whatsoever, which shall arrive at or depart from the said Island of Mauritius, shall be subject to the *same regulations* as such ships or vessels would be subject to, if arriving at, or departing from, any of His Majesty's Islands in the West Indies."

Since the West Indian islands had free ports, then Cooper argued Mauritius could have a free port regulated like the others in terms of section 4 of the Act. This section admitted to trade the ships of countries that had colonial possessions and which were prepared to admit British ships to similar privileges in their own colonies, or the ships of countries which had no colonies but which admitted the commerce and navigation of Britain on the basis of a most favoured nation, or the ships of countries admitted to part or all the privileges by Order in Council even though those countries did not fulfil all the requirements of the first two alternatives.[84]

The governor's Council recommended Cole to adopt Cooper's opinion, and the senior naval officer was asked to respect the application of such a policy until the local authorities had received an Order in Council or further instructions from the British Government.[85] The senior naval officer agreed subject to the approval of commodore Christian.[86] If Christian returned to the scene, Cole appreciated that the trade of the colony would be "kept in hot water" as long as he remained.[87] Cooper's opinion on the issue of a free port in Mauritius was obviously a legal nicety which lent itself to litigation. Cole told Bathurst that he hoped he would soon receive a new Order in Council to regulate the trade of Mauritius "for should Christian return here after the hurricane months, I much fear from what has already occurred, that endless difficulties and embarrassments will ensue".[88]

Meanwhile in Britain, James Stephen raised several technical difficulties which arose out of an Order in Council he had been asked to prepare to enable French ships to carry to Mauritius the same limited description of goods they were able to transport to the West Indian colonies in terms of an Order in Council of the 1st July 1826.[89] Stephen held that if the terms of this Order were simply extended to Mauritius such action would affirm that the British Government upheld the principle that the trade of Mauritius was subject only to rules contained in the Colonial Trade Act of 1825, and that the Order in Council of 1820 applying to Mauritius and the government regulations dependent upon it, were ultra vires. In consequence, the governor of Mauritius would be open to conviction because he had continued to act in terms of the Order although ordered to do so by the secretary of state. This was clearly undesirable. Furthermore, Stephen reasoned, if the proposed Order affirmed the general maxim of the parity of Mauritius with the West Indies, its proclamation would regulate the trade of Mauritius with any country exactly as if it were a West Indian island though this might not be desirable because of its geographic situation. The Colonial Trade Act, Stephen said, did provide for distinctions. Besides, he thought that the British Government should consider the possible embarrassment to other eastern colonies, such as the Cape of Good Hope, Ceylon, New South Wales and Van Dieman's Land, if express permission were given to French ships to import into Mauritius the same articles they could carry to the West Indian colonies. These other eastern colonies would be forbidden to trade with France without similar expressed sanction and there were no regulations for any of them framed in terms of the Colonial Trade Act of 1825 although the King in Council was empowered by the Act to make such regulations. Stephen concluded that an Order in Council specifically to regulate the trade of Mauritius with France would carry with it various indirect though important consequences with reference to the trade between Mauritius and other countries, the trade between the eastern colonies and France, and the general commercial relations of all those colonies.[90]

The problem was resolved by issuing an Order in Council for the temporary regulation of the trade of the Cape of Good Hope, Mauritius, Ceylon, New South Wales, and Van Dieman's Land. This Order proclaimed valid all the laws, rules, orders, and regulations operative on the 1st July 1825, in each colony provided they did not conflict with the terms of Huskisson's three acts of parliament or any Orders in Council made in terms of these acts.[91] This Order was followed in July 1827 by an Order in Council which embraced in one document the degree of freedom to trade with her colonies which Britain was prepared to give specified foreign countries. France, Russia, Prussia and several other German states, the United States, Mexico, and several South American Republics were included.[92]

The area of trade into which Mauritius was drawn was considerable by any standard, but the benefit of a free port at first eluded the colony. In November 1827, Huskisson informed Cole that it was intended to recommend the King to constitute Port Louis a Free Warehousing Port[93] but no Order in Council to this effect was signed until 2nd May 1832.[94] This, however, did not hold back the development of the colonial economy. The entrepôt trade had declined[95] and a different pattern of external trade had emerged. Imports consisted mainly of British manufactured goods and articles of consumption. Madagascar and the East Indies supplied Mauritius with rice; the United States of America, South Australia, Van Dieman's Land, and Valparaiso supplied corn; salt beef, fruit, and livestock, notably horses, came from the Cape. These purchases were paid for principally out of the export of sugar and its by-product, spirits.[96]

The equalization of the duty on Mauritian- and West Indian-grown sugar imported by Britain clearly stimulated the Mauritian sugar industry. This action reduced the duty levied on Mauritian sugar sold in London by ten shillings per hundredweight. Increased profitability naturally encouraged increased cultivation of sugar in Mauritius. The amount of land under cane increased from 27 800 arpents in 1825 to 57 000 arpents in 1830. The number of sugar mills increased too. In 1820 there were 106; by 1827 there were 171 sugar mills.[97] During the first ten years of the British administration of Mauritius (1810–1820) the annual average production of sugar was 11 700 tons. In 1826, the year after the British import duty had been equalized, sugar production almost doubled – 21 244 tons were produced. By 1830 production had reached nearly 34 000 tons.[98] According to Lamusse sugar exports from Mauritius to Britain soon increased sixfold.[99] This is reflected in the revenue derived in England from duty on Mauritian-grown sugar. In 1825 it amounted to only £106 205; but by 1828, even though the amount assessed was ten shillings per hundredweight less, £326 448 was collected in duty, and by 1832 the amount reached £631 600.[100] Prices of commodities like sugar, however, are notoriously sensitive to supply and demand and in 1823 Mauritian sugar had sold with difficulty on the London Market at twenty-six shillings per hundredweight; in 1827 the best grades of sugar from Mauritius fetched fifty-eight shillings per hundredweight.[101] This seems to have been due to a greater demand for sugar in Britain because the anticipated slump in sugar from the West Indies did not materialise. The higher price and the increased volume of sugar exported soon improved the fortunes of Mauritius although concentration on sugar put the island in an invidious economic position. Dependence on a single cash crop laid its economy open to the fluctuations of the world market. A demand for sugar meant high prices and a buoyant economy; when, however, there was a lesser demand for sugar there was over-production, low prices, and the economy was deflated. But in 1828, it must have seemed as if a new era had dawned. For the first time since 1810 the colonial government balanced its budget with a surplus. It was only a meagre £6 523, but it was a vast improvement on the deficit of £63 166 there had been in 1823. British imports of Mauritian sugar increased from 93 723 hundredweight in 1825 to 485 326 hundredweight in 1830.[102] Although this expansion of trade is reflected in favourable balances in the colonial revenue for 1829 and 1830, it also contributed to over-production of sugar and a severe fall in its price in Britain in 1830 and 1831.[103]

Cole was angered by assertions that economic recovery was the result of illegal importations of slaves. He told the colonists that he had assured the British Government of his firm conviction that the slave trade to Mauritius was extinct. He begged colonists to report any infractions to the government immediately so that offenders could be brought to trial and punished. He warned colonists that he was convinced that any resumption of the slave trade would incur the re-imposition of the extra duty on sugar as a reprisal.[104] Axiomatically it would end prosperity. The new economic measures therefore not only helped to balance the colonial budget but gave the colonial government additional strength in the maintenance of law and order.

The controversy over sugar duties, 1824–1825, shows that on occasion colonial problems had to be considered not merely in terms of principles and interests, but also in terms of the working of politics. Moreover, the interplay between the secretary of state and the governor illustrates their particular perspective of the problems of the Empire: the former had responsibilities to Parliament and the Empire as a whole, the latter adopted with discernment the particular problems of Mauritius. From the twentieth century point of view Cole may perhaps have over-emphasised the need to anglicize, but he certainly linked together the concepts of political loyalty and economic well-being. To some extent he was fortunate in that his stand on the question of sugar duties coincided not only with the trend of British economic policy, but also with the decline of the West India interest which was the main target of the anti-slavery campaign.

Many of Cole's tussles were small local combats, but it was often by such legal tournaments that the colonies scored a point which in retrospect is seen to have passed into the broad generalizations of imperial policy.

FOOTNOTES

1. A. H. Imlah, *Economic Elements in the Pax Britannica*, p. viii.
2. Quoted by A. Briggs, *The Age of Improvement*, p. 220.
3. A. Brady, *William Huskisson and Liberal Reform*, p. 73.
4. *Ibid.*
5. P.P. 1820, II, (300), pp. 367–379. This document has been published in V. Harlow and A. Madden, *British Colonial Developments 1774–1834*, pp. 295–299.
6. Created viscount Goderich in 1827 and earl of Ripon 1833. He was president of the Board of Trade, 1818–1823; chancellor of the exchequer, 1823–1827; secretary of state for War and the Colonial Department, 1827; first lord of the Treasury, 1827–1828; secretary of state for War and the Colonial Department, 1830–1833; lord privy seal 1833–1834.
7. The vice-president of the Board of Trade, 1818–1823.
8. The president of the Board of Trade, 1823–1827; secretary of state for War and the Colonial Department, 1827–1828.
9. 3 Geo. IV, c. 41, 42, 43, 44 and 45.
10. Imlah, p. 14.
11. S. G. Checkland, *The Rise of Industrial Society in England, 1815–1885*, p. 19.

12. 4 Geo. IV, c. 24.
13. 4 Geo. IV, c. 77, and 5 Geo. IV, c. 1.
14. J. H. Clapham, *An Economic History of Modern Britain*, p. 333.
15. 6 Geo. IV, c. 109.
16. These were: – masts, timber, boards, salt, pitch, tar, tallow, rosin, hemp, flax, currants, raisins, figs, prunes, olive oil, corn or grain, pot ashes, wine, sugar, vinegar, brandy and tobacco.
17. 6 Geo. IV, c. 110.
18. 6 Geo. IV, c. 114.
19. That area east of the Cape of Good Hope and west of the Straits of Magellan.
20. F. Armytage, *The Free Port System in the British West Indies.*
21. Huskisson's pamphlet on "The Depreciation of the Currency" (1810, re-issued in 1819). Quoted by S. Buxton, *Finance and Politics*, p. 17n; and by L. Woodward, *The Age of Reform*, 1815–1870, (2nd edition), p. 70.
22. C. Pridham, *England's Colonial Empire*, Vol. I, Mauritius and its Dependencies, p. 251.
23. See J. Steven Watson, *The Reign of George III, 1760–1815*, pp. 288–289.
24. 1 March 1817, see *B.F.S.P.*, Vol. IV, pp. 565–566; 28 May 1819, see *B.F.S.P.*, Vol. VI, pp. 1125–1126.
25. *B.F.S.P.*, Vol. VII, pp. 934–936.
26. C.O. 167/74, Cole to Bathurst, 28 December 1824.
27. C.O. 167/144, Report of the commissioners of inquiry, 14 January 1829.
28. C.O. 167/74, Cole to Bathurst, 28 December 1824.
29. P.P. 1825, XIX (236). The earliest petition was presented in 1817. Altogether five petitions were presented in the period 1817–1824.
30. C.O. 167/76, Memorial of J. Saunders on behalf of the planters of Mauritius to the lords commissioners of the Treasury, 18 August 1824.
31. See Chapter II, p. 37.
32. C.O. 167/72, Cole to Bathurst, 10 March 1824.
33. C.O. 167/72, Cole to Bathurst, 25 May 1824.
34. C.O. 167/72, Cole to Bathurst, 10 March 1824 and 18 April 1824.
35. C.O. 167/72, Cole to Bathurst, 25 May 1824. See Chapter II, p. 36.
36. C.O. 167/75, T. Lack to Wilmot Horton, 4 June 1824.
37. Copies of the resolution were sent to the earl of Liverpool, earl Bathurst, G. Canning, F. J. Robinson and W. Huskisson.
38. C.O. 167/75, Resolution of the Standing Committee of the West India Planters, 31 May 1824. See Chapter IV. pp. 69–71.
39. *Ibid.*, See also p. 50 and p. 54.
40. Armytage, p. 129.
41. See Chapter IV, pp. 64–69.
42. C.O. 167/76, Memorial to Bathurst from the agents of the West Indian Islands, 2 June 1824.
43. C.O. 167/75, T. Lack to Wilmot Horton, 4 June 1824.
44. C.O. 168/8, Bathurst to Cole, 5 June 1824.
45. Mauritian *Government Gazette*, 9 October 1824 to 6 November 1824.
46. M.A., R.A. 275, Cole to Barry, 21 November 1824.
47. P.R.O. 30/43/86, Cole to Wilmot Horton, 28 December 1824, Private and Confidential.
48. See p. 50 and pp. 52–53.
49. C.O. 167/74, Cole to Bathurst, 18 December 1824.
50. *Ibid.*
51. P.R.O. 30/43/86, Cole to Wilmot Horton, 28 December 1824, Private and Confidential.
52. C.O. 167/74, Cole to Bathurst, 28 December 1824.
53. 6 Geo. IV, c. 76.
54. 6 Geo. IV, c. 114.
55. See p. 59.

56. C.O. 167/78, Cole to Bathurst, 7 July 1825.
57. C.O. 168/8, Bathurst to Cole, 15 March 1825.
58. C.O. 167/80, Owen (the senior naval officer in Mauritius) to Cole, 2 July 1825.
59. C.O. 167/78, Cole to Bathurst, 7 July 1825.
60. C.O. 167/83, Cole to Bathurst, 26 June 1826.
61. C.O. 170/1, Minutes of Council, 5 April 1826.
62. 6 Geo. IV, c. 114.
63. C.O. 167/83, Cole to Bathurst, 26 June 1826.
64. C.O. 167/83, Minute of governor 17 June 1826, enclosed in Cole to Bathurst, 26 June 1826.
65. C.O. 167/83, Cole to Christian, 19 June 1826, enclosed in Cole to Bathurst, 26 June 1826.
66. C.O. 167/83, Christian to Cole, 19 June 1826, enclosed in Cole to Bathurst, 26 June 1826.
67. Christian complained to the Admiralty of the injustice of the case because the judge allowed him to be personally attacked in court. "I have been called in open court, a pirate, a robber, and a tiger, who for the gratification of his pride and vanity has been induced to commit an oppressive and tyranical act," he wrote. See Adm. 1/70, Christian to Croker, 28 November 1826.
68. An Order in Council, 10 March 1824, authorized the import of cattle into Mauritius from Madagascar in French vessels.
69. The *Gratidao* was restored to its owners, together with the cargo it had loaded in Port Louis, and that part for the original cargo which had been declared for export to a further destination. The seizer was allowed his costs, but demurrage for the protracted detention of the vessel was set off against them, and against the commodore's share of the forfeited goods. That share of the forfeited goods which accrued to the Crown and the governor was given up to the owners by a disclaimer put in on behalf of the colonial government. Small quantities of tea and other articles of Chinese produce were condemned. The Portuguese captain was fined £100.
70. Adm. 1/70, Christian to Croker, 13 July 1827.
71. C.O. 167/86, Cole to Hay, 11 November 1826, Private and Confidential.
72. C.O. 167/82, Cole to Bathurst, 13 April 1826.
73. C.O. 167/82, Cole to Bathurst, 24 February 1826.
74. C.O. 167/89, Stephen to Hay, 19 July 1826.
75. M.A., R.A. 363, Minute of the governor, 7/1827, 17 January 1827.
76. 6 Geo. IV, c. 109, 110 and 114.
77. Mauritian *Government Gazette*, 10 February 1827.
78. 6 Geo. IV, c. 110.
79. 6 Geo. IV, c. 114. Article II.
80. 6 Geo. IV, c. 110.
81. C.O. 167/91, Cole to Bathurst, 1 March 1827.
82. C.O. 167/103, J. Stephen to H. Twiss, 23 September 1828.
83. 6 Geo, IV, c. 114.
84. C.O. 167/91, Cooper to Blane, 8 February 1827, enclosed in Cole to Bathurst, 12 March 1827.
85. C.O. 167/91, Cole to Dunn (the senior naval officer in Mauritius), 11 February 1827, enclosed in Cole to Bathurst, 12 March 1827.
86. C.O. 167/91, Dunn to Cole, 19 February 1827, enclosed in Cole to Bathurst, 12 March 1827.
87. P.R.O. 30/87, Cole to Smith (agent for Mauritius), 10 April 1827.
88. C.O. 167/91, Cole to Bathurst, 12 March 1827.
89. Order in Council, 1 June 1826. See *B.F.S.P.*, Vol. XIII, p. 365.
90. C.O. 167/89, Minute of J. Stephen, 10 November 1826.
91. Order in Council, 30 April 1827. See *B.F.S.P.*, Vol. XIV, pp. 777–778.
92. Order in Council, 16 July 1827. See *B.F.S.P.*, Vol. XIV, pp. 666–671.
93. C.O. 168/11, Huskisson to Cole, 1 November 1827.
94. Order in Council, 2 May 1832, See *B.F.S.P.*, Vol. XIX, p. 1364.
95. See p. 51.

96. Pridham, Vol. I, p. 251.
97. M. J. R. Lamusse, *The Economic Development of the Mauritius Sugar Industry*, p. 81, unpublished B.Litt. thesis, Oxford, 1958.
98. *Ibid.*, p. 45.
99. *Ibid.*, p. 81.
100. Pridham, Vol. I, p. 390.
101. Lamusse, p. 81.
102. *C.H.B.E.*, Vol. II, p. 483.
103. *Ibid.*
104. C.O. 167/82, Cole to Bathurst, 1 March 1826, enclosing Cole's reply to Memorial of thanks from the merchants and planters of Mauritius "on the occasion of the passing of the new Mauritius Trade Bills".

CHAPTER IV

THE APPLICATION OF BRITISH SLAVE POLICY TO MAURITIUS, 1823–1828

British slave policy in the first three decades of the nineteenth century had a two-fold purpose: to prevent fresh importations of slaves and to improve the condition of the slave population as a prelude to emancipation. It was a difficult policy to implement because it touched the vital questions of private property, vested interests, and the supply of labour.

Abolitionists had believed that the termination of the slave trade in 1807 would itself lead to the gradual disappearance of slavery.[1] However, it soon became evident that supplementary measures were required if their policy was to be made effective. In order to extinguish the lucrative traffic in slaves the Slave Trade Felony Act[2] made slave trading an offence punishable by transportation. But there could be no adequate check on importations until there was a comprehensive registration of slaves. A start was made in Trinidad in 1812, where slave registration was required by Order in Council.[3] This policy was subsequently extended to other conquered colonies, including Mauritius,[4] and 1815 colonies with legislatures were also required to establish registers. Generally, the measures passed by the colonial legislatures were ineffective, so that in 1819 an act of the British Parliament established a Slave Registry Office to keep duplicate registers.[5] The officials in this office soon pointed out faults in the colonial registries, including those made by authority of an Order in Council.

Slave-owners were foolish to evade the law. It drew public attention in Britain to reports of the evils of slavery at a time when the reform of the criminal code was being considered, and when the first steps were being taken to regulate the employment of children in industry, to prevent cruelty to animals, and save pick-pockets from the gallows.[6] Thus not only the evangelicals but other members of parliament were disposed to treat the problem of slavery seriously. On the 15th May 1823 Buxton introduced a motion into the House of Commons for the gradual abolition of slavery. This motion was withdrawn when the government itself sponsored three resolutions which were passed nem con.[7] The House agreed, first, that it was expedient to adopt effectual measures for ameliorating the condition of the slaves in the colonies; secondly, that through a determined but judicious enforcement of such measures, the House looked forward to a progressive improvement in the character of the slaves such as would prepare them for full participation in civil rights; and thirdly, the House stated its concern to accomplish this with all the speed compatible with the well-being of the slaves, the safety of the colonies, and a fair consideration of the interests of private property.[8]

The British Government chose a policy of social evolution rather than social revolution. But in the colonies, slave-owners saw in the application of these principles only a threat to their economic and social position. In both conquered colonies and colonies with legislatures, the British Government faced the opposition of slave-owners. Governors had to obey instructions and keep the peace in their colonies. Colonial garrisons had been reduced so far as possible,[9] therefore governors had to resort to diplomacy to implement policy with the result that even ameliorative measures framed in the conquered colonies did not always reach the standard required by the British Government.

After the conquest of Mauritius by the British in December 1810, the existing statute to abolish the slave trade throughout the Empire[10] became applicable there though it was not immediately enforced by the local courts.[11] The importations of new slaves was reckoned by local planters to be the only means to recover fortunes lost in the war years.[12] More slaves were imported into Mauritius from Madagascar than was permitted by the capitulation agreement, and this had been overlooked by the courts. But the Slave Trade Felony Act of 1811,[13] registered in the courts of Mauritius in 1813, put an end to judicial leniency. A final check on fresh importations of slaves was intended by an Order in Council of the 24th September 1814 which provided for the registration of slaves in Mauritius on the pattern already established in Trinidad.[14]

The Order in Council established two categories of slaves for purposes of registration: plantation and personal slaves. A separate register had to be kept for each group, and the name, description and occupation of each slave recorded therein Obligation to register slaves lay with their owners. They had to submit a schedule of their slaves to a registrar of slaves especially appointed to receive it within three months of the publication of the Order in Mauritius. Owners had to pay a fee of ten shillings per schedule and one shilling per slave mentioned in the schedule on registration. Failure to register a slave, or slaves, incurred the penalty of forfeiture to the Crown of the slave, or slaves, concerned. Fraudulent registration carried the penalty of a £100 fine in addition to forfeiture, part of the fine accruing to any informer.

Once the initial registration was completed, the registers were made available to the public for two months so that inaccuracies could be detected and corrected. Thereafter owners had to make an annual return of their slaves noting, in particular, births, deaths, and changes in status, condition or ownership during the past year. Details of slave children were required: any change in appearance had to be noted, their height and distinguishing characteristics recorded, particular note being taken of bodily defects or deformities together with an explanation of how this condition had come about. Penalties for infringement of the law were similar to those applying to the original return.

The Order in Council was published in Mauritius in April 1815.[15] T. Bradshaw was appointed registrar of slaves and instructed to put the Order in Council into effect, but the failure of slave-owners to co-operate with him made it impossible to complete the registration within the three months prescribed. Governor Farquhar attempted to coerce slave-owners into co-operation. He publicly warned them that if slaves were not registered by due date, they would be confiscated. He was, however, obliged to extend the time limit a further month. Even then, not all the slaves were registered.[16] In September 1815, however, Farquhar reported to Bathurst that he had reason to believe that most proprietors had registered their slaves. Opposition, he said, only came from "a portion of the lower class of inhabitants".[17] Thirteen months later he admitted the extent of opposition encountered. "Not a single proprietor or inhabitant of note" had registered a single slave.

The explanation for the opposition was vague. Farquhar now admitted a strongly marked disinclination on the part of the slave-owners to the application of the law because they feared the introduction of "innumerable evils".[18] He thought that insufficient time had been allowed for registration, and that slave-owners had failed to co-operate because of the expense in which slave registration involved them. Farquhar thought that the capitation tax was already as high as most slave-owners could afford and that they considered the additional expense oppressive. In order to lighten the financial burden on slave-owners Farquhar had agreed to a request from the registrar of slaves to receive promissory notes to cover the cost of registration to exempt those who obviously could not afford it.[19] But even this palliative did not work.

Delays in the initial registration made it impossible to take a new census in 1816, but in any case, a further Order in Council in September that year provided for a triennial return of slaves in place of the annual return. This meant that the next return was not due in Mauritius until 1819. Registration was just as much a failure when it took place on that occasion.[20] By way of remedy the acting governor, Major General Darling,[21] attempted to revive the annual census. This did not work either. Proclamations requiring registration, and others allowing for an extension of time, followed one another with regular monotony until the early years of the governorship of Sir Lowry Cole. Cole soon grasped the deficiencies of the registry in Mauritius. He told Bathurst that it was useless as a device to detect new importations of slaves and recommended a complete revision.[22]

Meanwhile officials in London had come to the same conclusion as Cole after an examination of returns made in 1815 and 1819. Thomas Amyot complained that he had found the returns for 1815 available when the Slave Registry Office opened in 1819 while the returns for 1819 only arrived in 1823[23] and those of 1822 only reached London in 1826. Conclusions drawn from a comparison of the first two returns were proof enough of their shortcomings. The registration of 1815 showed 5 761 separate returns comprising a total of 85 423 slaves, whilst that for 1819 showed only 2 088 returns and recorded only 20 948 slaves.[24] A drop in number of this magnitude suggested gross error. One official, Bataille, a clerk in the registry office in Mauritius was discovered to have made numerous alterations in the original registers, and himself owned vessels engaged in the slave trade.[25]

The position was hardly better in the dependencies: similar irregularities had occurred there in registering the slaves, and similar frauds appear to have been committed. In the Seychelles Islands, for example, the tax rolls for 1810 record 2 533 slaves, but in 1815, 6 950 slaves were registered of whom 4 960 were males and 1 990 were females. The increase was phenomenal, and illicit importation was the obvious deduction. The number and topography of the islands facilitated the introduction and concealment of negroes, and for several years the government agent had insufficient staff to enable him to effect a seizure in the face of resistance.[26]

The returns from Mauritius for 1822 merely confirmed the defects of the registration. This time there were only 1 169 returns comprising 7 485 slaves in all.[27] But by the time these figures had become available, the British Government had decided that a complete revision was necessary. The evidence of the earlier figures had been enough to call into question the validity of the earlier returns and had demonstrated the impracticability of using them to check the slave trade.

James Stephen was entrusted with the task of drafting a new Order in Council which would exclude the possibility of past errors. All the correspondence between the secretary of state and the successive governors was sent to Stephen.[28] In all there were 34 letters which contained several voluminous enclosures. Two acting governors, Hall[29] and Darling, blamed the failure of registration partly on the incompetence of the registrar, and partly on the inveterate dislike and consequent opposition of the inhabitants to the measure itself. Stephen also learned from the correspondence that it was possible that some slave-owners registered many more slaves than they actually possessed in order that the gangs when increased by illegal importations might correspond with the entries in the registry. It was thought, and subsequently proved by the commissioners of inquiry, that such illegal importations did take place.[30] A strict application of the law would have led to wholesale confiscation of slaves. This could have proved extremely embarrassing to the colonial government. Judge Smith[31] suggested that the earlier registration be forgotten and a new start made. While Stephen appreciated the practical value of this suggestion, he did not think it was possible because it would sanction the continued detention in slavery of negroes illegally imported into the colony. If illegality could be proved, the law had to be upheld. Stephen maintained that re-registration of the slaves was only possible in the light of that proviso.[32]

Since the errors of the former general registration were attributed to the prejudice, ignorance, or fraud of the persons making the returns, Stephen proposed to transfer the responsibility for registration from the proprietors to paid permanent officials. He recommended the appointment of several assistant registrars to assist the registrar of slaves in the country districts. He suggested that slave-owners should make returns to these officials in the first instance, but advised the personal inspection of the slaves by the officials to check the returns. He thought that when the returns were completed they could be transcribed into registers in the manner prescribed in the earlier Order in Council.[33]

Stephen pointed out to officials in the Colonial Department that the registrar of slaves in Mauritius had one peculiar difficulty not experienced by registrars in other colonies. In the West Indies, he explained all "alienations of slaves" were matters of record, and therefore changes of property could be readily traced. No such records existed in Mauritius. Changes of ownership were proved by oral testimony. "The absence of this solemnity on the sale of slaves by increasing the facility of such transactions, has a direct tendency to multiply their number," Stephen observed. He proposed, therefore, that sales of slaves should become a matter of legal record.[34]

As a practical measure of compromise between annual and tiiennial returns, Stephen recommended that the new Order in Council should provide for a biennial return.[35]

Stephen's proposals were accepted and included in the new Order signed by the King on the 30th January 1826. In a despatch forwarding the Order to Cole, the secretary of state instructed him to fix a day for the inspection of the whole slave population. Domestic slaves had to be brought before the registrar or one of his assistants at some convenient place in the quarter where they normally resided; plantation slaves had to muster on the estate to which they normally belonged. Printed blank forms had to be left at every house and plantation in the island together with printed instructions to explain how to complete them.[36]

On receipt of the instructions from Britain, the colonial government set to work with all haste. Bradshaw was removed from the office of registrar of slaves[37] and Colonel Draper was appointed in his place.[38] Both governor and registrar were military men, and the operation of re-registration was tackled with the thoroughness and skill of well seasoned campaigners.

Instructions for filling up the forms were issued in a government notice of the 4th October 1826. This was followed by two proclamations on the 11th October: one reduced the fees levied on registration to the nominal figures of one shilling, the other gave details about the examination and inspection of the slaves which was to take place between the 16th October and the 16th December.

The requirement of personal inspection necessitated a change of accommodation for the office of the registrar. Hitherto his department had been housed in the barracks. It was regarded as inconvenient and objectionable for large gangs of slaves to be assembled within the barrack walls. The registrar was therefore empowered to hire a house for the three months the inspection was expected to take.[39]

Additional staff had to be added to the registrar's establishment. Cole doubted his ability to find competent persons to serve as assistant registrars. He therefore secondedt he civil commissaries[40] in six districts to serve in this capacity, and replaced them by upgrading their suppleánts.[41] In Savanne, however, Cole appointed the suppleánt to the civil commissary as assistant registrar because he considered him better qualified for the office. But in Grand Port, where the ordinary duties of the civil commissary and his suppleánt were too heavy to permit of the expediency of drawing on these officials, he appointed a clerk in the Slave Registry Department as assistant registrar for that district. Additional clerical staff was required too: two clerks were added to the personal staff of the registrar, and four experienced clerks were detached from the government offices in Port Louis to assist the assistant registrars in the more heavily populated districts of Pamplemousse, Rivière du Rempart, Flacq, and Grand Port. Furthermore, the registrar and his eight assistants were authorized to employ two messengers each throughout the period of registration.[42]

The governor estimated that the registration of the slaves would increase the colonial expenditure by £1 728 per annum, in addition to a temporary expense of £105.4.0d. per month while the work was being done.

Registrations commenced according to plan on the 16th October. Cole warned the assistant registrars that "the greatest attention, exactitude and activity was expected from them, and that any remissness of duty on their part will at once subject them to the serious displeasure of Government".[43] The registrar and his assistants had an exacting task to perform. It took time to examine, measure, and note the marks of every slave. The registrar estimated that he registered an average of 179 slaves a day in a working day of seven to eight hours. He declined assistance with personal inspection because it might have led to the application of double standards. Fortunately the slave-owners were co-operative. This may well be explained by the attention given to slavery in the colony by the controversy over the equalization of the duty on Mauritian-grown sugar imported into Britain with that from the West Indies.[44] However co-operative they were, the slave-owners still made mistakes in filling up their returns even though printed instructions were issued. Sometimes the returns had to be done a second or third time because slave-owners made repeated errors in describing the families of their slaves. Sometimes the officials had to make out the returns for the owners. Not surprisingly, therefore, the registrar had to apply to the governor for more time to complete the registration.[45] Cole readily concurred because he was anxious that the job should "not be done lightly, nor with precipitation". The period of registration was extended by one month, and the task was completed in that time except in one district, Flacq, where the assistant registrar died during the work. Some returns he left incomplete had to be verified by his successor.[46]

On the 28th January 1827, Cole was able to report to Bathurst that slave registration in Mauritius itself was complete. A few people had failed to register their slaves. They had made plausible excuses which had to be investigated. But the returns from the dependencies were still outstanding.[47] Those from the Seychelles were forwarded to Britain a few months later.[48] Delay was greater in the other dependencies of Mauritius. Cole explained to the secretary of state that he could not send an assistant registrar to the islands until the end of the hurricane season in April. Because of the difficulty in communicating with those islands and the general deficiency in knowledge about them, Cole decided to ask the official he chose to go there to make a general report on them when registering the slaves.[49] It was January 1828 before Cole was able to report any figures.[50]

A hard task had been successfully accomplished. There were 69 004 slaves in Mauritius itself,[51] 6 522 in the Seychelles,[52] and 782 in the minor dependencies.[53] This did not necessarily correspond with the number of slaves on the tax roll of the collector of taxes. There were about 62 000 slaves on the tax roll. Cole told the secretary of state that the difference between that number and the return of the registrar of slaves, that is, 7 000 slaves, was equal to the number of government slaves, old invalid slaves, and children, none of whom were liable for the capitation tax.[54] Henceforth slave-owners were relieved of the necessity of making an annual return of their slaves for tax purposes. These figures were calculated on returns submitted by the registrar of slaves to the collector of internal revenue on the 31st January each year.[55]

Though the field work was completed, there was still a lot to do. The returns had to be written up and copies prepared for the Slave Registry Office in London. Minor administrative problems caused some delays but Cole knew that he now possessed the information he needed to check illicit importations of slaves. Until this point the government had not been able to prove illicit importations, or slave-owners disprove it. In London, a Parliamentary Select Committee in 1826–27, and in Mauritius, the commissioners of inquiry from 1827 to 1829, investigated allegations that there had been a continual importation of slaves from the beginning of the occupation in 1810 until at least 1822. The former investigation tended to discredit the charges; the latter showed that there was circumstantial evidence to support the allegations but, because of the distance in time and the refusal of witnesses to give evidence, it was impossible to bring home charges against individuals or to estimate the number of negroes imported.[56]

The proximity of Mauritius to the slave traffic lanes of the Indian Ocean, and the inadequacy of naval patrols certainly facilitated an illicit trade in slaves. Two squadrons of the Royal Navy – one stationed at the Cape and the other in the East Indies – were responsible for policing a vast area[57] with comparatively few ships.[58] Indeed doubt has been cast on whether the preventive cruisers ever captured more than 10% of the shipping involved.[59] The position was aggravated, moreover, by the refusal of the French Government[60] and the British Admiralty[61] to agree to any reciprocal right of search until 1833.[62] Consequently vessels of the Royal Navy had sometimes to stand-by helplessly while a slaver sailed past flying French colours.[63] Occasionally slavers escaped because the naval ships were too old and too slow.[64] But besides the inadequacy of the ocean patrols, there were no vessels small enough to negotiate the coral reefs and rocky creeks of the islands, especially those of Mauritius.

The Navy Board had been advised to provide Mauritius with an establishment "similar to the preventive or waterguard in Great Britain".[65] Cole endorsed this recommendation shortly after he arrived in Mauritius,[66] and the Admiralty were instructed to place four long-boats at the disposal of the senior naval officer in Port Louis.[67] Meanwhile a former slaver was refitted at colonial expense.[68] This was fortunate, because when the long-boats arrived they were pronounced "wholly unfit" for the service for which they were intended.[69] Useful though the former slaver was, it too proved to be too large for the coastal service, and after a few years it was sold and replaced by two smaller vessels.[70] But inter-departmental wrangling led to the sale of these ships too.[71] However, the Admiralty was eventually persuaded to send an additional sloop to the Cape station.[72]

Given the difficulty of policing a sea known to carry a heavy traffic in slaves, and given the faulty registration of slaves in Mauritius, it would seem a reasonable assumption that slaves were smuggled into Mauritius. However, Governor Farquhar reckoned the best check was to seal the trade at its source. He therefore negotiated treaties with the Ovah King Radama of Madagascar[73] and the Imam of Muscat[74] for this purpose. These treaties aided by the naval patrols, were sufficiently successful for Cole to report soon after his arrival in Mauritius that he understood that the direct traffic in slaves had ceased, but that slaves were still brought into Mauritius through the circuitous route of the Seychelles Islands.[75] This view was confirmed by the senior naval officer[76] and independently reported to Bathurst, through Wilberforce, by a former official in Mauritius, the Chevalier de Marcenay.[77] It was subsequently proved that Madge, the government agent in the Seychelles, was implicated in buying slaves known to be illicitly imported for which he was dismissed from the government service.[78] Meanwhile slaves could be transported from the Seychelles to Mauritius merely on Madge's description of them and certification that they came from the Seychelles.[79]

Cole acknowledged that the slave trade persisted in the Seychelles but he thought it was "much diminished". He noted, however, that a vessel with slaves on board had touched at one of the islands of the Seychelles to repair damages and remained several weeks before it sailed again. Because of the "unconnected situation of those islands" the event was not known in Mahé, where the government agent lived, until after the vessel had sailed again. This suggested to Cole that the slave trade could not be stopped in the Seychelles until a small armed cruiser was stationed there. Meanwhile he assured the secretary of state that all slaves who came to Mauritius from the Seychelles were seized unless they agreed with their description on their recensements. In any case he did not think that the matter was important because the number of slaves transferred from the Seychelles to Mauritius amounted to only 1 054 in five years – from 1818 to 1823.[80]

The Consolidated Slave Trade Abolition Act of 1824[81] circumscribed the freedom of individuals to transfer slaves from one island to another. Henceforth transfers could only be made with the governor's licence.[82] The obvious solution in the case of the Seychelles and Mauritius was for the governor to desist from granting any more licenses. When the commissioners of inquiry recommended this course, Cole opposed it. He argued that when slaves were brought to Mauritius from the dependencies their lot was likely to be improved because they would be brought "under the eyes of government" instead of being left "to the absolute authority of the overseer". In any case, he considered, the new registration of slaves made it scarcely possible for new slaves to be introduced.[83] When Cole subsequently discovered that his licence was abused, he immediately declined to grant any more licences until he had received the instructions of the secretary of state on the point. When these came, they ordered the governor to abstain from granting licences until the commissioners of inquiry had reported.[84]

In spite of the possible evasion of the law through the Seychelles, Cole confidently asserted that the slave trade to Mauritius was at an end. He wrote privately to Wilmot Horton that he feared that exaggerated reports about the slave trade were occasionally sent to Britian by officers of the navy serving on the Cape station. "In their zeal and anxiety for the suppression of this traffic", he wrote, "it appears to me that they are too much disposed to credit mere rumour, which on enquiry, as I frequently find myself, proves to be unfounded, and especially as regards the irregular introduction of slaves into this island from the Seychelles".[85] To Major Colebrooke, one of the commissioners of inquiry, Cole wrote in confidence, "I am rather incredulous in respect to naval reports on the subject of the slave trade in these seas, as mere suspicion with them is frequently conviction".[86] Hence Cole was unmoved by allegations made in Britain during and after the debates in parliament on the equalization of the sugar duties that slaves were still clandestinely imported into Mauritius. The point could not be proved one way or the other. The registration of slaves completed in 1827 made it easier to check further illicit imports.

More difficult for the governor than stopping the slave trade itself was the implementation of the policy of amelioration required by the House of Commons in terms of its resolutions of the 15th May 1823.[87] Copies of the resolutions and the speech Canning made in support of them were immediately sent to the governors of the West Indian colonies.[88] Two months later, copies of the despatches sent to the governor of Demerara and lieutenant-governor of Essequibo were forwarded to Cole so that he should be fully informed of the policy of the British Government. He was invited to make suggestions for applying the policy in Mauritius, and asked to make arrangements to facilitate, if not anticipate an Order in Council to give effect to the policy.[89]

The governor and lieutenant-governor of the two South American colonies had been urged to restrict Sunday markets and encourage the religious instruction of slaves, and had been recommended to abolish the flogging of female slaves, define regulations for the flogging of male slaves, and abolish the use of the whip by slave-drivers as a stimulus to labour. Indeed, Bathurst had recommended that the whip should no longer be carried into the field and displayed there by the driver "as an emblem of his authority or employed as the ready instrument of his displeasure". To assist the introduction of these measures, the governor of Demerara and lieutenant-governor of Essequibo had been told to maintain a strict censorship of the press to prevent the publication of articles written, or speeches made "in a spirit of angry feeling".[90]

The policy outlined in the correspondence embarrassed Cole. He wrote and told Bathurst that the colonists were already informed by the overseas press of the debates in the British Parliament and in the colonial assemblies of the West Indies concerning the amelioration of the conditions of the slaves. They were also aware of the disturbances in some of the West Indian colonies resulting from the application of the measures recommended. This in itself had led to hasty sales of property in Mauritius. Cole's discretion therefore suggested the propriety of keeping the intentions of the British Government secret. There were only "two weak regiments" in the colony to keep the peace, hence he perceived that he would have to proceed with caution if he was to avoid a wholesale confrontation of the merchants and planter community against the colonial government. Cole told Bathurst that any hasty or compulsive measure would be ruinous to the island. It would, he said, "have the effect of reducing the planter to absolute penury, and would be no less detrimental to the true interests of the slaves". Besides, he pointed out, the time was not politically opportune because of the distress caused by two severe hurricanes in February and April 1824, and the economic restrictions he thought would be caused over the abolition of paper currency and the resumption of specie in December that year. He claimed that he always had the improvement of the slave population in mind, but from his experience in Mauritius the slaves were not nearly ready for emancipation. "Generally speaking the slaves are idle and indifferent, insensible to habits of industry and disinclined to labor except from obligation", he wrote. His view was strengthened by the fact that the free people of colour made up the majority of the paupers of the colony. These people, he wrote, would "rather beg or steal than cultivate the soil". However, he did request Foisy, the government advocate, to draw up a report on the Code Noir so that he could see what modification he could make in the interests of the slaves. But Foisy was an old man in poor health which, in addition to "the habits of indolence almost unavoidable in Tropical Climates", caused delay even though urgency had been requested and speedy compliance promised. In any case, Cole was anxious to delay revision of the Code Noir until Bigge, one of the commissioners of inquiry who had legal experience in the West Indies, had arrived in the colony.[91]

Perhaps fortunately for Cole the matter was left in abeyance for some time. The British Government decided to leave the commissioners of inquiry to recommend adaptation of the local laws and customs of Mauritius to the new policy which had been spelt out in an Order in Council of the 10th March 1824 and sent to the governor of Trinidad.[92] This Order not only forbade the carrying of the whip in the fields and the whipping of female slaves; it also revived two articles of the Spanish code – the institution of a protector of slaves and recognition of the right of slaves to purchase their freedom from their masters at a price which, if not settled by mutual consent, was to be determined in the last resort by a disinterested third party.[93]

The commissioners of inquiry were delayed at the Cape longer than was intended. Consequently, to avoid further delay, the British Government decided that the governor and the Council should prepare an ordinance modelled on the Trinidad Order in Council. The draft of this ordinance the governor had to submit to the Crown for approval before promulgation. Bathurst wanted it to appear as though the initiative for the legislation had come from the colonial authorities. He sent Cole a printed copy of a despatch he had written to the governor of Demerara stating that:

> "the object might have been more speedily accomplished by issuing an Order in Council; but the adoption of that measure would have been attended with the loss of the important advantage of shewing to the slave population that the chief authorities in the colony are the immediate authors of the beneficial change which it is proposed to accomplish in their situation".

This did not mean, however, that the colonial authorities were entitled to vary the Trinidad Order in its local application. "His Majesty's Government cannot be satisfied with anything short of a complete compliance with the propositions that were detailed in that despatch," Bathurst told the governor of Demerara.[94]

Before Cole had time to act on his instructions, Commissioners Colebrooke and Blair had arrived in Mauritius.[95] A few months later they reported to Bathurst that some of the barbarous punishments sanctioned by the Code Noir had fallen into disuse but that some objectionable practices had remained. For example, fugitive slaves no longer had their ears cut off, but masters still chained their slaves without restriction. The punishment of slaves in Mauritius was harsh, but would be restrained, the commissioners thought, if a protector or guardian of slaves were appointed. They submitted that this officer was all the more necessary because the new register ignored the previous ones. One case of a master whose slaves had disputed his title had come to their notice and they argued that among the more ignorant slaves other cases would no doubt be discovered were there some person to advise them. A protector or guardian would be able to champion the rights of slaves in the courts, hence they recommended that the officer appointed should have some legal training.[96]

The governor was totally opposed to a witch-hunt based on the defective registers of the past. "No man's property would be safe", he wrote to Colebrooke, "and those of many of them who are now in affluence would be totally ruined – and nineteen out of twenty of the blacks anything but benefited by the change". Cole was convinced that only misery could ensue if "everything which has been done contrary to Law is to be stirred up and acted upon in the Colony". The governor was content to let bygones be bygones in return for present and future obedience to the law. So strongly did Cole feel about it that he was prepared to resign his office if the commissioners carried their point.[97] Cole understood far better than the commissioners the ramifications of their policy. One colonist, Rondeaux, reputed to have considerable influence in the colony, told the colonial agent in London that he was afraid the appointment of a protector or guardian for the slaves would endanger the tranquillity of the colony.[98] Criticism notwithstanding, a protector of slaves was appointed though the peace of the colony was not threatened until the appointment of J. Jeremie as procureur général in 1832.[99]

Meanwhile the colonial authorities began to undertake the required reformation. As a matter of tactics and diplomacy, Cole made every endeavour to carry the slave-owners with the government in reform. In line with the British Government's desire that the initiative for improving the welfare of slaves should seem to come from the colonial government, Cole wished such initiative to appear to proceed from the free-will of the masters rather than from any compulsive measure.[100]

Several slave-owners collaborated. A. D'Epinay prepared a paper on the new slavery laws published in the other British colonies, and the owners formed a committee to discuss the most appropriate means of reconciling the views of the British Government with the interests of the colony. This committee reckoned that improved conditions for the slaves had to rest on two fundamental propositions: first, that they should not alter the right of ownership; and secondly, that they should emanate from the colonists themselves.

After a detailed examination of the Trinidad Order in Council of the 10th March 1824 the committee argued that the appointment of a protector of slaves in Mauritius was superfluous. Provision for the protection of slaves, they said, was laid down in the French laws. The procureur général had to defend them in court and members of the bar had to give them assistance if called upon. Besides, they thought, the appointment of an official to champion the cause of the slaves would be impolitic. He would not be seen as the defender of the rights of the slaves but as "his blind protector, his friend and consequently the enemy of slavery, the enemy of our institutions, the enemy of the colony". The very existence of a protector, they thought, would lead to unrest. They noted that the arrival of the commissioners of inquiry in Mauritius had caused some indiscipline among slaves. Older slaves remembered the visit of a commission of the National Convention to Mauritius in 1796 bearing a decree for the general emancipation of slaves,[101] and had obviously expected a similar concession from the British commissioners.

Among other considerations, the committee questioned the wisdom of a twenty-four hour delay before corporal punishment was inflicted. They agreed that in theory it was wise not to whip slaves in the heat of the moment, but considered this was off-set by the unpleasantness the victim would suffer contemplating his punishment. They thought he would have to be imprisoned to prevent his running away. Thus the victim would suffer two penalties (imprisonment and lashes) instead of one, and the master would lose the value of his labour for a day. The committee also opposed the recording of punishments in a special book because many slave-owners could not write. Moreover, they objected to the slaves being given any right to buy their freedom because it would encourage them to acquire money by theft, brigandage, and, in the case of women, by prostitution.

In the committee's opinion, the first step was to teach the slave Christian principles and morals and to recognize their duties. They proposed to persuade slave-owners to remedy abuses which still existed, undertook to keep a strict watch on the area in which they lived, and individual members promised to correspond with the committee on all matters concerning the improvement of the slaves. The committee noted the example of the governor who, they thought, had gone a long way to improve the condition of the slaves without recourse to law.[102]

Cole had attempted to carry through reforms by executive action. In a circular to commandants and civil commissaries of the districts, he begged them generally to tone down the punishment of slaves and discontinue the whipping of female slaves. In spite of his directive, he did not approve of the immediate abolition of corporal punishment for female slaves. He agreed abolition was desirable, but he told Bathurst that because male slaves far out-numbered female slaves in Mauritius "a very general promiscuous intercourse prevails" which so debased the women that their conduct was quite as bad as the worst male slaves. In any case Cole hoped that tact and executive pressure within Mauritius would anticipate the requirements of the British Government so that when the new legislation was published in Mauritius it would only make legal what was already fact.[103]

But Cole was prepared to go further than the requirements of the law to improve the lot of slaves. He attempted to lead the way in small improvements significant to individuals. For example, it had been the practice for all slaves irrespective of age to receive the same ration of meat. The governor gave instructions for the meat ration to be increased, but he also wanted more attention paid to the age of the recipient. He noted that infants could not consume a full ration, and that in the past the excess was frequently disposed of by their parents or guardians to procure liquor or for other purposes which, instead of being beneficial, were injurious to the parties concerned. He therefore recommended a reduction in the ration for young children, and a corresponding increase in their clothing allowance or other comfort better suited to their own wants or those of their mothers.[104]

Cole was sometimes disappointed by individual slave-owners who neglected his regulations. He was very angry when he discovered that on some estates in the district of Plaines

Wilhems the bell was rung to call slaves to their work at 4 o'clock in the morning, that evening corveés worked until a late hour, and that the slaves had to work on Sunday. The commandant and civil commissary of the district was admonished because he did not compel owners to comply with regulations. The governor ordered that the morning bell was not to be rung until half an hour before sunrise, on weekdays work had to stop a quarter of an hour after sunset, and no slaves were to work on Sundays. Gendarmes were required to make regular calls to ensure the enforcement of the governor's instructions.[105]

Further improvements were written into a new ordinace[106] which prescribed the weight of the chain, fetters and iron rings which masters were entitled to put upon their slaves by way of punishment. The same ordinance prevented masters from punishing slaves returned to them by "a competent authority" after the slave had lodged a formal complaint against his master. Other legislation[107] fixed the maximum weight which a slave was permitted to carry. No ordinance was introduced regulating the condition of slaves on the lines of the Trinidad Order in Council until February 1829 after Cole had left Mauritius for the Cape.

Cole had played for time during which he maintained a diplomatic pressure on influential sections of the community to move them in the direction of local improvement of the condition of the slaves. Had he been given time, he might have succeeded.

The newly founded *Anti-Slavery Monthly Reporter*[108] was critical of slavery in Mauritius even though it focused mainly on slavery in the West Indies. The administration of Sir Robert Farquhar was vigorously attacked in retrospect, and Cole's administration received unsympathetic comment. The *Anti-Slavery Monthly Reporter* of November 1828 asked:

> "Can Sir Lowry Cole have been weak enough to imagine that a few impotent recommendations of this sort,[109] addressed to commissaries, all of whom are slaveholders or slave-drivers, would have any other result than that of exciting their rage or their ridicule?... Besides, was it only in December, 1826, that he discovered, for the first time during a residence of three or four years in this island, that men and women were cruelly and excessively flogged; that, even while at work, their limbs might be loaded with chains and fetters, and their necks so surrounded with three-pronged collars, as to prevent the sufferers from extending themselves on the earth? Was it then he first discovered that slaves were forced to work night as well as day with scarcely an interval of rest; and to work on Sundays just as on other days; and that their clothing was insufficient to cover them, and their food to sustain them? He might have known all this, and denounced it in 1823 as well as in 1826, and thus perhaps spared the miserable wretches under his government at least some small part of those sufferings, which the very terms of his circular so forcibly depict."[110]

On general lines there were some grounds for criticism. The attitude of slave-owners towards their slaves was not easy to remould. When Indian labourers were brought to Mauritius after slaves were emancipated in 1833, Governor Nicolay[111] found he had to inform prospective importers of this labour that Sunday work, unlimited hours, and corporal punishment were illegal.[112] Since administrative coercion was not possible in Mauritius, he stressed the need to win co-operation. Hence the comments made for example in the *Anti-Slavery Monthly Reporter* of November 1828, are rather beside the point.

FOOTNOTES

1. R. Coupland, *The British Anti-Slavery Movement*, p. 112.
2. 51 Geo. III, c. 23.
3. Coupland, p. 115.
4. Order in Council, 24 September 1814. The main provisions of the Order in Council are published in R. R. Kuczynski, *Demographic Survey of the British Colonial Empire*, Vol. II, pp. 716–721.
5. *C.H.B.E.*, Vol. II, p. 311.
6. Coupland, p. 117; N. Gash, *Mr. Secretary Peel*, p. 308 says that enforcement was less severe than the law.
7. *Parliamentary Debates*, published under the superintendence of T. C. Hansard, New Series. Vol. IX, c. 360.
8. *Parliamentary Debates*, published under the superintendence of T. C. Hansard, New Series, Vol. IX, c. 285–c. 286.
9. *C.H.B.E.*, Vol II, p. 809.
10. 47 Geo. III, c. 36.
11. C.O. 167/126, Report of the commissioners of inquiry on the slave trade in Mauritius, 12 March 1828.
12. G. S. Graham, *Great Britain in the Indian Ocean, 1810–1850*, p. 59.
13. 51 Geo. III, c. 23.
14. The first attempt at registering slaves had been made in Mauritius in April 1753 on instructions from the French East India Company. Subsequent registrations had been made from time to time, but carelessness, as well as a desire to evade taxes calculated on the number of slaves which slave-owners possessed made returns inaccurate and incomplete. D'Unienville, who spent many years assembling all the statistics available in the island, thought the commonly accepted figure of a 25% margin for omissions was too high. See Kuczinski, Vol. II, pp. 707–712.
15. Kuczinski, Vol. II, p. 721.
16. *Ibid.*
17. C.O. 167/26, Farquhar to Bathurst, 18 September 1815.
18. C.O. 167/29, Farquhar to Bathurst, 20 October 1816.
19. Kuczinski, Vol. II, p. 723.
20. *Ibid.*
21. Darling was commander of the troops in Mauritius from 1818 to 1823. He acted as governor from 6 February 1819 to 6 July 1820 because Farquhar was away on leave, and again for a few weeks in 1823 between the departure of Farquhar and the arrival of Cole. From 1825 to 1831 Darling was governor of New South Wales.
22. C.O. 167/82, Cole to Bathurst, 2 February 1826.
23. C.O. 167/80, Amyot to Wilmot Horton, 2 May 1825.
24. *Ibid.*
25. C.O. 167/126, Report of the commissioners of inquiry, 12 March 1828.
26. *Ibid.*
27. C.O. 167/89, Amyot to Hay, 22 March 1826.
28. C.O. 167/80, Stephen to Hay, 23 December 1825.
29. Hall was appointed commander of the troops in Mauritius in 1817 and acted as governor from 19 November 1817 to 10 December 1818.
30. C.O. 167/126, Report of the commissioners of inquiry, 12 March 1828.
31. The chief justice, 21 October 1814 to 13 August 1823.
32. C.O. 167/80, Stephen to Hay, 23 December 1825.
33. *Ibid.*
34. *Ibid.*
35. *Ibid.*
36. C.O. 168/8, Bathurst to Cole, 26 February 1826.
37. C.O. 168/8, Hay to Bradshaw, 23 December 1825.
38. C.O. 168/8, Bathurst to Cole, 18 January 1826.
39. C.O. 167/85, Cole to Bathurst, 31 October 1826.

40. Government officials in the country districts who had magisterial powers.
41. i.e. deputies to the civil commissaries.
42. C.O. 167/85, Cole to Bathurst, 31 October 1826.
43. *Ibid.*
44. See Chapter III, pp. 52–55.
45. C.O. 167/86, Cole to Bathurst, 23 December 1826; enclosure Draper to Blane, 6 December 1826.
46. C.O. 167/91, Cole to Bathurst, 28 January 1827.
47. *Ibid.*
48. C.O. 167/93, Cole to Bathurst, 14 May 1827.
49. *Ibid.*
50. C.O. 167/99, Cole to Huskisson, 9 January 1828.
51. C.O. 167/91, Cole to Bathurst, 28 January 1827.
52. C.O. 167/93, Cole to Bathurst, 14 May 1827.
53. C.O. 167/99, Cole to Huskisson, 9 January 1828.
54. C.O. 167/91, Cole to Bathurst, 28 January 1827.
55. Kuczinski, Vol. II, p. 729.
56. M. K. Jones, "The Slave Trade at Mauritius, 1810–1829", unpublished B.Litt., thesis, Oxford, 1936.
57. Instructions issued in 1822 defined the two stations as follows:
    (a) The Cape station extended in the Atlantic as far west as the equator; in the Indian Ocean the northern limit was again the equator (i.e. just north of Mombasa) and the eastern limit 60°E (thus including Mauritius and the Seychelles, but not the Chagos Islands). The southern boundary was the Antarctic circle.
    (b) The East Indies station included everywhere north of the equator on the east side of Africa, the seas south of the coast of Asia, together with the China Sea and all the coasts of the East Indies, Australia and New Zealand extending as far east as 170°W (i.e. roughly from the Bering Strait to the Antarctic Circle.) See C. Lloyd, *The Navy and the Slave Trade*, appendix D, p. 285, and G. S. Graham, *Great Britain in the Indian Ocean, 1810–1850*, pp. 455–59, for details of changes in the two boundaries from time to time.
58.

Year	1823	1824	1825	1826	1827	1828
Number of ships on the Cape station	7	4	3	4	4	5
Number of ships on the East Indies station	8	7	8	12	14	9

See Lloyd, appendix C, pp. 280–281.

59. Lloyd, p. xii.
60. *Ibid.*, p. 48.
61. Graham, p. 66.
62. Lloyd, p. 49.
63. *Ibid.*, p. xi. See also Adm. 1/69, Nourse to Croker, 7 November 1822.
64. Lloyd, p. xi.
65. C.O., 167/75, Barrow to Goulburn, 20 November 1820, enclosure W. Shield to Navy Board, 20 November 1820.
66. C.O., 167/67, Cole to Bathurst, 11 August 1823.
67. C.O. 168/7, Bathurst to the Admiralty, 18 February 1824.
68. C.O. 167/67, Cole to Bathurst, 11 August 1823.
69. C.O. 167/73, Cole to Bathurst, 18 November 1824.
70. C.O. 167/91, Cole to Bathurst, 30 January 1827.
71. C.O. 168/11, Goderich to Cole, 6 August 1827.
72. C.O. 167/97, Croker to Hay, 26 July 1827.
73. A treaty was signed with Radama in October 1817, but Hall who acted as governor during Farquhar's absence on long leave declined to fulfil its terms. The treaty was renewed in 1820; and in 1823 it was made more effective by a further treaty which permitted British cruisers to seize slave-ships in Madagascar waters and prescribed the procedure of adjudication and confiscation.

74. This treaty was concluded in 1822 by Captain Moresby, R.N., after preliminary negotiations had been made by Farquhar.
75. C.O. 167/67, Cole to Bathurst, 28 July 1823.
76. C.O. 167/67, Cole to Wilmot Horton, 17 December 1823, enclosure Moorsom to Cole, 17 November 1823.
77. De Marcenay was formerly a substitute for the *procureur général* in Mauritius. He was dismissed by Sir Robert Farquhar and subsequently spent his time making tedious remonstrances and complaints. See C.O. 167/72, Cole to Wilmot Horton, 29 May 1824.
78. C.O. 168/11, Huskisson to Cole, 1 February 1828. Confirmed C.O. 167/113. Stephen to Twiss, 29 July 1829.
79. C. Pridham, *England's Colonial Empire: An Historical, Political and Statistical Account of the Empire, its Colonies and Dependencies*, Vol. 1, "The Mauritius and its Dependencies", p. 158.
80. C.O. 167/72, Cole to Wilmot Horton, 29 May 1824. The number of slaves transported from the Seychelles to Mauritius from the 1 November 1818 to 23 July 1823, was officially given as follows:

Year	Male	Female	Total
1818	5	2	7
1819	42	6	48
1820	131	13	144
1821	237	25	262
1822	335	61	396
1823	150	47	197
	900	154	1 054

C.O. 167/126, Report of the commissioners of inquiry, 12 March 1828, states that no registers were kept at the Customs House prior to 1818, therefore there is no means of ascertaining the extent of transfers prior to that date.

81. 5 Geo. IV, c. 113.
82. 5 Geo, IV, c. 113, Section 14.
83. C.O. 167/95, Cole to Goderich, 26 August 1827.
84. C.O. 168/11, Huskisson to Cole, 12 October 1827.
85. P.R.O. 30/43/86, Cole to Wilmot Horton, 20 November 1824.
86. P.R.O. 30/43/86, Cole to Colebrooke, 29 April 1827.
87. See pp. 64–65.
88. G. R. Mellor, *British Imperial Trusteeship*, p. 89.
89. C.O. 168/6, Bathurst to Cole, 28 July 1823.
90. C.O. 112/5, Bathurst to Murray and Beard, 28 May 1823.
91. C.O. 167/7, Cole to Bathurst, 30 September 1824.
92. C.O. 168/8, Hay to Cole, 13 March 1826, Private and Confidential.
93. See V. Harlow and F. Madden, *British Colonial Developments 1774–1834*; pp. 567–573, and *C.H.B.E.*, Vol. II, p. 320.
94. P.P. 1826, XXIX, p. 110, Bathurst to D'Urban, 9 July 1825.
95. September 1826. Bigge remained at the Cape to complete the commission's work there and only visited Mauritius briefly to finalise reports on the Cape, after which he retired from the commission of inquiry.
96. C.O. 415/1, The commissioners of inquiry to Bathurst, 22 November 1826.
97. P.R.O. 30/87, Cole to Colebrooke, 29 April 1827, Private and Confidential.
98. C.O. 167/103, Smith to Leveson Gower, 3 April 1828.
99. See A. F. Madden, "The attitude of the Evangelicals to the Empire and imperial problems, 1820–1850", pp. 240–241, unpublished D.Phil. thesis, Oxford, 1950.
100. C.O. 167/86, Cole to Bathurst, 24 December 1826.
101. See R. Coupland, *East Africa and its Invaders*, p. 194; and P. J. Barnwell and A. Toussaint, *A Short History of Mauritius*, pp. 98–100 and p. 112.

When it was discovered that the commissioners were serious in their intent to free the slaves, the white colonists forced them to flee from the colony in the face of a rebellion. Slavery and the slave trade persisted throughout the period of French administration in Mauritius.

102. C.O. 167/96, Observations on the Order in Council, 10 March 1824, on the possibility of its adoption in Mauritius, on the advantages and inconveniences which result from it, and on the means of managing without violence or danger to conciliate its dispositions with the colonial interests; and an extract from the deliberations of 31 May 1827.
103. C.O. 167/86, Cole to Bathurst, 24 December 1826 in which a copy of Cole's circular is enclosed.
104. M.A., R.A. 307, Governor's Minute 77/1826, 4 July 1826.
105. M.A., R.A. 364, Governor's Minute, 97/1827, 14 October 1827.
106. Ordinance 20.
107. Ordinance 33.
108. First published in June 1825.
109. See pp. 74–75.
110. B.M., P.P. 1046, *Anti-Slavery Monthly Reporter*, Vol. II, number 42, November 1828, p. 336.
111. Governor of Mauritius, 30 January 1833 to 20 February 1840.
112. I. M. Cumpston, *Indians Overseas in British Territories, 1834–1854*, p. 13.

CHAPTER V

THE CHALLENGES AND RESPONSIBILITIES OF A NEW ENVIRONMENT:

COLE'S TRANSFER FROM MAURITIUS TO THE CAPE OF GOOD HOPE

In 1828 Sir Lowry Cole was transferred to the Cape of Good Hope. The post presented him with new challenges. In some respects the Cape did resemble Mauritius: both colonies possessed ports which in the hands of an enemy could be used as strategic bases to attack British shipping,[1] hence their harbours rather than their hinterland were valued; both were valued; both were located in areas in which the East India Company had privileged trading rights;[2] and both were inhabited by well-established European communities of non-British stock, a community of free coloured people, and a substantial slave population. But there the similarity ended. Though both Mauritius and the Cape were retained in the post-war settlement, historical development as well as geographical location made the contrast more striking than the similarities.

The British had discovered in 1781 that an enemy squadron stationed at the Cape could prove very inconvenient to British merchant shipping,[3] and this had motivated the British occupation of the Cape in 1795. Though the Cape was restored to the Dutch in the Peace of Amiens, 1802,[4] the renewal of war between Britain and France in September 1803 again highlighted the importance of the Cape. The re-occupation of the Cape was demanded by British politicians as necessary for the security of British possessions in India. Consideration of economy, which was later to become a matter of great importance to the British Government, was over-shadowed by the problem of a major war. It was argued that occupation of the Cape was "even more material as depriving the enemy of the best intermediary position between Europe and India, for assembling a large European armament for service in the East Indies".[5]

In the second half of 1805, a British fleet sailed south carrying Major General Baird and 6 700 troops.[6] A landing was effected at Blaauwberg in December 1805. The weak forces of the Dutch governor, Janssens, divided. One group fell back on Cape Town, the other, led by the governor himself, withdrew to the Hottentots Holland Mountains. The force in Cape Town was the first to capitulate. Janssens held out in his mountain fortress for another nine days, but appreciated the hopelessness of his situation, and finally capitulated with all the honours of war on the 18th January 1806.

The articles of capitulation[7] reflect British concern to control the Cape as a defensive measure. The British Government wanted political and military power and was not concerned with carrying through a social revolution like the one planned by the Batavian Government.[8] Although all the rights and privileges held and exercised by the Batavian Government at the Cape were surrendered to the British, private ownership of property, including that of men who had been civil or military servants of the Batavian Government, was respected. Moreover, the Dutch troops were repatriated to Holland at British expense. The burghers and other inhabitants[9] were preserved in all the rights and privileges they had hitherto enjoyed. Existing forms of public worship were continued without hindrance, and the legal distinction between the burghers and other inhabitants was recognized and consequent restrictions acknowledged.

Britain's title to the Cape was made permanent when the war was over. Castlereagh conducted negotiations on Britain's behalf in the post-war settlements of 1814–1815. The key-stone of his new balance of power in Europe was the creation of a strong Netherlands.[10] If it was to be an effective buffer state against future French aggression, its economy had to be strengthened, not weakened. This explains the decision to restore to the Netherlands all those colonies in America, Africa and Asia taken from her by Britain since 1793, with the exception of the Cape of Good Hope, Demerara, Essequibo and Berbice.[11]

When the peace treaties were signed in 1814–1815 Britain and Holland agreed to settle the problems of the transfer of colonies by a Supplementary Convention. The new Dutch Government was glad to be freed of the expense of maintaining the Cape and instructed its envoy, Hendrik Fagel, to concentrate his efforts upon retaining the richer colonies in South America.[12] In this he was unsuccessful, but in another Supplementary Convention negotiated the following year the Dutch secured trading rights in Demerara, Essequibo and Berbice.[13] No reference was made to the Cape; the external trade of the Cape therefore continued to be regulated by Order in Council as it had been since 1806.[14]

The Cape is on the southern extremity of a vast continent and covered in the early nineteenth century an area of approximately 200 000 square miles. The climate is temperate and attractive to European settlers. Wine, wheat, cattle and sheep were the staple products of the Cape. The vineyards and grain farms were in the south-western region where the landholdings were comparatively small and the community relatively compact. Cattle and sheep were raised to the north and east. Stock farms were large, hence the population was widely dispersed. The farmers (boers) were whites of predominantly Dutch descent while the labourers were people of colour.

Some of the labourers were slaves brought to the Cape from the Dutch possessions in the East Indies or descended from them, but few households possessed more than eight slaves.[15] The mainstay of labour in the colony was people of colour who were free. They were described in contemporary literature and documents as "Hottentots and other free persons of colour". Some of these were manumitted slaves but most of them were descendants of the Khoikhoi (Hottentot) population who inhabited the Cape when it was first visited by Portuguese sailors in the fifteenth century.[16] Some Khoikhoi had moved into the interior in the face of European penetration and, by the time Cole arrived, had settled beyond the north and north-eastern frontier of the colony.[17] Other Khoikhoi remained at the Cape but they had been decimated by three smallpox epidemics in the eighteenth century. This, together with their association with Europeans, partly explains the disintegration of their culture. By the nineteenth century there were very few of pure Khoikhoi descent within the colony. Khoikhoi blood was mixed with that of San (Bushmen),[18] Europeans and slaves in "various permutations and combinations".[19]

Though 29 545 slaves and 20 006 "Hottentots" were recorded in the census of 1805, and this increased to 35 698 slaves and 28 835 "Hottentots" by 1821,[20] the farmers complained that labour was in short supply. A potential source of additional labourers were the people who lived beyond the northern and eastern colonial frontiers. In addition to the Khoikhoi and other fugitives who for one reason or another had left the Cape, there were also among others the San and, more important, the Bantu[21] beyond the eastern frontier. Until 1828, however, the use of these people as labourers was discouraged by both Dutch and British administrators at the Cape.[22]

The question of frontier settlement was obviously a difficult one for successive governors. Legislate as they might, they had been powerless to stop expansion on the frontier until, in the east, colonists came into contact with the southward drift of Bantu migration. In 1778 the Dutch governor van Plettenberg had visited the frontier to fix a boundary between the colonists and the Bantu. Two years later the line of the Great Fish River had been proclaimed the eastern boundary of the colony.[23] The creation of a fixed line of demarcation stemmed for a time the dual tide of advance, but created tensions within each community on either side of the frontier.

The transfer of sovereignty from the Netherlands to Britain had important economic consequences for the Cape. The Netherlands was a declining commercial power, but Britain's commerce was growing. Britain's dominant maritime position and expanding interests in India, Malaysia, and the southern hemisphere offered better prospects for economic development and a different type of political control. Every effort seems to have been made to make the Cape economically viable. This would placate opposition in Britain to a permanent occupation of the Cape, and win the loyalty of the colonists to the new régime. In an effort to check inflation the issue of paper money was pegged: the governor was forbidden to make any further issues without special authority from the Crown, except to replace those worn out or defaced. Presumably this was intended to fix the exchange level of the rixdollar at the price when taken over from the Batavian authorities, that is, 3s. 4d. though nominally it was 4s.[24]

An act of 1806[25] gave the Crown the power to regulate the trade of the Cape by executive action. The act was continued from time to time by other short-term acts.[26] Practice established during the first British occupation was revived: internal trade was freed of restrictions hitherto placed on it by the Dutch East India Company, and external trade was regulated by an Order in Council of 1796. Goods imported from any part of the British dominions had free entry, while the goods of friendly foreign powers were admitted on paying a duty fixed by the governor. The only limitation upon this concession was the reservation of the East India Company's monopoly of trade to and from all parts east of the Cape.[27]

Trade with the African population was also encouraged in contra-distinction to previous practice at the Cape. The governor was asked to do his best to conciliate the affections of the Africans and induce them to trade with the colonists. He was required to report to the secretary of state on the nature and extent of trans-frontier trade, and suggest measures to extend and improve it. He was also asked to report on the possibility of cultivating timber, hemp or flax for the Royal Navy; and whether the colony had any valuable minerals such as gold, silver, iron and copper. An annual report had also to be submitted to the commissioners of the Privy Council for Trade and Plantations, through the secretary of state, on the state of the trade and fisheries of the colony. Precise details of the state of cultivation were required.[28]

A favourable balance of trade in the colony was clearly to Britain's advantage. It would ensure a good market for British products and it would help the colony to pay the costs of its administration because import and export duties were one of the colonial government's principal sources of revenue. The Cape, however, was unfortunate in that its products did not attract buyers. An attempt was made to improve the quality of wine for export, but in days before refrigeration it was impossible to export fresh meat, fruit and vegetables. The sale of these perishable commodities was restricted to the victualling of vessels passing through Cape Town. Thus the Cape government was more dependent upon other sources of revenue than it might have been had trade conditions at the Cape been more fortunate.

Land, of which there was plenty, was an obvious asset. It had provided an income for the colonial government since van Riebeeck[29] had established the quitrent system for the first Free Burghers in 1657.[30] When the British occupied the Cape they found established principles for acquiring revenue from land. A farmer had to pay 24 rixdollars (about £5) per annum for a grazing licence. The term used for this payment was "recognite" – the implication being that the licensee "recognized" the Dutch East India Company as the owner of his stock farm, though as a matter of fact he held it on an indeterminate lease. With the passage of time and the natural increase in the population there was a growing demand for more farms, hence new lands were brought under the hoof or plough. Administrative machinery did not have a corresponding rate of growth and consequently it became increasingly difficult to collect this revenue. Caledon's instructions, however, required him to take the necessary measures to ensure regular payment of the quitrent to avoid loss to the public revenue from an accumulation of arrears. He was also instructed to make himself familiar with the management and disposal of land by the Company, and advise the Crown as the successors of the Company on the future management and disposal of land.[31]

Concern for the colony's trade, the careful collection of quitrent, and an attempt to regulate the disposal of Crown land, however, did not mean that the colonial government received sufficient revenue to meet expenditure. In 1828, even after reductions had been effected, more than 62% of the total revenue for that year was paid out in salaries to government officials. Approximately another 4½% was paid in civil and military pensions.[32] Before Cole arrived at the Cape, colonists had criticised this expense and opposed further taxation to meet the deficit. In their opinion the administration was inefficient and could only be rectified by the termination of autocratic government.[33]

Whether the government of the Cape was autocratic or not, it is a fact that the Cape was a difficult colony to govern. The complex and rapidly growing population was a problem in itself. In 1806 there were 26 568 whites, and by 1825 there were 50 613. The average annual increase between 1825 and 1837 was 2½%, which means it probably exceeded 53 000 in 1828 – approximately double the figure of 1806.[34] This expansion of the white population can in part be explained by natural increase, and in part by immigration from Britain. Some British merchants naturally gravitated to Cape Town. The shortage of labour[35] had encouraged Benjamin Moodie to bring out 300 young Scots in 1817.[36] This was followed by a large-scale immigration sponsored by the British Government in 1820 to strengthen the eastern frontier by the settlement of a compact white community. Approximately 4 000 British settlers[37] were brought to the Cape and most of them were settled in the frontier of Albany.[38] In subsequent years there was a moderate stream of immigrants from Britain, which is estimated to have varied from 100 to 200 per annum.[39] In spite of the increases, the white population remained out-numbered by the non-whites. The total population in 1822 was estimated at 111 451. By 1830 this had grown to 124 455.[40] The precise number of slaves is not known but it can be safely estimated at approximately 35 000.[41] By deduction, therefore, the free coloured population must have been about the same figure.[42]

The scheme to settle Britons on the frontier in 1820 was a failure. Albany was not suitable for intensive farming. Crop failures and bad rapport between settlers and government officials caused concern in Britain.[43] Moreover, like Mauritius, attention was drawn to the Cape by the parlous condition of its finances and by humanitarian interest in the treatment of the slaves and the free coloured population. Thus the British Government decided to include the Cape, with Mauritius and Ceylon, in the terms of reference of a commission of inquiry they appointed in January 1823.

Among the problems referred to the commissioners was a memorial signed by 171 British settlers on the 19th March 1823,[44] in which they set out their complaints about conditions at the Cape. They pointed out that the 100 acre grants of land made to them were not large enough to support them and their families under South African farming conditions and observed that the farms granted to the Dutch farmers at the Cape were all about 4 000 acres. Their position was made more difficult by local officials who withheld part of the deposit money due to be refunded after they had occupied their holdings. As a result the majority of settlers did not have sufficient capital to change from agricultural to pastoral farming, for which the area was more suitable. But even had their position been improved there was no market for their surplus produce because artificial restraints were placed on their trade. The military provided the chief internal market, and this was monopolised by the colonial government which obtained supplies from the government farm at Somerset. All the external trade of the colony was confined to the port of Cape Town and although the settlers lived near Algoa Bay their external trade was subjected to the expense of transshipment in Cape Town.

Many settlers resented Somerset's decision to transfer the drostdy[45] from Bathurst to Grahamstown in 1822 in order to keep the civil and military headquarters of the district in close proximity. Their resentment was in part explained by investments in land made with the greater importance of Bathurst rather than Grahamstown in mind, and in part because of their general ill-feeling towards Somerset's government. They were also displeased because a garrison stationed at Fredericksburg beyond the frontier was withdrawn. They complained that reduced military protection had exposed the frontier to raids by Xhosa,[46] as a result of which cattle were taken and several murders committed within a few months.[47]

The memorialists alleged that attempts to redress their grievances were frustrated by local officials, and in particular they resented the refusal of permission to hold a public meeting to discuss their problems. On the day the meeting was to have been held, the 24th May 1822, the governor issued a proclamation reminding the settlers that public meetings held without his consent were illegal and punishable with severe penalties. They concluded their memorial by alluding to their objection to the system of government and laws to which they were subjected.

The recommendations of the commissioners of inquiry[48] and subsequent action by the British Government show that they were sympathetic to the problems of the settlers. The government farm at Somerset was sold, and the supply of produce for the troops was thrown open to the public.[49] Algoa Bay (Port Elizabeth) was opened to external trade.[50] Grahamstown remained the headquarters of the civil and military authorities, and soon became a thriving commercial centre for the eastern districts.[51] It was intended to appoint a lieutenant-governor for the eastern districts, and indeed one was appointed in the person of Major-General Bourke. Soon after his arrival in the Cape, however, he was sworn in as acting governor because of Somerset's return to Britain.[52] In view of the poor financial resources of the colony the British Government decided in 1828 to reduce the rank of the senior civil officer in the eastern districts to that of commissioner-general.[53] Meanwhile as early as 1825 some restraint was placed on the autocracy of the governor by the creation of a council of advice whose composition and powers were similar to those of the council created in Mauritius at the same time.[54] Substantial changes were also made in the colonial judiciary.[55]

The settlers were not satisfied by the administrative reforms. They constantly alleged that government from Cape Town was too remote to be effective in the eastern districts. Moreover, the office of commissioner-general did not prove to be a success. Andries Stockenstrom, who held the office from 1828 to 1833, resigned it in 1833 because he considered his position superfluous[56] and the office was abolished the following year without a successor ever being appointed. A separatist movement developed in the eastern districts which became at intervals a major political factor at the Cape for the next fifty years.[57]

Another problem with which the colonial government had had to grapple was the question of the relationship between the colonists and the people who lived beyond the frontier. In spite of Somerset's frontier agreement with Ngqika in 1819,[58] the segregation of Xhosa and colonists on the eastern frontier by a barrier of unoccupied land proved impracticable. The close settlement of white people to strengthen the frontier on the colonial side added to the population pressure in that area at a point when chain reaction from tribal warfare further north had its repercussions on the frontier chiefdoms. Tribal land became congested. Both Xhosa and colonists therefore pressed forward to occupy the empty lands. Close proximity soon led to complaints by colonists that Xhosa stole their cattle. In terms of an arrangement that Somerset had made with Ngqika in 1817,[59] burgher patrols could trace animals to a kraal and put the onus on a headman either to prove that the spoor led beyond his kraal or to return the stolen beast with compensation.

Contact between colonists and their neighbours was not confined to feuds about land and cattle. On the north and north-eastern frontier friction between the colonists and their neighbours was less intense than on the eastern frontier. No doubt this is partly explained by the fact that the political organization of the Khoikhoi, San and Mantatee[60] tribes who lived beyond that frontier was much looser than that of the Xhosa, and partly because the terrain was easier to cross. Trekboers often grazed their cattle and sheep round the waterholes and grasslands beyond the northern and north-eastern frontier. On occasion they gave presents of animals to San as a form of insurance against the theft of their livestock.[61]

Missionaries initiated more subtle contact between the colonists and the trans-frontier peoples because they were the harbingers of western civilization among the latter. Nosipho Majeke[62] claimed that they undermined the traditional political structure of the several chiefdoms, and prepared the way for subsequent annexation by Great Britain.[63] In part he is correct, but it is not the whole truth. On occasion the missionaries were used as agents of the colonial government but they disliked this rôle because their official duties sometimes lost them the confidence of the chief and the people among whom they worked.[64] However, even when they were not official agents they often found themselves acting as intermediaries between the colonial government and the chiefs because they were usually the only people who could understand both English and the African language in the area where they worked.

Perhaps more important than their rôle as intermediaries was the attack missionaries made on traditional African values where these conflicted with Christian principles. Chiefs would naturally be sceptical, even resentful, of men who undermined their power by condemning witchcraft, advocating monogamy, and proclaiming a message of peace and goodwill on earth. According to Majeke the teaching of Christianity was only a camouflage for sinister imperial expansion.[65] Traders always followed in the wake of the missionaries, hence Majeke asserts that "the Bible and the bale of Lancashire cotton became the twin agents of a revolutionary change".[66]

There is some justification for linking the work of the missionaries with temporal affairs. Dr. John Philip, the superintendent of the London Missionary Society in South Africa from 1820 to 1850, claimed that "while our missionaries, beyond the borders of the Cape of Good Hope, are everywhere scattering the seeds of civilization, social order, and happiness, they are, by the most exceptional means, extending British interests, British influence, and the British empire".[67] In material terms this meant the development of markets for British manufactured goods. Such was the case within the colony too. In pleading for improved conditions for the Khoikhoi in the colony Philip asserted that "a new and extensive market would be created for British goods".[68] Missionaries shared with Donkin[69] the view that trade had an educative and civilizing effect upon the Africans.[70] But to condemn the missionaries as the fifth column of economic imperialism, as does Majeke,[71] is to under-estimate the attraction of trade to those who buy as well as those who sell.

The colonial government's attempts to regulate trans-frontier trade through fairs, first in Grahamstown (1817), then at Fort Willshire (1824) and on the banks of the Tyhume River (1827), failed because of the greater profits traders could make by deeper penetration into tribal territory. Trans-frontier trade rescued the British settlers from their economic plight. Grahamstown which in the first instance had been selected as a focal point of frontier defence soon became an entrepôt where traders sold trans-frontier products like ivory, hides and skins and purchased worthless articles like glass beads and brass wire for purposes of barter.[72]

The expanding economy of the eastern districts was soon reflected in a shortage of labour. Logically this could be solved by utilizing the labour of the people who lived beyond the frontier. In 1828 the colonial government passed an ordinance[73] which permitted the entry of trans-frontier people into the colony to seek work on contract.

Within the colony Ordinance 50, promulgated on the 17th July 1828, gave a new deal to "Hottentots and other free persons of colour". This ordinance lifted restrictions and released these people from undertaking compulsory services for which white colonists were not liable. It restated the need for written contracts of service, specifically declared Khoikhoi and free coloureds able to possess freehold property, and generally pronounced all the King's subjects who were not slaves, equal in law. This ordinance, confirmed by Order in Council in 1829,[74] became the pattern for British Orders in Council for other colonies,[75] and laid the basis for the legal equality of colonists of whatever race in most colonies once the slaves were emancipated. Thus the improvement of the condition of slaves by Ordinance 19 of 1826[76] was also a signpost of the new direction of the relationship of the several population groups within the colony.

Arrangements made for the government of the colony were temporary, pending a final peace settlement. But no one seriously considered a second retrocession, hence there are threads of continuity which antedated 1815 and persisted. This shows in an interesting manner when the instructions to successive governors are examined.

The first civil governor, the earl of Caledon, took office on the 22nd May 1807.[77] Even though his commission[78] referred to the "temporary" government of the colony, the breadth of his instructions[79] suggests a far greater degree of permanence. Moreover, the instructions issued to Caledon's successors – Sir John Cradock[80] and Lord Charles Somerset[81] were substantially the same as Caledon's. Even the instructions issued to Cole were similar though they included provision for a council of advice which had been created in 1825 during Somerset's governorship.[82]

Pencil comments on the copy of Cradock's instructions kept in the Colonial Department show that they were used as a model by the officials who prepared those for Cole. Successive Cape governors were vested with considerable power. Indeed in broad terms there is some justification for the claim that until 1854 when the Cape was given a representative legislature they had despotic powers.[83] Professor Manning says that "the outstanding characteristic of the Government of the Cape Colony was the concentration of authority in the hands of the governor, whose powers were greater than in any other colony except New South Wales".[84]

Caledon was given autocratic powers within the colony: all the powers of government, military as well as civil, were vested solely in him. Warrants for the issue of public money for all public services could only be signed by the governor. But the authorities in Britain kept a careful check on him. There was no question of his deputing his powers to an agent for he was expressly forbidden to leave his command without formal leave of absence. He was obliged to keep the secretary of state for War and the Colonial Department fully informed on all matters concerning his government and he had to report everything he did. He had to submit all orders, regulations or laws for the secretary of state's approval, in a prescribed form which included a full preamble and marginal abstracts, and support them by a full statement on their necessity.

The governor's control of the public purse was carefully supervised by the Treasury in Britain. Caledon was required to keep an account of his receipt and expenditure of public money. He had to submit these accounts to the Treasury twice a year, or more frequently if the occasion required it. He even had to report fines and forfeitures in excess of £10 to the Treasury and could only dispose of the money on the specific instructions of the Crown.

A further limitation on the governor's power lay in his inability to make permanent appointments. Caledon could only make temporary appointments to vacancies. Moreover he was expressly forbidden to fill any office granted under the Great Seal of the United Kingdom to which appointment was usually made by warrant under the royal signet and sign manual. According to A. Berriedale Keith such offices might include the chief justice, attorney-general, secretary, surveyor-general, and receiver-general, but there was no fixed principle governing these matters.[85] Appointment to office in the colony depended upon influence in Britain rather than any nomination the governor might make on grounds of ability or competence.[86]

Caledon was charged with the temporary administration of justice and the police. He was instructed to exercise these powers in conformity with the procedure practised by the Dutch East India Company modified by regulations and improvements made during the previous British occupation. The courts had been reformed by the Batavian authorities in 1803,[87] and it was in fact the practice then established that the British continued. The judges were required to administer justice promptly and impartially in all the courts of the colony. Appeal lay to the governor who with the lieutenant-governor,[88] or separately, was empowered to form a Court of Civil Jurisdiction. In the exercise of his appellate jurisdiction the governor would hear and determine appeals in causes involving at least £200. When more than £500 was involved further appeal lay to the Crown in Council provided the appeal was made within fourteen days after sentence and good security was given by the appellant to cover costs. When a case involved duty payable to the Crown, or any established fees of office, or annual rents, for which there was no precedent, appeal lay directly to the Privy Council however small the sum. In all criminal cases in which fines amounted to £100 or more appeal was also allowed to the Privy Council provided adequate security was given.

The governor's commission as vice-admiral gave him other legal duties, particularly in respect of piracy and prizes. Until 1827 these powers were usually exercised independently of the civil judicial authorities but in that year they were transferred to the chief justice.[89]

To keep the authorities in Britain up to date with the state of the defence at the Cape the governor was instructed to report regularly to the secretary of state and the master-general of the ordinance on the state of the defences and the stores of war such as arms and ammunition kept not only in the public magazines but also by private persons. Moreover, he was instructed to make a survey of all the major rivers, landing places and harbours and to report what further fortifications were needed. As a further security measure he was authorized to disarm those who did not have his licence to keep arms. In addition, he had authority to banish from the colony suspected traitors and "such other persons the Continuance of whose residence you may have reason to imagine might be inconvenient or prejudicial to the Peace, Good Order and Security of the . . . Settlement".[90] Although the governor was forbidden to declare war without the King's specific command except in defence of the colony or unavoidable emergency, he was empowered to raise troops to maintain peace, order and good government in the colony.

The form of government in the colony was undoubtedly autocratic but it would be wrong to imply that the British Government intended it always to remain so. The Crown had reserved the powers of its prerogative not to entrench dictatorial authority but to leave the British Government free to manoeuvre in the light of experience.[91] Thus the structure of government, like policy, was revised when conditions changed.

The first overtures by Bathurst to Cole were made early in 1826 as soon as it became clear that Somerset might relinquish the governorship of the Cape. He had aroused the ire of the colonists and their complaints were taken up by politicians in Britain who seized the opportunity to attack Liverpool's ministry by attacking him. Somerset was charged in the House of Commons with the maladministration of the government of the Cape.[92] He returned to Britain to answer these charges. Bathurst surmised that Somerset would be successful in defending himself "in the most important parts" of the accusations against him.[93] Indeed a motion introduced into the House to test the accusations was abandoned.[94] But Bathurst appreciated that it would be difficult for Somerset to return to the Cape because of his personal unpopularity, the activities of his personal enemies, and the mismanagement of the Cape revenue and consequent financial embarrassment.[95]

The expenditure of the colonial administration was grossly in excess of revenue. Cuts in government expenditure had to be effected. Among these the British Government included the salary of the governor. The reduction in the governor's salary was expected to be about two or three thousand pounds, that is, a reduction from £10 000 per annum to £8 000 or £7 000. This reduction was expected to be distasteful to Somerset, a fact in itself which made his return doubtful. Thus Sir Lowry Cole was asked whether or not he would be interested if the Cape governorship should fall vacant.[96]

Cole had reservations about accepting the post at the Cape. He told Bathurst that he would leave Mauritius with regret but that he thought a move to a colder climate was in the best interests of his children. He cavilled at the reduction in salary and, though he accepted the offer of the post, he hoped that Bathurst would not be forced to reduce the salary below £8 000 a year,[97] which was lower than he received as governor of Mauritius.[98] Bathurst, however, was unable to refuse the recommendation of the commissioners of inquiry to fix the governor's salary at £7 000 in view of the financial circumstances of the colony and because he also proposed to appoint a lieutenant-governor who would have charge of the eastern districts of the colony. He was obviously not anxious to rush Cole into taking the post. In any case, he told Cole, he expected Somerset to go back to the Cape "just to show he is not recalled in disgrace, tho' he will certainly not like to remain after all these reductions both in authority and emoluments".[99] Correct though Bathurst generally was in these suppositions, he was wrong in one particular: Somerset chose to resign in June 1827[100] without ever returning to the Cape.

Cole, the family man, considered it necessary to remove his family from a tropical climate. He had already sent one child to the Cape for the recovery of her health. Thus he accepted the Cape governorship even though it was "less desirable than when first offered". He complained of the decision of the British Government to sell the governor's country house. He noted that the furniture in Government House in Cape Town belonged to Somerset, and hinted that in view of the reduced salary, Government House should be repaired and furnished at government expense.[101] Finally, he challenged the recommendation of the commissioners of inquiry to reduce the governor's salary. "I believe", he wrote, "there is no one who has had anything to say to a Colonial Council who will assert that it diminishes the labors of the Governor, whatever it may his responsibility".[102] Besides, the British Government had decided to suspend the division of the colony into two and not to appoint a lieutenant-governor.[103] Cole therefore argued that he could not see where the labours of the Cape governor had been reduced except in his judicial capacity.[104] This slight reduction of duties he thought was off-set by the changes made at the Cape on the recommendation of the commissioners of inquiry.

"Time will tell", he wrote, "how far so complete a revolution has been wise or prudent – but I confess I am far from being satisfied of the prudence of my accepting Lord Bathurst's offer of the government of the Cape. There will be plenty of work . . . without credit I fear, or even profit to recompense."[105]

Cole, in taking up the governorship of the Cape, faced problems far more exacting than those which had confronted him in Mauritius. A substantial number of British settlers was added to the complex population of alien white people and free and slave non-white people. The economy of the Cape, unlike Mauritius, had no valuable cash crop. Cape wine, though protected by preferential duties when imported into Britain, could not compete with European wines on the world market. The victualling of ships was an inadequate market for the produce available, and, in any case, was subject to the fluctuations of world trade.

When Cole arrived at the Cape the economy was depressed, and was made more so by retrenchment in the government service and reduction in government expenditure. Reduced financial circumstances caused discontent, especially among the white land-owners and merchants. Their privileged position, moreover, had been threatened by legislation to improve the conditions of the slaves, and subsequently by Ordinance 50 which had given all free people of colour in the colony legal equality with white.

The vast distances at the Cape were a new experience for Cole. The difficulty of governing the island dependencies of Mauritius were exchanged for the perplexity of controlling a large colony with hundreds of miles of inadequately guarded land frontiers beyond which lived people whose society was imperfectly understood by both government officials and colonists.

At the point of Cole's entry into Cape affairs the first British extra-territorial demonstration in southern Africa had just taken place. In July and August 1828 a commando under Colonel Henry Somerset[106] went as far as Umtata to defend Xhosa chiefdoms against the Zulu aggressors. About the same time the Ngwane[107] attacked the Cape Thembu. Apparently the colonial authorities did not realise that the Ngwane and the raiding Zulus were quite unconnected, consequently they thought they had fought the Zulus when in fact they had fought the Ngwane. The latter were defeated in two decisive battles, whilst the Zulu impi[108] returned to their own country without a shot being fired at them by British soldiers.[109]

Such unrest clearly had repercussions. The more sparsely settled land within the colonial boundaries attracted encroachment. The problem had been tackled by Cole's predecessors without great success. Cole attempted to solve the problem by minor amendment to previously fixed boundary lines.[110] He was fortunate in that while he was governor there was no major frontier conflagration. The war which broke out in December 1834, some sixteen months after Cole left the colony, could not be attributed to him alone but rather to the gradual eastward movement of the colonial frontier itself. Even had Cole wanted to reverse earlier policy, it was too late to be practical politics. He continued the policy of his predecessors and attempted to enforce the separation of the colonists from their neighbours.

The years of Cole's governorship of the Cape (1828–1833) were crucial ones for the colony. Steps were taken to improve the economy, but even so the colonial treasurer had to struggle to balance the books. Reductions were again made in the government service and public works were curtailed.[111] Moreover, measures drafted in Britain to improve the condition of the slaves further met with stiff opposition from the white colonists. Firm action on the part of Cole prevented any serious disturbance of the peace but increased the opposition of white colonists to government from Britain by British officials.[112] The white colonists proposed constitutional reforms which would transfer legislative power to a legislature elected by themselves.[113] Judicial reforms introduced in 1828, however meritorious in most respects, had nevertheless provided for trial by jury in criminal cases. The qualifications prescribed for jurymen were so narrow as almost to fix a permanent panel of white jurors in some districts, if indeed a jury could be assembled at all. The decisions of the white jurors were not without racial bias.[114] This suggests that had legislative power been put into the hands of the white colonists all the efforts of the British government to improve the lot of the slaves and free coloured people would have been undermined. No doubt as legislators the white colonists would have tackled the question of the frontier[115] with a policy which might well have amounted to one of subordination of the Bantu.

FOOTNOTES

1. See D. M. Schreuder, *Gladstone and Kruger*, pp. 7–13 on the strategic importance of the Cape "in the geometry of imperial defence". See also *C.H.B.E.*, Vol. VIII, (2nd edition), pp. 169–170.
2. i.e. east of the Cape of Good Hope and west of the Straits of Magellan.
3. V. T. Harlow, *The Founding of the Second British Empire*, Vol. 1, pp. 106–135. A French fleet under Admiral de Suffren beat the British commodore, Johnstone, in a race for the control of the Cape. Walker, p. 104 says, "The Frenchmen virtually occupied Capetown for three years."
4. The Cape was not regarded as a commercial asset and seamen of such rank as Admirals Lord Nelson and Lord St. Vincent discounted its strategic importance. See *C.H.B.E.*, Vol. VIII, (2nd edition), p. 193, and G. S. Graham, *The Politics of Naval Supremacy*, p. 40, and G. S. Graham, *Great Britain in the Indian Ocean, 1810–1850*, pp. 27–28.
5. Graham, *The Politics of Naval Suremacy*, p. 40, quotes Castlereagh to Cornwallis, 10 September 1805 (enclosed in Castlereagh to the lords commissioners of the Admiralty, 10 September 1805), Adm. 1/4200.
6. Walker, p. 137.
7. W.O. 1/342, Articles of Capitulation signed by Lieutenant-General Janssens, the governor and commander-in-chief of the Batavian forces, Cape of Good Hope, 19 January 1806.
8. "Memorandum by Commissary J. A. de Mist, containing recommendations for the form and administration of government at the Cape of Good Hope, 1802": English version edited by K. M. Jeffreys and a preface by S. F. N. Gie; publication number 3 of the Van Riebeeck Society.
9. The term *free burgher* was first used in 1657 with reference to a handful of men who were discharged from service in the Dutch East India Company to farm on their own account. With the growth of the European population independent of the Company the more general term of *burgher* was used. In 1803 the Batavian authorities limited the right of burghership to those who had been born at the Cape or who had lived in the colony for three years and could give proof of good conduct. All who had not been born at the Cape or in Holland or procured a proper title of burghership were aliens who only had temporary rights of residence which could be withdrawn at the governor's pleasure. These arrangements of 1803 were continued by the British authorities after 1806, hence even British subjects who went to the Cape without the British Government's permission were obliged to get the governor's permission if they wished to remain in the colony. Presumably new Dutch immigrants were similarly placed. The distinction made in the articles of capitulation between "the burghers and other inhabitants" was to distinguish the burghers from the aliens. Presumably the free coloured people at the Cape were recognised as burghers in the articles of capitulation because the Batavian authorities had declared that "the Aborigines of this Colony, the Hottentots, were to be considered and treated as free people, who had a legal right of residence in the Colony and who were therefore the same as other free People to be protected in their persons, property and possessions". See report of J. T. Bigge on the courts of justice at the Cape, 6 September 1826, published in Theal, *R.C.C.*, Vol. XXVIII, pp. 33–38.
10. C. J. Bartlett, *Great Britain and Sea Power*, 1815–1853, p. 59.

11. *B.F.S.P.*, Vol. II, Convention between Great Britain and the Netherlands, 13 August 1814, Article 1.
12. *C.H.B.E.*, Vol. VIII, (2nd edition), p. 214.
13. *B.F.S.P.*, Vol. III, pp. 386–96. Convention between Great Britain and the Netherlands, 12 August 1815.
14. *C.H.B.E.*, Vol. VIII, (2nd edition), pp. 233–237.
15. See Chapter VII, p. 117 and Appendix B, p. 178.
16. For an account of the characteristics, distribution, social, economic and political organization of the Khoikhoi see M. Wilson and L. Thompson, (ed.), *The Oxford History of South Africa*, Vol. I, Chapter II.
17. See Chapter VI, pp. 102–103.
18. Professor Wilson points out that scholar's attempts to fit scientific classifications to popular usage have bedevilled discussion on hunters and herders. Skin colour and economy have been the basis of classification. *All* the yellow-skinned hunters were *San* to Khoikhoi herders and *Bushmen* to Whites. The Whites assumed that the *San* all spoke the same language because they all *clicked*, where as in fact they spoke a variety of languages. See M. Wilson and L. Thompson (ed.), *The Oxford History of South Africa*, Vol. I, pp. 41–47.
19. J. S. Marais, *The Cape Coloured People* 1652–1937, pp. 9–19.
20. Marais, p. 31, fn. 1. See also p. 84 and Chapter VII, p. 111 in which doubt is cast on the accuracy of the figure relative to slaves.
21. They are a congeries of people speaking the language of the Bantu subgroup of the Niger Congo language family, who inhabit most of Africa south of the equator. The term Bantu is primarily a linguistic one although Bantu-speaking peoples in specific areas, such as southern Africa, have strong cultural and physical affinities. The two major groupings of Bantu-speakers in southern Africa are the Sotho and Nguni. The former live in the interior, and the latter occupy the eastern coastal region between the Drakensberg and the sea. For an account of the Nguni and Sotho people see M. Wilson and L. Thompson, (ed.), *The Oxford History of South Africa*, Vol. I, Chapters III and IV.
22. See Chapter VI.
23. H. M. Robertson, "150 Years of Economic Contact between Black and White", Part I, *The South African Journal of Economics*, Vol. II, 1934, p. 404. See also J. S. Marais, *Maynier and the First Boer Republic*, pp. 5–6.
24. *C.H.B.E.*, Vol. VIII, (2nd edition), p. 197. See also M. Wilson and L. Thompson (ed.), *The Oxford History of South Africa*, Vol. I, p. 295. More paper money was issued between 1810 and 1815 which partly explains the decline in the value of the rixdollar to 1s.6d. by 1825.
25. 46 Geo. III, c. 30.
26. 49 Geo. III, c. 17; 56 Geo. III, c. 8; 1 Geo. IV, c. 11.
27. *C.H.B.E.*, Vol. VIII, (2nd edition), p. 182.
28. C.O. 49/9, Instructions to the earl of Caledon, 1 August 1806. Caledon was governor of the Cape of Good Hope, 22 May 1807–4 July 1811.
29. Commander, 7 April 1652–6 May 1662.
30. *C.H.B.E.*, Vol. VIII, (2nd edition), pp. 117–118. For the term *Free Burgher* see fn. 9 above.
31. After the British occupied the Cape, land not yet granted to any individual was usually called Crown land
32. C.O. 48/131. Total revenue for 1828 was £128 971.12.8$\frac{7}{8}$d, of which £80 220.14.16$\frac{1}{4}$d was paid in salaries and £5 925.16.11$\frac{1}{4}$d was paid in pensions.
33. See Chapter IX, pp. 147–149.
34. C. G. W. Schumann, *Structural Changes and Business Cycles in South Africa*, p. 38.
35. See pp. 81–2.
36. *C.H.B.E.*, Vol. VIII, (2nd edition), p. 238.
37. Estimates vary between 3 475 and 4 320 settlers because lists do not tally, see U. Long (ed.), *The Chronicle of Jeremiah Goldswain*, Vol. 1, p. xvii. The most recent list is that of E. M. Jones, *Roll of the British Settlers in South Africa*, Part I, "Up to 1826", which gives the total number of settlers as 4 320.
38. That part of the district of Uitenhage called the Zuurveld was proclaimed the district of Albany in 1814. It became a separate drostdy in 1820. See fn. 45 below.
39. Schumann, p. 41.
40. A. Wilmot and J. C. Chase, *History of the Cape of Good Hope*, appendix iii.
41. See Chapter VII, p. 111.
42. Calculation in approximate figures: total population 125 000 less 54 000 whites and 35 000 slaves, leaves 36 000 free people of colour. Compare figures given Chapter VIII, p. 138, fn. 8.

43. See I. E. Edwards, *The 1820 Settlers in South Africa*, Chapter V.
44. Theal, *R. C. C.*, Vol. XV, pp. 305–311.
45. The term *drostdy* applies to the unit of local government at the Cape under the supervision of a landdrost – an official who had both administrative and magisterial duties. The seat of the landdrost was also called the *drostdy*. In this case the area of the drostdy was unchanged but the seat of the landdrost was transferred from one township to the other.
46. The term X*hosa* is a general one applicable to the tribal cluster of people who lived between the Keiskamma and the Umtamvuna Rivers. The chiefdom immediately beyond the frontier was the *Ngqika*. Several small chiefdoms, among them the *Ndhlambe*, actually occupied territory west of the Keiskamma. Attempts by the colonial government to remove them were subsequently the cause of considerable friction. In contemporary nineteenth century literature and documents the Xhosa are usually called the *caffres* or the *Kaffirs*. Originally these terms were not derogatory. They are derived from an arabic word meaning 'non-believer' and were used in the colony as a colloquial synonym for 'pagans'.
47. G. Cory, *The Rise of South Africa*, Vol. II, Chapter IV.
48. Theal, *R. C. C.*, Vol. XXI, pp. 279–326 for the report of the commissioners of inquiry to Bathurst upon the "Address of the Principal Settlers in the Albany District," 25 May 1825; and P.P. 1826–7, XXI (371), pp. 89–97, for further observations of the commissioners to Bathurst, 24 December 1825.
49. *C.H.B.E.*, Vol. VIII, (2nd edition), p. 245.
50. *Ibid.* See also Chapter VIII, p. 135.
51. K. S. Hunt, "The Development of Municipal Government in the Eastern Province of the Cape of Good Hope with special reference to Grahamstown 1827–1862", *Archives Year Book for South African History*, 1961, p. 149.
52. Bourke was acting governor of the Cape of Good Hope, 5 March 1826 to 9 September 1828.
53. Andries Stockenstrom was appointed to the post. See Chapter VI, p. 96.
54. See Chapter II, pp. 39–40, and Chapter IX, pp. 141–146.
55. See Chapter X, pp. 156–157.
56. C. W. Hutton (ed.), *The Autobiography of the late Sir Andries Stockenstrom, Bart.*, Vol. I, p. 407. See also J. L. Dracopoli, *Sir Andries Stockenstrom*, pp. 90–91.
57. D. B. Sole, "The separation movement and the demand for resident government in the Eastern Province (comprising a record of political opinion in the Province during the half century 1828–1878)", unpublished M.A. thesis, Rhodes University College, 1939.
58. Theal, *R. C. C.*, Vol. XII, pp. 342–5. See also Chapter VI, p. 98.
59. Theal, *R. C. C.*, Vol. XI, p. 314, Minutes of a conference between Somerset and Ngqika at the Kat River on 2 April 1817, enclosed in Somerset to Bathurst, 24 April 1817. See Chapter VI, p. 97.
60. The word *Mantatee* as it appears in contemporary writings was used to describe any displaced marauding group of tribesmen. It is a corruption of Mantatisi of the BaTlokwa who had been displaced by the Hlubi during the mfecane or "crushing" of tribes which followed the rise of Zulu military power after 1816. Mantatisi acted as regent for her son Sikonyela: her prowess as a warrior probably explains the colonial habit of describing all displaced groups as *Mantatees*. See W. F. Lye, "The Difaquane: the Mfecane in the Southern-Sotho area 1822–1824", *Journal of African History*, Vol. VIII, number 1 (1967), pp. 107–131.
61. J. S. Marais, *The Cape Coloured People*, 1652–1937, pp. 19–21.
62. The name Nosipho Majeke is a pseudonym. It is not known whether he is an African or European. It is clear from the contents of his book, *The Role of the Missionaries in Conquest*, that he is arguing from a Marxist standpoint.
63. N. Majeke, *The Role of the Missionaries in Conquest*, pp. 6–8.
64. D. Williams, "The missionary as government agent on the Eastern frontier 1818–1830", unpublished M.A. thesis, University of the Witwatersrand, 1953.
65. Majeke, pp. 6–8.
66. *Ibid*, p. 7.
67. J. Philip, *Researches in South Africa*, Vol. I, Preface, pp. ix–x.
68. Philip, Vol. I, p. 365.
69. Acting governor of the Cape of Good Hope in the absence on leave of Lord Charles Somerset from 13 January 1820 to 30 November 1821.

70. H. M. Robertson, "150 Years of Economic Contact between Black and White", Part I, *The South African Journal of Economics*, Vol. II, 1934, p. 410.
71. Majeke, p. 8.
72. Hunt, *Archives Year Book for South African History*, 1961, p. 153.
73. Ordinance 49 of 1828, see Chapter VI, p. 99.
74. H. A. Gailey Jr., "John Philip's Role in Hottentot Emancipation", *Journal of African History*, Vol. III, number 3 (1962) pp. 419–433.
75. For example, Order in Council for Trinidad, 18 March 1829; for St. Lucia, 16 June 1829; and Mauritius, 22 June 1829. A. Burns, *History of the British West Indies*, p. 625 says "In 1828 all legal disabilities connected with colour were abolished in the Crown Colonies by Order-in-Council", but no such Order/s in Council could be traced in the Privy Council Register for 1828. See also W. L. Mathieson, *British Slavery and its Abolition*, 1823–1838, p. 195, fn. 1.
76. See Chapter VII, pp. 113–114.
77. During the first sixteen months of the second British occupation the commander of the forces acted as governor.
78. C.O. 49/9, Commission dated 30 July 1806.
79. C.O. 49/9, Instructions dated 1 August 1806.
80. The Colonial Department's copy of Cradock's instructions dated 9 April 1811 can be found in C.O. 49/10. He was governor of the Cape of Good Hope, 6 September 1811 to 6 April 1814.
81. The Colonial Department's copy of Somerset's instructions dated 2 November 1813 can be found in C.O. 49/10. He was governor of the Cape of Good Hope, 6 April 1814 to 5 November 1826 though he only resigned in June 1827 while he was on leave in England.
82. See J. C. Beaglehole, "The royal instructions to colonial governors, 1783–1854: a study in British colonial policy", summary of a Ph.D. thesis, published in *The Bulletin of the Institute of Historical Research*, Vol. VII, (1929–30), pp. 184–187.
83. A. K. Fryer, "The Government of the Cape of Good Hope, 1825–54: The Age of Imperial Reform", *Archives Year Book for South African History*, 1964, Vol. I, p. 27.
84. H. T. Manning, *British Colonial Government after the American Revolution*, p. 418 quoted by Fryer, p. 27.
85. A. Berriedale Keith, *Constitutional History of the First British Empire*, pp. 195–196.
86. *C.H.B.E.*, Vol. VIII, (2nd edition), p. 201.
87. See Chapter X, pp. 153–154.
88. See p. 85.
89. Walker, p. 163.
90. C.O. 49/9, Instructions to Caledon, 1 August 1806, clause 29.
91. See Chapter 1, pp. 19–20.
92. See G. McC. Theal, *History of South Africa since 1795*, Vol. I, Chapter XVIII, and G. Cory, *The Rise of South Africa*, Vol. II, Chapter VII. Cory is particularly critical of Somerset, but recent research has come to his defence: see A. Kendal-Miller, *Plantagenet in South Africa:* M. Hughes, "Lord Charles Somerset in South Africa: a re-assessment", unpublished Ph.D. thesis, Liverpool University, 1964; and G.C.O. Key, "A Critical Study of the administration of Lord Charles Somerset during the period 1820–1826", unpublished M.A. thesis, Rhodes University College, 1935.
93. P.R.O. 30/43/96, Bathurst to Cole, 26 February 1826.
94. A. Kendal-Miller, pp. 240–250. See also M. Roberts, "Lord Charles Somerset and the 'Beaufort Influence' ", *Archives Year Book for South African History*, 1952, Vol. II.
95. P.R.O. 30/43/96, Bathurst to Cole, 26 February 1826.
96. *Ibid.*
97. P.R.O. 30/43/96, Cole to Bathurst, 24 August 1826.
98. See Prologue, p. 14.
99. P.R.O. 30/43/96, Bathurst to Cole, 15 January 1827.
100. Roberts, *Archives Year Book for South African History*, 1952, Vol. II, p. 33.
101. P.R.O. 30/43/96, Cole to Bathurst, July 1827.
102. P.R.O. 30/43/87, Cole to Hay, 30 March 1828.
103. See p. 85.

104. See Chapter X.
105. P.R.O. 30/43/87, Cole to Hay, 30 March 1828.
106. The commandant of the eastern frontier (1825-1839) and lieutenant-colonel commanding the Cape Mounted Rifles (1839–1851). He was a son of Lord Charles Somerset.
107. At the beginning of the nineteenth century the Ngwane, of whom *Matiwane* was chief, lived in the valley of the White Mfolosi River in northern Natal. They were displaced in 1818 by Tshaka, chief of the Zulus from 1818 to 1828. Thereafter they wandered southward and lived by plunder. In 1828 they attacked the Thembu who were close neighbours of the colony.
108. Technical term for Zulu soldiers.
109. N. J. van Warmelo, "History of the Matiwane and the amaNgwane Tribe", *Ethnological Publications*, Vol. VIII. Department of Native Affairs, Union of South Africa, 1938.
110. See Chapter VI.
111. See Chapter VIII.
112. See Chapter VII.
113. See Chapter IX.
114. See Chapter X.
115. See Chapter VI.

CHAPTER VI

THE PROBLEMS OF THE CAPE FRONTIER

Neither the Dutch nor the British colonial governments at the Cape of Good Hope proved equal to the task of controlling the expansion of the area of the colony. Colonists migrated into the interior in northerly and easterly directions from Cape Town. For administrative purposes the boundary was divided into a northern frontier and an eastern frontier. Each frontier posed a distinct problem. They differed in topography and in the socio-political organization of the people who lived beyond them.

The commissioner-general for the eastern districts[1] was especially charged with the supervision of the eastern frontier and the vital eastern part of the northern border. In all cases of urgency, in which the delay of a reference to Cape Town would be prejudicial to the public interest, he could take decisions and instruct civil commissioners and other subordinate officials of the frontier districts.[2] Andries Stockenstrom was the man chosen for the post when it was created in 1828. He had wide experience of the frontier. The son of a landdrost of Graaff-Reinet, he had eventually held that office himself. As a young ensign he had taken part in the military operations of 1811, and was present when the verbal frontier agreement was made in 1819.[3]

In 1780 the entire length of the Fish River had been proclaimed the eastern frontier of the colony, but it only became so in fact in 1811–12. Until the latter date, Xhosa had been in occupation of the land between the Fish and the Sundays Rivers – an area known as the Zuurveld. Colonel Collins,[4] however, had advised the governor that it was in the best interests of the security of the colony to drive the Xhosa out of the Zuurveld and establish a military force on the frontier to prevent further incursions of Xhosa into the colony.

The country to the east of the Fish River is hilly, even mountainous, and traversed by numerous rivers. Normally it receives good soaking rains in the summer, though on occasion it can be ravaged by drought. This region was populated by Xhosa chiefdoms which blocked the path of the eastward progression of the colonists, just as the colonists checked the gradual migration of the Xhosa into south-western Africa. Indeed the ejection of the Xhosa from the Zuurveld was the first step in reversing the traditional direction of Xhosa expansion.

An essential of Xhosa society was the availability of plenty of land. Political tensions were sometimes resolved by the subdivision of a chiefdom. Dissatisfaction with a chief was a common cause of fission. Recalcitrants, often led by a relative of the chief, would hive off to new lands and only keep a tenuous link with the original chiefdom.[5] The circumscription of movement dictated by a European frontier created tensions among the Xhosa which neither colonists nor their government could understand. Segregation was the focal point of government policy because it was reckoned that peace could only be maintained by keeping the races apart. Driving the Xhosa east of the Fish River, however, did not bring tranquillity to the eastern frontier because the Xhosa displaced in 1811–12 were thrown back onto already occupied land. Moreover, the removal took place just when Zulu aggression in the north triggered off a series of wars and new migrations.

The military frontier established in 1812 did not prevent Xhosa from entering the colony and taking cattle belonging to colonists. The latter were expected to see that their cattle were always guarded, but in this respect they were often found to be in default. As soon as losses were detected a farmer was entitled to pursue the thieves by himself or with the help of his neighbours and, in defence of his life or goods, if he could not secure the depredators for legal trial, he might kill them. Once the cattle had been driven beyond the frontier they could only be recovered by a commando[6] – a party of armed men under some authority usually a field cornet or his deputy – for which the authority of the landdrost was required or, preferably, the sanction of the colonial government.[7]

A commando was expected only to recapture stolen cattle, but the system was open to abuse. Motives of revenge could lead to unnecessary bloodshed and the claiming of cattle in addition to those stolen. Furthermore, it was not always very easy to trace cattle. Sometimes their spoor became confused with the traces of other animals and in wet weather the spoor was often lost altogether. Thus it is not surprising that colonists begged the government to take "strong" measures against those who took their cattle.[8]

Somerset decided to resolve the problem by enlisting the support of Ngqika whom the colonial government had for some time considered to have paramount authority over the Xhosa on the frontier. Accordingly a meeting was arranged between the governor and the chief at the Kat River on the 2nd April 1817.[9] The meeting was also attended by Ngqika's eldest son, Maqoma, his uncle, Jalousa, and two chiefs named Botumane and Nqeno. At this meeting Somerset officially acknowledged Ngqika as "the first chief" and observed that the colonial government had never treated with any of the other chiefs, nor did they propose to do so in the future. Ngqika, however, was aware that the chiefdoms which made up the Xhosa tribal cluster were basically independent of each other and, although he accepted the rôle of first chief and hoped the other chiefs would mark the recognition, he advised the governor that in matters where control was required the other chiefs should be approached independently. No attempt was ever made to ascertain the views of the chiefs present let alone those who were not there. Ngqika's efforts to assist the colonial government to prevent cattle thefts soon cost him popularity with the Xhosa and weakened, rather than strengthened, his authority.[10]

At the Kat River conference the method Somerset proposed, and Ngqika accepted, for the recovery of stolen cattle recognized a doctrine of communal responsibility – a principle with which Xhosa legal tradition was familiar. Unfortunately another principle was ignored, namely, the right of a chief or headman of a kraal to prove that the spoor did not end in the neighbourhood of his kraal, but led through it or away from it. Thus when cattle were lost all colonists had to do was trace the spoor to *any* Xhosa kraal and take cattle from the inhabitants to the value of their losses and leave the sufferers to indemnify themselves from the real thieves if they could find them.[11]

This system was even more open to abuse than the previous one. Any trail which led to a kraal where there were cattle was evidence enough for colonists in pursuit of stolen cattle. An unscrupulous colonist could trump up a charge of theft and might claim more cattle than he ever owned, or even blame Xhosa for cattle stolen by thieves in the colony, or taken by wild animals, or strayed and lost. Moreover, instead of an equal *number* of cattle being recovered from Xhosa, it became general practice to claim cattle of equal *value*. According to Reyburn, "the colonists made the valuation, and five to one was sometimes regarded as a fair balance."[12]

It is no wonder that many Xhosa chiefs took up arms against Ngqika whom they considered the friend of the colony. He was soundly beaten in battle on the plains of Amalinde in 1818. Troops stationed on the frontier were sent to support him. They recovered some cattle for him, but they did not subdue the Xhosa chiefs. Before they could do so, in April 1819, the Xhosa chiefs attacked Grahamstown in an attempt to recover "their land", that is, the Zuurveld.[13] It was the action of a desperate people, but it was doomed to failure because of the British army's superior weapons.

The war brought Somerset to the frontier again. At a further meeting with Ngqika, the Xhosa were driven yet another step east. Unfortunately no minutes of the conference were taken and there is some doubt about the terms Somerset laid down because the official communiqué in the *Gazette* and the governor's despatch to the secretary of state are incomplete.[14] Apparently Somerset confirmed his recognition of Ngqika as first chief and exhorted the other chiefs to acknowledge him as such. Somerset then told Ngqika that because of the ease with which thefts took place from the forests near the Fish River, he had decided to make the Keiskamma River the boundary of the colony. All Xhosa who lived between the Fish and the Keiskamma Rivers were required to withdraw east of the new boundary. At Ngqika's special request he was allowed to occupy the valley of the Tyhume River, a tributary of the Keiskamma.[15] The boundary was therefore declared to run along the Keiskamma River from the sea to its junction with the Tyhume, and from the Tyhume along the ridge of the Kat River Hills where it touches that river to where it joins the chain of the Winterberg. In explanation of this statement it was added that the waters which flowed from the ridge of the Kat River Hill into the Tyhume should belong to Ngqika and those which flowed into the Kat Valley should belong to the colony.[16]

Somerset proposed to keep the land ceded to the colony unoccupied except for the militia. This must have emphasized the hardship of the dispossessed Xhosa. The fertile land they vacated stood empty whilst they had to find land to cultivate and graze their livestock in the more congested area east of the Keiskamma. It is not surprising that first Donkin, then Somerset himself, made concessions to the Xhosa. Some chiefs and their people returned to the coastal area of what was called in official contemporary documents, the ceded territory.[17] More important for future events, in 1821 Maqoma had led his people back into the fertile valley of the Kat River.[18] Meanwhile colonists were also permitted to settle in the valley of the Koonap River, a tributary of the Fish, very near to the Kat River, whilst other colonists sought temporary grazing for their cattle on the territory's open grasslands.

Lord Bathurst seems to have been quite happy with the way in which colonial authorities were handling the situation on the frontier. In a despatch to Bourke he asserted that he had no doubt of the competence of the colonial government to occupy the ceded territory and was content to concede to the Xhosa "the temporary indulgence of grazing their cattle".[19] No doubt both secretary of state and governor must have felt that contact between the colonists and Xhosa could be controlled.

An attempt was certainly made to regulate trade between the Xhosa and the colonists, through trade fairs. Initially they were a success, but they collapsed when individual traders discovered that more lucrative results were obtainable from deeper penetration into Xhosa territory. One settler records that by 1828 traders' wagons reached as far north as Delagoa Bay.[20] Meanwhile in 1824 a small group of traders had out-flanked the Xhosa and set up shop in the neighbourhood of Port Natal. These men were anxious for this territory to be annexed by Britain, but their requests aroused little interest either in Somerset or Cole.[21]

Further contact between colonists and Xhosa on the frontier was encouraged by Ordinance 49 of 1828. The British settlers had been specifically debarred from using slave labour. Khoikhoi provided an alternative, but inadequate, labour force. Hence the settlers cast their eyes beyond the frontier in their search for labourers. Ordinance 49 provided for the admission of "native foreigners" to work in the colony and prescribed regulations for their employment. Those who came from beyond the colonial frontiers[22] could not work for more than one month unless they entered into a formal contract in the presence of a magistrate or other authorized official. A maximum length of service was fixed at twelve months, but renewal of the contract was permitted. Adequate food and clothing was recognized as an essential part of a worker's remuneration, but neither a ration of liquor nor tobacco was permitted as part payment of wages. Any attempt to detain a labourer in employment against his will was made subject to a penalty of £10 or six months imprisonment. Xhosa who took jobs in the colony were subject to the laws of the colony while they lived within its boundaries. Vagrancy was subject to a penalty of twelve months imprisonment.

The Xhosa chiefs were suspicious of the intentions of Ordinance 49. They thought its object was to lure their people into the colony and correspondingly weaken their forces. More particularly they objected to colonists penetrating tribal territory to recruit labourers. Stockenstrom attempted to explain to the chiefs that Ordinance 49 was expressly designed for the safety of their followers, but he decided that to press the point would only aggravate the situation and that practice alone would overcome their suspicions and jealousies. Besides, Stockenstrom told the chiefs, there was no necessity to entice Xhosa into the colony because he was sure that the famished people on the northern border[23] would oversupply the labour market for some time. And, he pointed out, those Xhosa who could not find subsistence in their own lands, were now entitled by law to find an honest means of livelihood instead of resorting to plunder for food.[24]

Increased contact between the colonists and their neighbours was taking place just at a time when the repercussions of Zulu aggression threatened to upset the stability of the tribal clusters in the neighbourhood of the colony. In 1828 the Ngwane, a chiefdom displaced by Tshaka, threatened to invade the Cape Thembu who lived in the Tarka district to the north-east of the frontier. Unrest among the chiefdoms obviously threatened the stability of the frontier. Bourke, therefore, decided to send a military force into the troubled area to restore peace.[25] The secretary of state approved his action but urged Cole, who arrived at the Cape at this juncture, to cultivate a good understanding with the Zulu chief "by any means short of a grant of money or warlike stores".[26] An embassy to Tshaka was planned,[27] but before it left the colony news was received of his assassination.

Tshaka's death, however, did not immediately ease the situation on the frontier. Militant Xhosa wandered through the ceded territory, frontier farmers frequently reported thefts of cattle, and two soldiers of the 55th Regiment were killed on patrol. In an effort to check lawlessness, Stockenstrom decided to see as many of the chiefs as he could.[28] This decision was an important one because it marks a break with past practice. It suggests that the colonial authorities had at last awakened to the necessity of negotiating directly with individual chiefs. The new approach may possibly be explained by the death of Ngqika in

1828, and the succession to the chieftainship of the young Sandile for whom Maqoma was Regent. Stockenstrom probably appreciated that if Ngqika's authority over the chiefs had been slight, that of Sandile and Maqoma would be negligible.

Accompanied by Lieutenant-Colonel Somerset, the commandant of the frontier, Stockenstrom set out on a tour of the border country in October and November 1828. He addressed gatherings of chiefs at Fort Willshire and Grahamstown. He told them of the government's displeasure with recent depredations, and warned them that they stood to be the losers if they continued to antagonize the colonists. The chiefs gave their assurance that they would make every effort to discover and punish offenders and return stolen property to the colony. However, Stockenstrom was not impressed by these promises because, he claimed, they had been too often repeated and broken to be relied upon.[29] It was not long before his point was proved.

Less than three months later, on the 25th January 1829, Maqoma, who had attended the Fort Willshire gathering, and 400 of his men attacked the Cape Thembu. The Thembu fled into the colony for protection. Some twenty miles inside the colonial boundary they were overtaken by Maqoma's forces. Several Thembu were killed and their entire herd of 3 000 head of cattle taken. This wanton aggression by people who lived in the ceded territory at the government's pleasure called for a show of strength.

Cole, on Stockenstrom's advice, decided to eject Maqoma and his people. Two months were allowed them to restore the Thembu's cattle, gather in their crops, and remove themselves beyond the Keiskamma River.[30] At first Maqoma made no attempt to comply, but when the military were ordered to enforce removal the chief and his people withdrew from the colony without incident. The opportunity was taken to make effective the boundary line established in 1819. Assertions that the occasion was used to extend the boundary to include the upper reaches of the Tyhume and Kat Rivers are questionable.[31] The absence of any formal proclamation altering the boundary, or any report to the secretary of state that an addition had been made to colonial territory, suggests that officials at the Cape did not consider themselves as exceeding the area delimited in 1819.

The expulsion of Maqoma was made the occasion to alter the commando regulations. The changes foreshadowed the later Commando Ordinance (No. 99 of 1833.)[32] The practice of following the spoor of stolen animals had been a recognized procedure since the late eighteenth century.[33] Governor Somerset's method of retrieving lost property was open to abuse,[34] and on two occasions the commandant of the frontier himself attacked the wrong village. In an effort to avoid injustice, Acting Governor Bourke had forbidden patrols to cross the boundary unless the stolen cattle were in sight.[35] Chiefs were expected to discover and punish offenders, but in fact they did not. Patrols were generally unable to recapture cattle before they crossed the boundary because of the time lost before a report of theft could be made to the nearest post. Furthermore, there were occasions when frontier patrols were outwitted by Xhosa who returned some of the cattle they had stolen which they claimed to have recovered from the thieves,[36] and then kept the rest. Ngqika and several other chiefs had told the commandant of the frontier that they would welcome a return to Somerset's policy.[37] Stockenstrom agreed it was senseless to forbid patrols to cross the boundary and follow spoor wherever it might lead but asserted that action should be taken immediately a crime was detected. He recommended that patrols should be led by a military officer or a carefully selected civilian. These patrols should only be allowed to retrieve stolen property. Compensation, he said should be forbidden.[38]

Cole decided to adopt Stockenstrom's recommendations.[39] The secretary of state regretted that Bourke's milder policy had not succeeded but accepted the opinion of men on the spot.[40]

Meanwhile Stockenstrom had perceived that the removal of Maqoma and his people would create a vacuum which the Xhosa would refill the moment the military force was diminished unless remedial measures were taken. In a lengthy minute he suggested that the lands vacated by Maqoma's tribe in the valley of the Kat River should be immediately occupied by Khoikhoi. He pointed out that experience had shown that no better troops could be assembled for commando service and that the creation of a Khoikhoi location would absorb many Khoikhoi who had been unemployed since the "Hottentot Corps" (sic) had been disbanded in 1827.[41] Such a policy, he wrote, would secure the frontier, prevent the vagrancy of which colonists complained, bind the Khoikhoi to the soil, and link them irrevocably to the colony. Stockenstrom recommended that initial settlement should be provisional only so that reference could be made to the British Government for its approval. Moreover delay in finalizing arrangements would give the local authorities time to determine individual capabilities.[42] Cole agreed to the plan, but the British Government's approval only came after Cole had reported that progress in the settlement had exceeded his "most sanguine expectations".[43]

When Goderich resumed the secretaryship of state for War and the Colonial Department,[44] he suggested it might be wise to open up the ceded territory to respectable settlers – "Englishmen and Hottentots, but not Boers". This, he thought, would overcome the shortage of good agricultural land within "the ancient limits of the colony", encourage immigrants whose industry and capital would yield a profitable return, and secure the colony against further invasion by the Xhosa whose civilization the settlers would develop by "judicious arrangements".[45]

Politic though the new measures seemed, they did not bring peace to the frontier. In only a few months Xhosa were reported to have re-occupied the upper reaches of the Kat River. They were driven out of the area without bloodshed but numerous Xhosa continued to inhabit the "ravines and fastnesses" of the country and committed constant depredations.[46] Others made their way into the colony. The civil commissioner of Albany reported that 754 passes were issued to Xhosa in terms of Ordinance 49 in nine months, and that approximately 250 other Xhosa had entered the colony without following the correct procedure. Very few Xhosa were actually employed by farmers in either of the frontier districts of Albany or Somerset.[47] Some came to satisfy their curiosity, others to procure skins, but the majority came to steal iron and other portable goods.[48] Several farmers deduced that these Xhosa were responsible for the numerous stock losses they suffered.[49] By way of precaution the governor, with the advice of the Council, suspended Ordinance 49 insofar as it concerned Xhosa.[50] He also decided to visit the frontier and examine its problems on the spot. Much of the alarm had died by the time he reached the troubled area in September 1829, but he was told that the number of cattle carried off shortly before his visit was on a scale unprecedented. In five months more than 5 000 head of cattle were alleged to have been carried off and only 1 500 were recovered.[51]

Cole decided to address the chiefs whose people remained in the ceded territory. He told them that the boundary of 1819 was fixed irrevocably, that they could continue to occupy the land on which they lived subject to good behaviour, and that they were required to assist in the restoration of stolen cattle and bring offenders to justice. He informed them that he had suspended Ordinance 49, but had withheld more stringent measures because he understood that they had not countenanced the improper conduct of their people. He said that in due course he would lift the suspension of Ordinance 49 but that thereafter Xhosa would only be able to enter the colony with a pass from their chief, and the chiefs would be held responsible for the good conduct of their people. If chiefs incurred the government's displeasure they would be ejected like Maqoma.[52]

Cole regretted that the Xhosa had ever been allowed to re-occupy part of the ceded territory. Because of government ineffectiveness they had settled on the best lands which they claimed to occupy by right rather than on sufferance. Cole recognized that it was impossible to dispossess them without considerable irritation, much bloodshed, and possible loss to the people of Albany.[53] The secretary of state was sympathetic to the views of the governor and endorsed his policy.[54]

It was unfortunate that the close co-operation of governor, commissioner-general and commandant of the frontier did not persist. Stock losses continued. Stockenstrom strove to maintain peace through the goodwill of the chiefs. Somerset used patrols to recover stolen animals. In July 1831 Cole authorized a commando without first referring to Stockenstrom because he thought that Stockenstrom was away from the scene of action. But Stockenstrom was on the spot and disapproved of the commando. Experience had taught him that the colonists were careless with their herds and frequently allowed them to graze unguarded and cattle wandered off unchecked, yet all losses were blamed on the Xhosa. Stockenstrom claimed to be able to prove "the backward state of improvement of the Border Colonists as well as the Caffres".[55] He observed that Cole's injuction, that no cattle owned by the Xhosa should ever be taken as compensation, was ignored. He had discovered the root of the frontier problem: ferment among the Xhosa was maintained by depriving them of their means of subsistence.

Cole for his part discovered that oral agreements with Xhosa chiefs were unsatisfactory. On occasion chiefs complained that the colonial government did not honour its word. If friction were to be avoided, Cole realised that future agreements would have to be set down in writing. Accordingly he gave instructions that henceforth all the articles of each compact were to be recorded in detail, and signed by the contracting parties in the presence of witnesses who were required to testify that the language of the document declared the real meaning and intention of the contracting parties. Three copies of the document were to be made immediately: one for the commissioner-general, one for the commandant of the frontier and one for the chief. The original document had to be forwarded to the office of the secretary to the colonial government where it was filed. Cole claimed that this procedure would ensure that a chief could always ascertain his exact position through any one of the missionaries whom he cared to consult.[56] In his last weeks in office, therefore, he set the points for a new approach to the problems of the eastern frontier.

The northern frontier, like the eastern frontier, was frequently shifted to accommodate the colonists' desire for more land, but, unlike the eastern frontier, it was devoid of natural lines of demarcation. Stockenstrom was partly responsible for a new delimitation that was made between 1822 and 1824. The Zwart Kei and Klaas Smits Rivers and the Stormberg

Spruit was fixed as the boundary in the north-east. From the confluence of the Stormberg Spruit with the Orange River the boundary followed the course of the Orange as far as longitude 24°20′ east, then cut straight across to the Pramberg, and then formed an irregular curve cutting the confluence of the Zak and Riet Rivers and continuing westward to the mouth of the Buffalo River on the shore of the Atlantic.[57] This boundary was not properly surveyed and, as late as 1823, could not be accurately defined. In a letter to the secretary to the colonial government, the surveyor general commented that it was "very difficult to determine whether lands applied for are or are not in the Colony, whether Crimes (in those regions) are committed within or without the Colony – whether certain Boors (sic) can, or cannot claim a right of protection from the Colony".[58]

The commissioners of inquiry took Stockenstrom to task for his complicity in this extension of the colony on the grounds that land formerly in possession of the San had been incorporated into the colony. Stockenstrom defended himself on the ground that the land was very poor, and that the San had not been dispossessed, but lived, worked and hunted with the colonists.[59] In any case the San population must have been comparatively small. Stockenstrom said that they lived "in remote corners and rocks, and remove as often as they expect to find a part of the country more full of game".[60] This possibly explains why one missionary who crossed this country in 1813 reported that he did not meet any human beings except one family on the day his party entered it. He concluded that there must have been some inhabitants "from the remains of huts which we discovered in two or three places; but their number must be very small".[61]

Indeed across the sandy wastes to the north of the frontier lived small bands of Bastards,[62] Griquas, Namaquas, Koranas, San and Tswana – driven there to refuge from both white and black immigrants alike. These communities lived in small groups under a leader – sometimes called a kaptyn. They were semi-nomads whose very livelihood was determined by the viccissitudes of a harsh climate. Among them missionaries had struggled to make progress. By the third decade of the nineteenth century they could claim some success with the Griqua who, with centres at Griquatown, Campbell and Philippolis, had begun to resemble a settled community.[63] Consequently the Griqua shared with the colonists who lived near the frontier the terror of raids by marauding parties. The correspondence of missionaries reveals the existence of a lawless barbaric society.[64] Mantatee[65] and Tswana[66] fugitives plundered the Griqua and kept them in suspense for many years and gravely disturbed their unity and coherence.[67]

No professional militia guarded colonists on this frontier: it was protected by burgher patrols – a citizen force – called up to deal with crises as they arose. This was an inadequate force to cope with the long, open and barren frontier. Attempts at retribution were doubly difficult because it was often impossible to determine with certainty who was the agressor. Mutual jealousy induced the several African bands to accuse their opponents and, on occasion, the innocent would suffer for the guilty. But colonists sometimes courted disaster. Stockenstrom reported that it was not uncommon for a solitary family to migrate into the desert where they were easy prey for hungry natives who robbed them of their flocks, or murdered them all to procure ammunition. Others abandoned their farms for several months and left a defenceless Khoikhoi, San or slave in charge. They were always surprised to find their house burgled and the guardian murdered. Retributive action was impossible in such circumstances.[68]

At the point of Cole's arrival in September 1828, lawlessness beyond the frontier reached a new peak as a result of a drought which Stockenstrom described as the worst he had seen in his twenty years' experience of the frontier. Conditions were so bad that he reported to the government that even if it were necessary to raise a commando it would be impossible to do so because the horses were so starved.[69] Colonists anxious to find food and drink for their animals flagrantly disobeyed colonial laws intended to confine them to the boundaries of the colony. They were attracted to the water-holes and pastures in the lands beyond the Orange River. These were lands of which the San had not long been dispossessed by Griqua under their kaptyn, Adam Kok. Disputes between colonists and Griquas threatened border harmony. Kok formally complained to the governor that numerous colonists crossed the farms of Griqua, ruined the crops the Griqua had sown, and occupied land where Griqua habitually grazed their cattle. He contended that experience had taught the Griqua to guard against encroachment on their lands. However, he did not wish to forbid colonists to enter the territory, but requested that their movement through the land should be restricted to a route fixed by the Griqua, and that they should be subject to reasonable regulations to ensure the peace and security of the natives. Kok did suggest though that the colonial migrations would upset the balance of nature[70] in the area. Colonists travelled some 70 miles beyond the colonial boundary and shot game – which, according to Kok, was the natural food of the Basuto who, he said, were "in a very impoverished and destitute state". The Basuto thus deprived would in all probability resort to plunder – and Kok anticipated that the Griqua would be the first to suffer.[71]

The government was anxious to prevent the migration of the colonists. Stockenstrom admitted that in the particular circumstances of the drought it would have been cruel to stop them crossing the boundary in search of pasture for their flocks, yet Stockenstrom instructed the civil commissioner of Graaff-Reinet to prevent the precedent of 1828 leading to annual migrations or permanent residence beyond the Orange River.[72] But the drought persisted through 1829 and the migrant colonists made no attempt to return. Kok, on a visit to Grahamstown, complained to the commandant of the frontier of "the most cruel and oppressive treatment" colonists inflicted upon Griquas.[73] Cole suspected that the long residence of the migrants beyond the frontier would disturb the peace. The murder of two San in December 1829 indicates that he was right. Stockenstrom was asked to discuss with the civil commissioner of Graaff-Reinet measures to enforce the return of the migrants in order to prevent a crisis which Cole feared might arise.[74]

At first it seemed as though the problem would resove itself for, as so frequently happens in the interior of southern Africa, drought was followed by floods. Heavy rains fell in February 1830 and drew the colonists back to their farms within the colony. In their impatience to return one wagon was lost and a white man and a Tswana child were drowned whilst attempting to cross the swollen Orange River.[75] The hazards of a return trek must have suggested to many a colonist the advantages of permanent residence in the lands beyond the frontier. Although strict instructions were given to frontier field cornets not to permit further migrations without reference to the governor,[76] by July 1830 colonists were again leading their flocks across the Orange River.[77]

The prevention of migrations was clearly impossible. The governor doubted the possibility of affording protection to the native tribes because colonial jurisdiction ceased at the frontier.[78] Stockenstrom took the view that Griquas committed worse crimes against the

San than did the colonists, and argued that it would be in the best interests of all those who lived beyond the northern frontier, if they were brought under British administration. In Stockenstom's opinion it was only a matter of time before the migrant colonists settled permanently beyond the Orange River. Hence he recommended that the lands beyond the river should be systematically colonized, even though he knew that the British Government would not approve. But, he prophesied, that territory would have to be annexed, "after much mischief shall have been done, and when the task will be more colossal".[79]

Stockenstrom's recommendation was probably the only solution to a difficult problem but Cole made no attempt to persuade the British Government to adopt it – he must have been only too well aware of their desire to curb expansion in southern Africa. Just before he left the Cape in August 1833, conditions beyond the frontier deteriorated again. This time Tswana sought protection in the colony from Bastards and Koranas who had attacked them. Cole recommended an ad hoc solution which typifies his whole approach to the problem of the northern frontier: the Tswana were to be driven out because they were a danger to the colony, and the Bastards and Koranas were to be told that they would be punished if they did not desist from aggression.[80] This was no permanent solution to the problem. Statements collected beyond the boundary indicate that the people who lived there wanted what was, in fact, needed – a power strong enough to apportion the land fairly, maintain justice, and keep the peace.[81] Only the British could have provided that power at that time and in that place.

It was then against a background of strife that Cole, with the support of the Council of Advice, passed the Commando Ordinance (No. 99) in June 1833. Constant raids had tried the patience of colonial frontiersmen. They resented being called away from their work on their farms to undertake military duties. They argued that as they paid the same taxes as other colonists they were entitled to expect the colonial government to defend their farms and families and the nearby boundary without their personal assistance. One field commandant actually resigned his office because he was unable to persuade his men to take up arms and was therefore incapable of performing his duty. But the colonial government did not have the financial resources to maintain a permanent army on this frontier.[82] There was no alternative but to continue the past practice of relying on a citizen force for frontier defence.

Ordinance 99 was no revolutionary measure. It restated a proclamation made in 1797 which required colonists to go on commando when ordered to do so by the landdrost. Cole's measure extended the authority for calling out a commando to more junior district officials including field cornets, or provisional field cornets. Defaulters were made liable to a fine of from £5 to £20 for a first offence, and, for subsequent convictions, a similar fine was prescribed together with imprisonment up to a maximum period of three months. Field cornets were entitled to call on the assistance of neighbouring field cornets who were liable to a fine of from £10 to £30 if they declined to give such assistance. Resident magistrates were authorized to try offences.

But stories of the cruelties of the commando system had reached the Colonial Department. These were supported by statements by "several writers on South Africa".[83] Lord Stanley, the secretary of state wrote to Cole:

> "These expeditions have been represented as a system of military execution, inflicted upon the natives sometimes to prevent or to punish their hostile incursions

> into the territory wrested from them by the European settlers, but more frequently as a means of gratifying the cupidity or the vengeance of the Dutch and English farmers, and further, as being marked by the most atrocious disregard of human life, and by cruelties alike disgraceful to those who sanctioned and destructive to those who endured them."[84]

Cole agreed that if the commando system was used as a means of "aggression and atrocious cruelty" then it merited the utmost reprobation. But he did not think this was the case. It was resorted to "as the only possible means, to prevent or punish incursions into colonial territory the whole of which must have been originally wrested from the aborigines". He suggested that it suited the views of some writers to castigate the colonial government and the colonists "as the authors and abettors of a system of the most diabolical atrocities, and to represent the native tribes as the most injured and innocent of human beings". But Cole argued, atrocities were rare, and when they occurred offenders received just punishment if they could be traced. Indeed Cole pointed out that colonists were in such dread of the criminal law that they were even afraid to defend their persons and property lawfully. The cupidity of the colonists, Cole denied; their vengeance, he admitted, though this, he said, was "more frequently defeated than gratified". In the last analysis, however, he asserted that unless the frontier colonists stood together to defend themselves, they would fall before "their savage and remorseless invaders".[85]

In Cole's view the commando system was a basic necessity for frontier defence in the absence of a professional militia. Though he often grappled with the problem he admitted he was unable to suggest an alternative system. He did, however, raise one major issue which was fundamental to the whole problem of the colonists' trans-frontier patrols: the jurisdiction and processes of the colonial courts were confined within the boundaries of the colony, and British subjects once across the border could commit any crime then return to the colony with impunity.[86] Thus it was with Cole that the idea originated of extending the jurisdiction of the colonial courts beyond the boundaries of the colony, and this was effected in the Cape of Good Hope Punishment Act in 1836.[87]

In spite of Cole's supplications, Ordinance 99 was disallowed. The secretary of state told Cole's successor, Sir Benjamin D'Urban, that the commando system had been a fearful scourge to the native population and he objected to the requirements of an ordinance which entitled "the sword . . . to be drawn against whole bodies of people, at the bidding of a provisional constable". Instead he instructed D'Urban to find some other means to protect the colonists against unprovoked aggression and recommended that agents of the colonial government be stationed in proximity to the kraals of the chiefs. Many chiefs, Stanley thought, would become responsible for the peaceful conduct of their followers in return for small presents, and would ultimately appreciate the advantages of authorized barter.[88] On the same day that this opinion was written, Stanley wrote privately to D'Urban stating it was impossible to increase the military force at the Cape. He added that should "the pressure of public danger on the frontier" threaten the safety of the colony, D'Urban could submit his own estimate of the extra troops needed.[89]

Cole's approach to the problems of the frontiers was conservative: on his own admission he could not see how it could be changed. What he did was to take things as he found them and try to make them work efficiently. His Commando Ordinance did not pretend to do more than this. To reject it was to reject a fundamental part of the whole pattern of frontier control and defence. The disallowance of the Ordinance was an indication of new thinking in Great Britain. The British Government adopted Cole's proposal that formal treaties should be negotiated and signed with each of the chiefs, but before this could be put into practice another frontier war[90] had broken out. This was a war which the commando system and armed patrols had precipitated, and was a natural consequence of the eastward thrusts of the colonists.

FOOTNOTES

1. See Chapter V, p. 85.
2. C.O. 49/19, Bathurst to Bourke, 14 June 1827.
3. See p. 98.
4. Caledon appointed Collins to the temporary office of "Civil and Military Commissioner" to ascertain the means of inducing the Xhosa to retire from the colony and to acquire information concerning the means of resistance they possessed, the best means of pacifying the San, and, generally, of improving the internal conditions and external relations of the colony. He reported to the governor in 1809.
5. W. D. Hammond-Tooke, "Segmentation and Fission in Cape Nguni Political Units", *Africa*, Vol. XXXV, number 2, April 1965, pp. 157–166.
6. Ever since the Dutch East India Company had recognized free burghers in 1657, it was regarded as axiomatic that all white men able to carry arms could be called upon to defend the colony. They were formed into militia units under their own officers. A group of these units was occasionally called up for defensive purposes or, more commonly, to round up stolen cattle and stock thieves. The term *commando* was applied to the force as a unit and to the military operation.
7. C. W. Hutton, (ed.), *The Autobiography of the late Sir Andries Stockenstrom, Bart.* Vol. I, pp. 100–101.
8. *Ibid*, pp. 101–105.
9. The minutes of the conference are published in Theal, *R.C.C.*, Vol. XI, pp. 310–316.
10. H. A. Reyburn, "Studies in Frontier History", V, "Reprisals", *The Critic*, Vol. IV, number 1, October 1935, pp. 52–59.
11. *Ibid.*, pp. 54–55.
12. *Ibid.*, p. 56.
13. Reyburn, "Studies in Frontier History", VI, "From Amalinde to Somerset Mount", *The Critic*, Vol. IV, number 2, February 1936, pp. 105–113.
14. *Ibid.*, p. 114.
15. *Ibid.*
16. Theal, *R.C.C.*, Vol. XII, pp. 342–345.
17. The terms *neutral belt* or *ceded territory* are used indiscriminately by historians to describe this land. A pencilled comment in Somerset's handwriting in the margin of the Cory Library copy of Cowper Rose, *Four Years in South Africa*, p. 82, says: "If it was called the Neutral Ground it was a nickname not recognised by the Government". Somerset never used the term *neutral territory* in the official despatches. See D. Williams, *When Races Meet*, p. 26, fn. 45. A chart prepared by the military (C.O. 700 Cape/10) also refers to "the country *ceded* by the Kaffir Chiefs to the British Crown . . . on the 14 th October 1819".
18. G. Mc C. Theal, *History of South Africa from 1795 to 1872*, Vol. I, p. 382.
19. C.O. 49/19, Bathurst to Bourke, 26 October 1826.
20. A. Keppel-Jones (in consultation with E. K. Heathcote), *Philipps, 1820 Settler*, p. 371.
21. See E. H. Brookes and C. de B. Webb, *A History of Natal*, Chapter III.
22. The precise terminology of the Ordinance is "Native foreigners".
23. See p. 103.
24. C. A., C. O. 366, Stockenstrom to Bell, 22 November 1828.

25. See Chapter V, p. 90.
26. C.A., G.H. 1/15 Murray to Cole, 29 September 1828.
27. C.O. 48/130, Cole to Murray, 31 January 1829.
28. C.A., C.O. 336, Stockenstrom to Bell, 22 November 1828.
29. *Ibid.*
30. C.A., G.H. 23/8, Cole to Murray, 14 June 1829.
31. G. McC. Theal, *History of South Africa from 1795 to 1872*, Vol. V, pp. 242–243, states under the heading *Extension of the Cape Colony*, "in April 1829 without a formal proclamation it is extended to the watershed between the upper Tyumie and Kat Rivers, and an irregular line from the Tyumie to the Kat a little below Fort Beaufort, and the Kat River to its junction with the Fish".
E. A. Walker, *Historical Atlas of South Africa*, pp. 14–15 fn. 3, gives the following reference for an alteration of the boundary in 1829: "No. 617 (C. Archives) 17 April 1829". An attempt to trace Walker's reference in the Cape Archives was unsuccessful. In a letter to the author, Professor Walker has pointed out that the reference was given to the document "many years ago" and the archives have since been moved and re-catalogued. This reference appears to have been re-catalogued in the Cape Archives as C.O. 367 No.'s 13 and 14. Both these documents are signed by A. Stockenstrom, Commissioner General for the Eastern Districts and dated 17 April 1829. Neither document is a formal proclamation.
32. See pp. 105–107.
33. J. S. Marais, *The Cape Coloured People*, pp. 16–17.
34. See p. 97.
35. *C.H.B.E.*, Vol. VIII, (2nd edition), p. 302.
36. C.A., C.O. 367, Stockenstrom to Cole, 6 February 1829.
37. C.A., A.C. 4 December 1828.
38. C.A., C.O. 367, Stockenstrom to Cole, 6 February 1829.
39. C.A., G.H. 23/9, Cole to Murray, 14 June 1829.
40. C.A., G.H. 1/16, Murray to Cole, 15 October 1829.
41. The "Hottentot Corps" was initially raised by the British in 1796 for service in the interior of the colony. It was enlarged by the Batavian authorities and again by the British in 1807, but it proved objectionable to white colonists and was disbanded in 1817. It was replaced by the Cape Corps – a corps of coloured and Khoikhoi which by 1823 numbered 260 cavalry and 250 infantry. The infantry were disbanded in December 1827, but the cavalry remained in service.
42. C.A., C.O. 367. Minute for the secretary to government by A. Stockenstrom. 17 April 1829.
43. C.A., G.H. 23/9, Cole to Murray, 2 February 1830 and C.A., G.H. 1/16, Murray to Cole, 6 May 1830.
44. 22 November 1830.
45. C.A., G.H. 1/17, Goderich to Cole, 26 May 1831.
46. C.O. 48/131, Cole to Murray, 2 September 1829; enclosure Somerset to Dundas 12 August 1829.
47. C.O. 48/131, Cole to Murray, 2 September 1829; enclosure Campbell to Bell, 21 August 1829.
48. C.O. 48/131, Cole to Murray, 2 September 1829; enclosure Campbell to Bell, 14 August 1829.
49. C.O. 48/131, Cole to Murray, 2 September 1829; enclosure Campbell to Bell, 21 August 1829.
50. The term used in the proclamation was "Caffre". Bantu other than Xhosa continued to be admitted to the colony. The proclamation, dated 25 August 1829, was published in the *Government Gazette* on 28 September 1829.
M. Donaldson, Ph.D. thesis in course of preparation on the minutes and appendices of the Council of Advice at the Cape of Good Hope with special reference to the Eastern Cape 1825–1834.
51. C.A., G.H. 23/9, Cole to Murray, 2 February 1830.
52. *Ibid.*
53. *Ibid.*
54. C.A., G.H. 1/16, Murray to Cole, 6 May 1830.
55. C.A., C.O. 390, Stockenstrom to Bell, 14 July 1830.
56. C.A., C.O. 4903, Acting secretary to government to acting commissioner-general, 2 August 1833.
57. G. McC. Theal, *History of South Africa from 1795 to 1872*, Vol. I, pp. 393–394.

58. C.A., C.O. 403, Michell to Bell, 6 December 1832. Quoted by L. C. Duly, *British Land Policy at the Cape 1795–1844*, p. 115.
59. C. W. Hutton (ed.), *The Autobiography of the late Sir Andries Stockenstrom, Bart.*, Vol. I. pp. 222–232.
60. *Ibid.*, p. 226.
61. Rev. John Campbell quoted by H. A. Reyburn, "Studies in Cape Frontier History", IV, "Tooverberg", *The Critic*, Vol. III, number 4, July 1935, p. 204.
62. In the eighteenth century the term *Bastard* came into general use to denote people of mixed European and Khoikhoi blood. Some of the unions between Europeans and Khoikhoi were permanent, but were "irregular" in the sense that they had not been solemnised by either the Church or the State. Because they were socially unacceptable, several Bastards sought asylum in more remote parts. See J S. Marais, *The Cape Coloured People, 1652–1937*, pp. 10–12.
63. W. M. Macmillan, *Bantu, Boer, and Briton*, pp. 53–54.
64. See correspondence in the Archives of the London Missionary Society.
65. See Chapter V, p. 93, fn. 60.
66. Most official records and contemporary newspapers do not distinguish the various Tswana groups – Batlapin, Barolong, Bapedi, Bahurutsi, Bamangwato, Bakwena, Bangwaketse – but described them generally as Bechuanas.
67. Macmillan, p. 56.
68. C.A., C.O. 336, Stockenstrom to van Ryneveld, civil commissioner of Graaff-Reinet, 22 October 1828, enclosed in Stockenstrom to Bell, 22 October 1828.
69. *Ibid.*
70. This could refer to both the overgrazing of the pasture and to the destruction of game which Griqua, San, Basuto and others hunted for food.
71. C.A., C.O. 367, Memorial of Adam Kok and his counsellors to Sir Lowry Cole, 23 January 1829, enclosed in Stockenstrom to Cole, 26 February 1829. A copy of this document is in the Archives of the London Missionary Society, Cape, Box 11, Folder 3, Jacket A. It seems safe to assert that the document was drawn up by missionaries.
72. C.A., C.O. 336, Stockenstrom to van Ryneveld, civil commissioner of Graaff-Reinet, 22 October 1828, enclosed in Stockenstrom to Bell, 22 October 1828.
73. C.A., C.O. 373, Stockenstrom to Bell, 19 January 1830.
74. C.A., C.O. 4899, Bell to Stockenstrom, 30 December 1829.
75. C.A., C.O. 373, Stockenstrom to Bell, 27 February 1830.
76. C.A., C.O. 373, Van Ryneveld (civil commissioner of Graaff-Reinet) to Stockenstrom, 15 May 1830.
77. C.A., C.O. 373, Stockenstrom to Bell, 19 July 1830.
78. C.A., C.O. 4900, Bell to Stockenstrom, 28 May 1830.
79. C.A., C.O. 373, Memorandum by Stockenstrom, 30 November 1830.
80. C.A., A.C. 20 August 1833.
81. C.A., A.C. 30 December 1833, appendix F. pp. 26–53.
82. C.A., G.H. 1/20 Cole to Stanley, 15 November 1833, enclosed in Stanley to D'Urban, 27 November 1833.
83. This statement is probably derived from a letter written by Thos. Pringle to T. Fowell Buxton, 19 August 1833 and forwarded to the Colonial Office and bound in C.O. 48/152. Pringle listed the references on the commando system in several publications "with a view to bring it under Mr. Stanley's notice in as brief a space as possible".
    It included:
    Philip's *Researches in South Africa*, Vol. I, pp. 36–61; Vol. II, Chapters 1, 2, 3, & 14 – and especially pp. 285–290;
    Dr. Sparrman's *Travels* (anno 1775) Vol. I, pp. 202–206, 241; Vol. II, pp. 142–145, 311;
    Thurnberg's *Travels* (anno 1772–4) Vol. I, pp. 131, 173, 264, 304; Vol. II, pp. 156, 198, 304 etc.
    Barrow's *Travels* (anno 1797) Vol. I, p. 226;
    Report of the commissioners of inquiry on "The Hottentot Population", P.P. 1830, Vol. XXI (584), pp. 2–3;
    Publication by T. Pringle on "Our commando and some atrocities connected with it", and correspondence in *S.A.C.A.* in November and December 1832.
84. P.P. 1836, XXXIX (279), Stanley to Cole, 13 November 1833.
85. C.A., G.H. 1/20. Cole to Stanley, 15 November 1833, enclosed in Stanley to D'Urban, 27 November 1833.

86. C.A., G.H. 1/20, Cole to Stanley, 15 November 1833, enclosed in Stanley to D'Urban, 27 November 1833.
87. 6 & 7 Will. IV, c. 57. See Chapter X, pp. 162–164.
88. C.A., G.H. 1/20, Stanley to D'Urban, 27 November 1833.
89. C.A., G.H. 1/10, Stanley to D'Urban, Private and Confidential, 27 November 1833.
90. Sixth Frontier War, 1834–1835.

CHAPTER VII

APPLICATION OF BRITISH SLAVE POLICY TO THE CAPE

The policy for the amelioration of the condition of slaves required by the resolutions of the House of Commons in May 1823[1] was implemented at the Cape of Good Hope over a period of eight years by five Orders in Council, four ordinances and fourteen proclamations.[2] This legislation illustrates the extra-ordinary difficulty of translating lofty principles into workable rules applicable to the conditions of a colonial society.

Slaves were brought to the Cape of Good Hope soon after the first European settlement was made there in 1652. Mozambique and Madagascar were the principal sourses of supply, but other slaves came from India and Batavia.[3] After 1806 importations ceased.[4] The registration of slaves was ordered by a proclamation of Lord Charles Somerset in 1816, but, like the Mauritians, the Cape colonists were opposed to it. The opgaaf (tax) roll recorded fewer slaves than were on the register – in 1825, there were 32 830 on the former and 35 509 on the latter. Verification of the number of slaves was impossible because no provision was ever made at the Cape for personal inspection. Such a measure was certainly contemplated,[5] but it would seem that it was overlooked.[6] The discrepancy was not large, and the Colonial Department was possibly so busy supervising regulations for the amelioration of slave conditions in several colonies that it never caught up with the omission.

An analysis of the distribution of slaves at the Cape shows that the majority lived in and around Cape Town and Stellenbosch and that numbers tended to decrease the further the distance from these areas.[7] The distribution pattern reflected the degree of sophistication of slave society too. In the towns slaves provided a useful skilled labour force: in Cape Town the most skilled slaves were allowed to trade on their own account and to reside in houses apart from their masters to whom they paid a fee for the indulgence.[8] Some slaves acquired considerable reputation as craftsmen and it was not unknown for a slave to take on white youths as apprentices.[9] Generally, however, slaves were employed in viticulture or agriculture or as herdsmen. The wine industry depended upon semi-skilled slave labour but the agricultural and pastoral farmers to the north and east did not require the same degree of skill from their slaves. In the interior where vast distances separated one farm from another, conditions were more primitive and slaves were thrown more upon the mercy of their masters. It is not surprising to discover that slaves showed a distinct preference for employment in town – a fact which not only gave townsmen additional power over their slaves, but effectively transferred to the country the slaves of worst character and conduct.[10]

As early as April 1814, Cradock had drawn the attention of the secretary of state to the miscarriage of justice at the Cape in several cases which involved the maltreatment of slaves and people of colour.[11] The bi-annual reports of the protector of slaves show that occasional cases of wanton cruelty persisted until slavery was abolished. Even the reform of the courts in 1827 did not sufficiently safeguard the slaves.[12] An article in the *Anti-Slavery Monthly Reporter*[13] early in 1827 stated that slavery at the Cape was milder than in any of the other British colonies. In a later issue, however, it observed that the writings of Philip[14] and Pringle[15] proved that slavery at the Cape was as detestable as anywhere else. "The brutalizing influence both on master and slave", it commented, "may be equally witnessed in the corn-fields of the Cape as in the sugar plantations of Jamaica, or in the rice grounds of South Carolina".[16]

Slave-owners anxious to retain the gulf between master and slave have been held partly responsible for the failure of Christianity among slaves in the face of official encouragement. Some slave-owners erroneously believed that slaves who became Christian acquired a claim to freedom. Christian clergy complained that the wide dispersion of the slaves made it impossible for them to provide slaves with continuous instruction. This handicapped their efforts to convert them. Only 2 200 slaves regularly attended services in the 49 Christian Churches of the colony and, in the period 1816–1824, only 86 slaves were baptized.[17]

From 1823 onwards the colonial government made a more positive effort to win slaves for the Christian religion: tax exemption was offered to slave-owners who caused their slaves to be baptized, and Christian principles were taught to slave-children who could attend a school. In Cape Town, a society called "The Bible and School Commission" directed the education of 1 115 slave-children in 1823, the Wesleyan Methodists had 30 slave-children on their register, and the Government Slave School 17 in the same year. Outside Cape Town, however, school attendance was far less impressive: only 73 slave-children were recorded on the rolls in Stellenbosch in 1824. Numbers fell off drastically in 1825, to a total in the colony of 390, because of a government declaration which limited education in the Government Schools to the children of Christian slaves, presumably in an effort to encourage Christianity. These figures indicate the comparatively small number of slaves who became Christian.[18]

By contrast, Malay priests had considerable success in Cape Town converting slaves to Mohammedanism. Bigge found that there were 846 male slaves and 422 female slaves in the Mohammedan congregation in Cape Town, and a school kept by one of the Malay priests was attended by 372 slave-children. Outside Cape Town the Mohammedan influence was insignificant – there were only 42 male slaves and 16 female slaves who were Mohammedan.[19]

Bigge suggested that the appeal of Mohammedanism lay in a basic precept of the faith which taught that Mohammedans could not be slaves. The Malay priests at the Cape interpreted this to mean that although the bodies of slaves were held in bondage yet their souls were free and that they must trust in Allah (God) to make them free when they died.[20]

Slave society at the Cape of Good Hope posed a problem for British administrators quite different from that in the other colonies of the British Empire. The tropical islands of the West Indies and Mauritius were small compact colonies financially sustained by sugar. A plantation economy requires a substantial labour force, and the sugar plantations were worked by gangs of slaves. In the West Indies these gangs were supervised by managers of frequently absentee landlords. By contrast, the temperate climate of the Cape, the varied agricultural pursuits of the colonists, the direct relationship of master and slave, the demand for skilled and semi-skilled labour, together with religious complications, developed a society which was more complex. It was obviously desirable, therefore, that plans made in Britain to ameliorate the condition of slaves should provide for the particular circumstances of the Cape.

The first steps to improve the condition of slaves at the Cape were taken by the colonial government. Somerset, perhaps in an effort to forestall the British Government, issued a proclamation in March 1823 which anticipated the resolutions of the House of Commons in May of the same year.[21] The proclamation was not received with any enthusiasm by the secretary of state because it was more limited in its scope than was desired by the British Government.[22] Thus Somerset, like the governors of other colonies of conquest where there were slaves, was instructed to formulate legislation for the colony he governed modelled on an Order in Council for Trinidad.[23] The task of framing this measure at the Cape was entrusted to the chief justice, Sir John Truter, who was one of the leading slave-owners in the colony.[24] Edwards says that the ordinance he drafted was conditioned by a conscious desire to protect the interests of the slave-owners and to omit regulations in the Trinidad Order which were not suited to the particular circumstances of the Cape.[25]

Ordinance 19 of 1826,[26] like the Trinidad Order, provided for the appointment of a guardian (or protector) of slaves with assistants in the country districts to look after the interests of slaves; slaves' competence to own property was legally recognized; their evidence was accepted in court on a parity with freemen; Sunday was prescribed a day of rest, and masters were forbidden to work their slaves on that day except as domestic servants, or for defined work of necessity such as supervision of livestock, or field labour during periods of high pressure in the agricultural year, or in times of emergency. Sunday markets were abolished save for the sale of foodstuffs; and slaves were to be encouraged to attend Divine Service. A slave was entitled to raise a presumption of guilt against his master by an accusation of illegal punishment accompanied by an exhibition of his person in a state of laceration. Complaints which proved frivolous, or unfounded, rendered the slave liable to punishment. The ordinance permitted the sale of slave children independently of their mothers after their tenth birthday instead of their sixteenth birthday as required by the Order. The reason given was that the expense of training slaves began at the earlier age. Interest on deposits in a Savings Bank established for the benefit of slaves was fixed at four per cent instead of five per cent, in conformity with local interest rates.

The ordinance ignored several provisions of the Order considered impracticable in local circumstances. These included the prevention of superintendents from carrying or using a whip while on duty, the delay of twenty-four hours between the commission of an offence and the infliction of punishment for it, the necessity for the presence of a free person as a witness to punishment, the abolition of corporal punishment for females, the recording of full particulars of all punishments in a special book, and the requirement of a substantial bond for all slaves gratuitously manumitted who were young, aged, or infirm.

The British Government approved the ordinance, but required some additions and amendments to it. An additional article was required to delay domestic punishment for twenty-four hours after the commission of an offence so as to avoid forced labour "by direct and instant bodily suffering". Since the evidence of slaves was admitted in the courts Huskisson, the secretary of state, thought it was unnecessary for a slave to raise a presumption of guilt against his owner for illegal punishment, and he disapproved of the clause which subjected slaves to punishment if their complaints proved frivolous or unfounded. In this latter case, he asserted it was the responsibility of the owner to lay and prove a special charge against his slave, and he thought that the nature of the punishment of the slave, if convicted of the offence, should be defined by law and not left to the discretion of the court. The secretary of state agreed to compromise on the difference in age at which a slave child could be sold separately from his mother, and ordered an amendment to substitute the age of fourteen for ten years. Huskisson also pointed out some inaccuracy of expression with respect to interest paid by the Colonial Treasury to slaves who purchased their liberty under the authority of the court.[27]

Bourke did not proceed immediately to carry through amendments to Ordinance 19. The ordinance had been bitterly resented by the slave-owners because it struck at the roots of their vested interests. Slave-owners argued that the right of slaves to buy their freedom would encourage dishonesty among slaves. They pointed out that since slaves could only earn wages for work done on Sundays they would never be able to accumulate enough money to purchase their manumission unless they obtained it by false means. Thus, they reckoned, those slaves who applied for manumission would be those of the worst character.[28] In response to a statement of Lord Liverpool, that colonists could best work out how to ameliorate the condition of their slaves,[29] the slave-owners at the Cape took steps to consider the gradual abolition of slavery. In Cape Town and Graaff-Reinet committees were elected to formulate plans. Nothing really practical came of these moves. In Cape Town the repeal of Ordinance 19 was regarded as a necessary preliminary to all schemes of reform. When it was discovered that the colonial government had no intention of suspending the ordinance, interest in schemes for emancipation waned.[30] Clearly the slave-owners were more interested in removing Ordinance 19 from the statute book than they were in considering measures to abolish slavery.

In the course of time much of the strong opposition of the slave-owners to Ordinance 19 had abated, but Bourke appreciated that amending legislation to meet the secretary of state's requirements would re-arouse it. This Bourke wished to avoid. At the time when he received Huskisson's instructions to amend the ordinance, the colony was faced with the frontier crises of mid-1828,[31] and the colonial government was dependent upon the military support of the slave-owners. Bourke suggested, therefore, that amendments and additions to the ordinance should be left to a more convenient time.[32] Thus it was that Cole had to deal with the unpopular measures after he had taken over the government of the colony.

Cole placed a draft ordinance before the Council of Advice in November 1828. The Council thought that such legislation was inexpedient. They argued that the ferment created by the original ordinance had begun to subside, and the new measures would only antagonize the slave-owners without improving the condition of the slaves. Such technical amendments as the secretary of state required, the Council thought, could be met by executive instruction to the officials concerned. They held that Ordinance 19 as it stood was beneficial to the slaves, that they, the Council, were watching its progress carefully, and when conditions justified it, they would consider amendments. And for those reasons they rejected the draft ordinance.[33] The governor submitted the opinion of the Council to the secretary of state, and suggested that if the British Government insisted on the measure in spite of the opposition of the Council, then it should be enacted by the British Government.[34] But the British Government had a much more comprehensive measure in mind than legislation for a particular colony – they sought to bring some uniformity into the slave code of the colonies of conquest.

An Order in Council was passed on the 2nd February 1830. It was based on the legislation of several of the colonies of conquest.[35] Local legislation was revoked and its place was taken by the provisions of the Order which were of general application. Masters, managers, or overseers were prohibited from carrying a whip in the field as a stimulus to labour or as an emblem of authority. The punishment of male slaves by whipping was limited to twenty-five stripes administered in the presence of a free person, or six slaves, at least twenty-four hours after the offence was committed. Corporal punishment for female slaves was prohibited. Imprisonment or confinement in the stocks was recommended as adequate punishment for them. Owners and managers of slaves employed in agriculture or manufacture were required to keep a book in which they had to write a detailed account of every punishment they inflicted on their slaves and by whom it was witnessed. Every six months these books had to be taken for inspection to the protector, or assistant protector, before whom the owners or managers had to swear to the accuracy of the record. Those who could not write could get somebody to do it for them. Defaulters were liable to a minimum fine of £10, and a maximum fine of £50.

The Order left numerous details pertaining to local circumstance to the discretion of governors. Among these, for example, was a definition of such work of necessity as slave-owners could expect of their slaves on a Sunday. Cole was told that he could only sanction such work which, if neglected, might lead to "serious and irreparable injury". He was asked to take care in framing the definition to see that there was no unnecessary encroachment on keeping Sunday as a day of rest for slaves.[36] No discretion was left to governors to delay implementation of the Order. They had to publish it within one month of receiving it and it became law fourteen days thereafter.

The British Government recognized that in the general repeal of local legislation some local regulations beneficial to slaves might have been abolished, hence Cole was authorized to re-enact such measures as there might be at the Cape, provided they were not inconsistent with the Order itself.[37]

The governor's attention was drawn to the absence of any mention in the Order of slaves' conditions of work. The secretary of state thought they were overworked, underfed, and insufficiently clothed. The protector of slaves was ordered to inquire and report on the subject, and local medical practitioners were to be invited to comment on the report. On the basis of this information the governor was asked to recommend any regulations he thought would effectively check or prevent abuse.[38]

The Order became law at the Cape on the 26th August 1830 – exactly six weeks after its receipt by the governor. The speed with which it had to be promulgated was severely criticized by Cole. He complained that there was neither time to digest it and deliberate on local legislation framed in terms of it, nor to acquaint the numerous illiterate slave-owners who lived in remote and isolated parts of the colony of the law before it became effective. They would, therefore, become subject to heavy penalties for disobedience to regulations of which they could not reasonably have been apprized.

Cole was equally unhappy with some of the terms of the Order. He wrote to the secretary of state that he understood that in all slave colonies – and it certainly was the case in the two colonies of which he had had experience – female slaves of bad character were more depraved than the men, and that Sunday, far from being a day of rest, was a day of great debauchery and dissipation. Such activity, he thought, lowered the female character far more than corporal punishment, the abolition of which he opposed. Weekday imprisonment would deprive a master of his slave's labour, and to Cole it was irrational that the master should suffer for the sins of his slave. Cole's proclamation therefore provided for the imprisonment of female slaves on Sunday for offences committed on Saturday, that is, without a twenty-four hour delay. He attempted to rationalise his deviation from instructions on the grounds that the commission of an unpunished fault would only tempt the guilty slave to absent herself on Monday to avoid the punishment she deserved. The original offence would thus be aggravated. Besides, Cole argued, if the punishment of a guilty slave was delayed from Sunday to Monday slave-owners would be placed "in the unchristianlike position of passing the day of worship and rest in the resolution of commencing the next day by inflicting punishment on his offending slave".[39] Cole also attempted to alleviate the full impact of the Order on masters through a broad definition of "work of necessity". He listed all the activities associated with peak periods in the agricultural calendar and in the manufacture of wine – and left a loophole which covered all cases of urgent and unavoidable necessity. Weekly markets, however, were fixed on Wednesday instead of Sunday.[40]

Ordinance 75 of 1830 revived provisions in Ordinance 19 omitted by the Order in Council. It enacted that the food of slaves should be "sufficient and wholesome", their clothes "good and sufficient", and their lodgings "dry and comfortable". Provision for the education of slaves was not re-enacted as Cole preferred to delay legislation on this point until he knew whether the British Government intended to enforce the attendance of Mohammedan slave-children at Christian schools and places of worship, or compel slave-owners to send their Christian slave-children to school even though there was no legislation to compel freemen to educate their children.

The Order had, moreover, omitted to take into account that, in the particular case of the Cape, the guardianship of slaves had been divided in 1828 to provide a separate official for the eastern and western districts of the colony. The chief justice of the Cape held it was contrary to the new law to permit the continuation of the two offices however desirable this may have been. The long journeys into the interior and arduous nature of the office of protector made it imperative that two officers should be retained. Cole requested a supplementary Order in Council to legalize the position.[41]

Cole's measures to implement the Order in Council met with a mixed reception by the secretary of state. Goderich, who had replaced Murray at the Colonial Department, opposed Cole on several points. He critized Cole's departure from the strict letter of the Order with respect to the imprisonment of female slaves on Sunday. He argued that if the morals of female slaves were as bad as Cole alleged then it was due to their social condition, and to place them in solitary confinement on "the day appropriated to instruction and repose" would aggravate rather than improve the position. He also over-ruled Cole's objection to owners suffering for the misdeeds of their slaves. He pointed out that their suffering induced a reluctance to punish which was the best possible security against an arbitrary use of power. He also rejected Cole's assertion that it was unchristian for a slave-owner to spend Sunday contemplating the punishment of an offending slave. "If the punishment be merited", he wrote, "I cannot discover why the fixed purpose of inflicting it should be regarded as unchristian, and if unmerited, or if inflicted merely for the motive of revenge, it is alike contrary to the principles of religion, on whatever day of the week it may take place".[42]

Goderich also thought that Cole's definition of work of necessity was too loose and vague. He conceded that in a climate like the Cape's suspension of irrigation even for a day could prove inconvenient, but he thought that to provide generally for work on Sunday at times of high productivity would altogether abolish Sunday as a day of rest. Criticism of vagueness was also applied to Ordinance 75. Goderich insisted on a statement of minimum specifications for food, clothes and lodgings for slaves. Cole's criticism that several colonists would default through ignorance of the law simply because of the speed with which it came into operation met with sympathetic understanding. Goderich admitted the propriety of great indulgence "in every case of real or presumable ignorance". But, he asserted, a large part of the Order was a simple repetition of enactments long in force – a statement more true of the island colonies than of the Cape. Goderich set aside for further consideration the division of the office of protector of slaves in the eastern and western districts. Meanwhile he ordered Cole to amend the colonial legislation in the light of his criticism.[43]

In the colony the governor was faced with criticism of a different kind. Four clauses of the Order in Council especially irritated slave-owners. They complained of the restrictions placed on their punishment of female slaves, of the necessity to keep a record of punishment administered, of the necessity of witnesses for corporal punishment, and of restrictions placed on the employment of slaves on Sunday. Cole explained to the colonists that it was out of his power to alter the law but that he would forward to the British Government any petitions they might care to submit. He urged them meanwhile to comply with the law so far as possible and refrain from acts of violence.

Petitions were presented and forwarded as promised, but the governor realised that in any event slave-owners intended to defy the law with respect to the maintenance of punishment record books. In order to avoid public disregard for the law Cole discussed with the Council the advisability of suspending that part of the Order, but it was agreed that he could not do so. The judges, however, agreed with the governor that several of the provisions of the Order, including the maintenance of the punishment record books, were impracticable at the Cape. They pointed out that distances were so great and the population so scanty that it was impossible to assemble the number of witnesses required by the Order for the punishment of slaves – a requirement made doubly difficult when drought forced a farmer to trek into the interior in search of pasturage for his cattle. Farms were sometimes as much as thirty miles apart, and it could cause considerable inconvenience if a neighbour had to be fetched to witness punishment. Very few slave-owners possessed the eight or more slaves necessary to provide a sufficient panel of six slave witnesses.[44] A further factor was not only the inability of slave-owners to write, but the impossibility for them even to employ somebody who could. Even supposing the books could be written up, bi-annual inspection of them was extremely inconvenient because of the long journeys, sometimes of several days duration, which it would necessitate. If a slave-owner was ill at the time of the inspection it was equally impossible for him to fulfill the instruction of the Order to submit a medical certificate. Medical practitioners usually lived in the principal towns and a visit which involved a long journey for the doctor was obviously very expensive for the patient.[45]

Armed with the wide support of the slave-owners and the judges of the colony Cole attacked the Order in Council in a despatch to his superior. He asserted that on the one hand the Order recognized the right of property in slaves while on the other hand it placed innumerable obstacles in the way of management of slaves which consequently rendered that type of property worse than useless. Moreover, he claimed that in their desire to assimilate the slave laws of the several colonies, the framers of the Order had entirely overlooked the great difference between the Cape and the other slave colonies. What was feasible in the West Indies or Mauritius was not necessarily feasible at the Cape. The fines stipulated in the Order, Cole wrote, illustrated the complete lack of understanding of local conditions. He pointed out that the usual minimum fine specified of £10 would not be felt in Mauritius but at the Cape it would be an imposition of considerable severity. Such was the ill-feeling generated amongst the colonists by the Order that Cole reckoned that if the British Government persisted with its enforcement rebellion was possible. In that event he did not consider he had sufficient forces at his command to contain it and added that more troops, including cavalry, should be sent to the Cape.[46]

In public the governor gave quite a different impression. He was sympathetic to the colonists but insisted on compliance with the law as far as practicable. His position was not made easier by the publication of two pamphlets by two civil servants,[47] both of whom argued in favour of the abolition of slavery though they arrived at this conclusion by contradictory arguments. The official situation of the authors suggested to the colonists that the colonial government desired to lead slave-owners to consider some general measure to abolish slavery. Several merchants of Cape Town and some slave-owners attempted to get permission to hold a public meeting to elect a committee to consider the subject and discuss other matters of general interest. Cole was suspicious of the real intentions of these people. He declined to sanction a public meeting but, in a notice that he promulgated, told the colonists that he wished neither to promote nor discourage consideration of the abolition of slavery. If, however, slave-owners could satisfy him that they were favourably disposed to it and desired to consider proposals to accomplish that end, then he would readily sanction a public meeting at which every slave-owner could declare his sentiments and subscribe to whichever plan he thought best suited to the purpose. He announced, moreover, that he was uninformed of the views of the British Government on the subject, and disclaimed any association with the pamphleteers.[48] This was a wise move. He seemed to have called the colonists' bluff for there was no immediate response to his offer, though there were groups of people who favoured abolition.[49]

Cole's official attitude was put to a more severe test when a disturbance took place in Stellenbosch in April 1831 on the first occasion punishment record books had to be brought for inspection. Several slave-owners attempted to comply with the law, but an unruly mob prevented them from doing so. The assistant protector of slaves in Stellenbosch called on the resident magistrate for assistance to quell the rioters. The resident magistrate ignored the request. He subsequently explained that his inaction was due to the weakness of the local constabulary and that he preferred to delay action until there was a specific breach of the peace. The uproar continued throughout the week set aside to inspect the books. Damage was minimal – only a few windows broken – but several people were deterred from obeying the law. Since the resident magistrate, who was well known in Stellenbosch, made no attempt to disperse the rioters nor communicate with the government in Cape Town, only 25 miles away, until the period set aside for the inspection had passed, Cole sent the attorney-general and the protector of slaves to investigate and report to him. The enquiry established that the resident magistrate's failure to act was caused partly by timidity and partly from sentiments similar to those hostile to the law.

Cole himself was critical of the British Order in Council but he would not condone dereliction of duty. What was essentially a local affair could have developed into a general crisis had it not been firmly handled at the beginning: other districts might have followed the example of Stellenbosch. In the circumstances Cole dismissed the resident magistrate from the government service.[50] At the next circuit court at Stellenbosch seven of the principal rioters were prosecuted and brought to trial. The governor frustrated rumours of a serious disturbance of the peace by giving orders for adequate precautionary measures to be taken. The presiding judge, after a suitable admonition, sentenced the prisoners to a mitigated penalty of £10 each and required them to find sureties to keep the peace for a sum of £20.[51]

There was no further disturbance of the peace until the following April when dissatisfaction among the slave-owners reached a new height. The colonial newspapers published two Orders in Council dated 2nd November 1831. One Order in Council revoked that of the 2nd February 1830, the other Order, of general application, imposed amended and additional regulations for the amelioration of the condition of the slaves in the colonies of conquest. These new measures were not forwarded to the governor of the Cape until another Order in Council[52] had been passed on the 6th February 1832. This latter measure modified the general Orders to meet the special circumstances of the Cape. But as things stood it appeared to the colonists as if the general Order in Council would be made applicable to the Cape.

The new general Order plugged loopholes in the earlier measures. The protector of slaves and his assistants were given unrestricted authority to enter premises occupied by slaves or land worked by slaves. The maximum number of strokes that could be inflicted on male slaves was reduced from 25 to 18, but the number of slave witnesses to punishment was reduced as well – from six to three. The Order defined more precisely "work of necessity" so as to exclude all agricultural labour and work associated with making wine. The ordinary working day of a slave was fixed at 9 hours and basic rations of food and clothes were prescribed. The Order made no alteration to the regulations for keeping punishment record books. Indeed, the Order suggested to colonists at the Cape that their representations had been in vain and they viewed with apprehension legislation which subjected them to greater controls.

There was dissatisfaction with the Order in Council in all the colonies where it was applicable.[53] At the Cape opposition crystallised around what Cole described as "a numerous political party" of Dutch colonists in Cape Town who controlled a bilingual newspaper called *De Zuid-Afrikaan*.[54] Cole alleged that this newspaper had alienated the great mass of Dutch inhabitants from the British Government.[55] It was certainly provocative. It published accounts of opposition, by slave-owners in other colonies, to the slave legislation, and asked rhetorically what would become of the Cape when the amended general Order was proclaimed there. It gave reply, "Ruin, total ruin: but this is what our enemies are aiming at, and what they will now very soon attain".[56] A week after this statement appeared in the newspaper a group of slave-owners of Koeberg, a village some 15 miles from Cape Town, met and passed several resolutions which, though not violent, pointed to future resistance.[57] The meeting was given publicity and support by *De Zuid-Afrikaan*.

Similar resolutions were passed in Stellenbosch and other districts prepared to follow.

Cole perceived the probability of dissatisfaction with the slave legislation developing into acts of open sedition or even rebellion. Recent accounts of unrest in other slave colonies suggested to him the wisdom of quick, firm action. As the law stood it was doubtful if any crime had yet been committed. Cole decided to prevent any further meetings and submitted to the Council a draft ordinance based on a proclamation of Lord Charles Somerset.[58] The proposed legislation prohibited public meetings without the governor's permission, or, in certain districts, without that of the civil commissioner. Even lawfully assembled meetings were prevented from considering petitions which might bring the British Government into contempt or weaken its authority at the Cape. Neither could lawful meetings be used to "stir up and excite discontent, disaffection or disorder", or "move, instigate, or encourage" colonists to resist the laws in force or those about to be put into operation. Publication of any statement made at any such meeting was also an offence. Offenders were liable to a penalty of imprisonment from four months to one year.

The Council divided three to two against the immediate promulgation of the ordinance. The majority considered it was impossible for them to take a responsible decision on so serious a subject without more time than the governor was prepared to allow. Cole held that speed was the essence of the measure if a general confrontation with the colonists was to be averted. He therefore took upon himself the responsibility of publishing the ordinance without the consent of the Council.[59] He coupled with it a proclamation in which he made it known that if these penalties were insufficient for the maintenance of order he would banish from the colony any person whose continued presence he considered threatened its stability.[60] This was not a revolutionary assumption of autocratic power but a restatement of a device used at the Cape since the early days of Company government to exclude agitators from the colony, and a power he possessed in terms of his instructions.[61]

The governor considered that his prompt action was supported by the better disposed colonists, but invective articles in *De Zuid-Afrikaan* suggest that his action cost him his personal popularity with the slave-owners. However, they were soon pacified by receipt of the news of the Order in Council of the 6th February 1832, applicable to the Cape alone.[62]

This Order shows that the British Government tried very hard to meet local criticism. Powers reserved for the chief civil judge in the other slave colonies were extended to all the judges of the Cape bench – and the circuit courts made the judges more readily accessible to country districts. Judges were permitted to halve minimum fines in the general Order in Council of November 1831. Slave-owners at the Cape were spared the necessity of making a written declaration either of provisions supplied to slaves or alternatively of seeds, implements, and land allotted to them. Slave-owners found to be in default of minimum requirements remained subject to the penalties set out in the general Order. Punishment record books remained subject to the general Order for those who lived within twenty miles of Cape Town, Grahamstown, or other principal town of a district. The governor was empowered to vary, suspend or modify regulations for punishment record books for those who lived beyond the twenty-mile limit.

Cole submitted a draft proclamation to the Council to provide a free distribution of blank record books for these people. After completion they had to submit their books to the nearest resident magistrate, justice of the peace or field cornet for inspection. The officials who inspected the book had to forward details to the protector or assistant protector of their district. Illiterate slave-owners were expected to employ a writer to fill in the book for them, but if they were unable to get a writer they were merely required to declare this on oath. Those who were sick at the time of the inspection were expected to make their declaration within ten days of their recovery without risk of penalty, or alternatively officials could go to the residence of the sick slave-owner and take his declaration there.[63]

Members of the Council made innumerable objections to the draft proclamation. Some did not like the extension of powers of protectors and assistant protectors to field cornets who were themselves slave-owners and united by blood and friendship with the people in their district. One member of council considered that the emphasis on looser control of slave-owners was put in the wrong place, arguing that the further removed slave-owners were from the surveillence of society the greater was the need to supervise the treatment of their slaves. Another contended that since slaves had unrestricted facility to lodge complaints, however trifling, the government could hardly be kept in ignorance of the domestic treatment of slaves, and that there was plenty of opportunity to redress unjust punishments. Yet another reckoned the very existence of punishment record books opened the door to fraud, perjury, and combinations between slave-owners to defeat the object of government. Not surprisingly, the proclamation was rejected by the Council.[64]

The slave-owners were given a chance to express their opinion at a meeting held with the governor's authority in Cape Town on the 17th September 1832.[65] The object of the meeting was to prepare a petition to the King in Council to repeal some clauses of the Order in Council of the 2nd November 1831 which, even though modified by the Order in Council of the 2nd February 1832, were considered "injurious to the slave interests in the Colony". The meeting drew up a series of resolutions in which the old arguments were restated, but added that it was absurd for the King's ministers in Britain to make laws and regulations for a colony whose condition they did not understand. In their opinion only a "Representative Legislative Assembly" could prepare legislation to ensure the peace and happiness of the colony. In exchange for this boon they stated they would be willing to co-operate with the British Government to ameliorate the condition of slaves, and finally abolish slavery at the Cape. Meanwhile they asked the governor to suspend the execution of the Order in Council, and elected a committee of 27 members who were instructed "generally to adopt such measures as may best secure the interests of all slave proprietors as affected thereby".[66]

The chairman of the meeting called on Cole at Government House to present the resolutions. Cole thought the meeting had gone too far: he objected to the election of a committee for any other purpose than to convert the resolutions into a petition to the King in Council and to support it to the best of their ability. Moreover, he said, he was powerless to suspend the Order because it expressly forbade the suspension of any of its provisions by local enactments.[67]

The position was intolerable for a governor anxious to meet the demands of his superiors in London and satisfy the genuine grievances of slave-owners, yet provide adequate protection for slaves. Cole was convinced that the fault lay in the desire for uniformity in ameliorative measures, and he was convinced that if the British Government persisted with that policy they would be defeated. "The slaves will gain nothing," he wrote, "by the well-intentioned, but . . . mistaken measures adopted for their good; and the slave proprietors will only become more and more disgusted with a law which in many cases requires the performance of impossibilities". Cole did not object to the policy of amelioration itself, but "to the petty vexatious details to which it descends". The law as it stood, he thought, was probably perfectly applicable to a sugar island and might even suit all sugar islands, but was quite inapplicable to the Cape. ". . . I think Your Lordship will discover at last," Cole wrote to Goderich, "that it will be necessary to pass an Order in Council for this Colony alone, the draft of which, preserving all the great principles of the present law, should be prepared by this Government and transmitted for His Majesty's approval."[68]

The Order in Council of the 6th February 1832 which gave the Cape the right to deviate from the general Order in some respects, suggests that the British Government had begun to appreciate that the position at the Cape in respect of slavery was different from that in the other colonies where there were slaves. But by the time this Order was given effect at the Cape, rumour of the probable emancipation of the slaves had reached the colony, and was confirmed a few months later.

Goderich committed the British Government to the abolition of slavery in June 1832.[69] Contrary to expectation the news excited no open discontent whatever. The slaves were neither turbulent nor disorderly. There were increased complaints of insolence to masters, but this was not important because anything less than servile submissiveness to orders would be reckoned as disrespect by a slave-owner. However, the slave-owners were resigned to their fate. They received the news with "a dogged gloomy silence". It would seem that slave-owners preferred abolition of slavery to the multifarious regulations of amelioration. There was genuine fear of increased vagrancy and a shortage of labour, and general lack of confidence in the good faith of the British Government to meet its obligations with respect to the amount and prompt payment of compensation.[70]

It is perhaps an ironic commentary on the labyrinth of legislation designed to ameliorate the condition of slaves that its principal achievement was to intensify the divisions of white society at the Cape. *The South African Commercial Advertiser*, edited by the liberal Fairbairn, attempted to counter the criticism of government policy in *De Zuid-Afrikaan*. Editorial comment in the former newspaper and letters to its editor suggest a fair amount of support for British slave policy. The success of a Philanthropic Society at the Cape who in four years bought the freedom of 102 female slaves,[71] increased voluntary manumission of slaves,[72] even the occasional consideration of emancipation,[73] indicates that there was at the Cape a hard core of individuals anxious to do what they could to overcome the social and economic problems created by slavery.

It would seem though, that the colony as a whole was not politically acclimatized to develop the policy of amelioration beyond the terms of Ordinance 19 of 1826, and in part this can be explained by the precarious financial position of the colonists, and the wine farmers in particular.[74] In the opinion of members of the council, Ordinance 19 did improve the lot of slaves at the Cape.[75] Subsequent legislation apparently added very little to that improvement, and paved the way for emancipation only because increased amelioration regulations exasperated slave-owners. Cole's suggestion that local officials should frame a draft Order in Council was never put to the test, but the objection of members of the Council to Cole's draft proclamation of 1832 indicates that local officials would have found it equally hard to frame legislation to meet the difficult and complex situation at the Cape.

The root of the problem lay in the mere existence of slavery. Cole himself had written, "The very name of slavery is abhorrent to an Englishman and rouses every generous feeling in our nature". The topic engaged the minds of many great men, so that Cole considered it was not for him to contribute to any discussion of abstract principles but only to point out practical difficulties to the implementation of policy. Cole was aware of the miseries created by slavery and its tendency to debase human nature. He regretted it was ever introduced into the Cape where obstacles to the employment of white labour did not exist as in tropical climates.[76] But slavery did exist and the attempt to mitigate its evils failed largely because the principle of slavery itself was iniquitous. Abolition was the only answer.

FOOTNOTES

1. See Chapter IV, pp. 64–65.
2. C.A., G.H. 23/10, Wade to Stanley, 6 December 1833.
3. C.A., G.H. 1/18, Report of J. T. Bigge, one of the commissioners of inquiry, 5 April 1831, enclosed in Goderich to Cole, 11 August 1831.
4. Only one illegal importation is known to have taken place after that date. The case was brought before the colonial court and condemned.
5. C.A., G.H. 1/18, Goderich to Cole, 11 August 1831.
6. *C.H.B.E.*, Vol. II, p. 271, fn. 1.
7. Return of the Registrar of Slaves, 31 October 1829 accounts for the number of slaves in districts as follows:
   Western Province: Cape and district 11 929, Clanwilliam 791, Simon's Town 197, Stellenbosch 8 619, Swellendam 2 924, Worcester 3 937, Total 28 397.
   Eastern Province: Albany 116, Somerset 1 505, Uitenhage 1 181, Graaff-Reinet 2 115, Beaufort 515, George 2 105, Total 7 537.
   Grand Total 35 934.
8. C.A., G.H. 1/18, Bigge Report, 5 April 1831.
9. *C.H.B.E.*, Vol. VIII (2nd edition), p. 271.
10. C.A., G.H. 1/18, Bigge Report, 5 April 1831.
11. Theal, *R.C.C.*, Vol. X, pp. 1–60, Cradock to Bathurst, 15 April 1814, and enclosures.
12. See Chapter X, p. 161.
13. *Anti-Slavery Monthly Reporter*. Vol. I, number 20, 31 January 1827.
14. i.e. Rev. John Philip, superintendent of the London Missionary Society in South Africa, and author of *Researches in South Africa*, published in April 1828.
15. i.e. Thomas Pringle who contributed two articles in the *Anti-Slavery Monthly Reporter*, see Vol. I, number 20, 31 January 1827 and Vol. II, number 32, January 1828, and author of *Narrative of a Residence in South Africa*. The latter, however, was only published in 1834.
16. *Anti-Slavery Monthly Reporter*, Vol. III, number 54.
17. C.A., G.H. 1/18, Bigge Report, 5 April 1831.
18. *Ibid.*
19. *Ibid.*
20. *Ibid.*
21. I. E. Edwards, *Towards Emancipation: A Study in South African Slavery*, p. 91.
22. *Ibid.*, p. 94.
23. See Harlow and Madden, *British Colonial Developments, 1774–1834*, pp. 567–573.
24. An unpublished article for the South African Historical Society entitled "A Short History of Slavery at the Cape" by G. E. C. (i.e. Sir George Cory) and retained in the Cory Library, Rhodes University, Grahamstown, p. 8, gives a list of the principal slave-owners and the number of slaves they possessed in 1826. Truter had 49 slaves of whom 25 were males, 12 were females and 12 were children.

25. Edwards, p. 97.
26. See Theal, *R.C.C.*, Vol. XXVI, pp. 468–491.
27. C.O. 49/21, Huskisson to Bourke, 21 October 1827.
28. Edwards, p. 155.
29. *Ibid.*, p. 90.
30. *Ibid.*, pp. 156–157.
31. See Chapter V, p. 90.
32. C.O. 48/124, Bourke to Huskisson, 29 July 1828.
33. See Chapter IX, pp. 143–145. The subject raised an important constitutional issue.
34. C.A., G.H. 23/9, Cole to Murray, 20 March 1829.
35. Trinidad, Berbice, Demerara, St. Lucia, the Cape of Good Hope and Mauritius.
36. C.A., G.H. 1/16, Murray to Cole, 19 March 1830.
37. *Ibid.*
38. C.A., G.H. 1/16 Murray to Cole, 20 March 1830.
39. C.A., G.H. 23/9, Cole to Murray, 28 August 1830.
40. C.A., G.H. 23/9, Proclamation by the governor, 12 August 1830, enclosed in Cole to Murray, 28 August 1830.
41. C.A., G.H. 23/9, Cole to Murray, 28 August 1830.
42. C.A., G.H. 1/17, Goderich to Cole, 18 December 1830.
43. *Ibid.*
44. See Appendix B, p. 178.
45. C.A., G.H. 23/9, Cole to Goderich, 1 April 1831.
46. *Ibid.*
47. One was by T. Miller, the other by J. C. Chase. They were enclosed in Cole to Goderich, 6 April 1831, C.O. 48/142.
48. C.A., G.H. 23/9, Cole to Goderich, 6 April 1831.
49. *S.A.C.A.*, 9 and 12 February 1831.
50. C.A., G.H. 23/9, Cole to Goderich, 3 July 1831.
51. C.A., G.H. 23/9, Cole to Goderich, 4 December 1831.
52. See p. 120.
53. W. D. Jones, *Prosperity Robinson*, p. 223.
54. At this time *De Zuid-Afrikaan* was controlled by a syndicate of eighty shareholders. Among them were Advocates C. Brand, J. de Wet, J. Hofmeyr, Messrs. C. H. Neethling, M. L. Neethling and P. A. Brand. No fixed editor was appointed, and as the articles were written by various hands, the lack of continuity led to some loss of popularity. See J. H. Hofmeyr (in collaboration with F. W. Reitz), *The Life of Jan Hendrik Hofmeyr*, pp. 42–43.
55. C.A., G.H. 23/10, Cole to Goderich, 19 June 1832.
56. *Z.A.*, 18 May 1832.
57. C.A., G.H. 23/10, Cole to Goderich, 19 June 1832.
58. See Chapter V, p. 84.
59. C.A., G.H. 23/10, Cole to Goderich, 19 June 1832.
60. *Government Gazette*. 8 June 1832.
61. See Chapter V, p. 88.
62. C.A., G.H. 1/18, Goderich to Cole, 29 February 1832, enclosing Order in Council, 6 February 1832.
63. C.A., A.C. 7 August 1832.
64. C.A., A.C. 13 August 1832.
65. *S.A.C.A.*, 1 September 1832.
66. *S.A.C.A.*, 26 September 1832.
67. C.A., C.O. 5302, the secretary to government to M. van Breda, 20 September 1832.
68. C.A., G.H. 23/10, Cole to Goderich, 18 March 1833.
69. W. D. Jones, *Prosperity Robinson*, p. 224.

70. C.A., G.H. 23/10, Wade to Stanley, 6 December 1833.
71. *C.H.B.E.*, Vol. VIII, (2nd edition), p. 274.
72. *S.A.C.A.*, 2 February 1831, published a list of names of eight prominent slave-owners who declared their intention to free all children born to their slaves after 8 April 1831. Among them they owned 116 slaves. Their names were Hon. J. W. Stoll, Hon. Sir J. A. Truter, Hon. A. Stockenstrom, P. G. Brink, R. Crozier, J. G. Brink, Rev. A. Faure, J. N. de Villiers.
73. C.O. 48/142., Pamphlets by T. Miller and J. C. Chase.
74. See Chapter VIII.
75. C.A., A.C. 4 December 1828 and opinions read to the Council 3 January 1829.
76. C.A., G.H. 23/10, Cole to Goderich, 15 March 1833.

CHAPTER VIII

PROBLEMS OF INCOME AND EXPENDITURE

It was unfortunate that the legislation to improve the condition of the slaves and the Khoi-khoi and other free persons of colour was introduced at a time when the Cape was in financial difficulties. The white colonists regarded the reforms with suspicion and resentment because they appeared to them to threaten the labour force upon which they were so dependent. Indeed it must have seemed to many a Cape farmer that the British Government was more concerned for the welfare of the non-white population than the whites. The Trade Act of 1825[1] had narrowed the preferences hitherto enjoyed by Cape wines sold on the British market. Moreover, a general recession in Britain towards the end of the third decade of the nineteenth century was responsible for a reduction in the number of ships that called at Cape Town for supplies.

The *South African Commercial Advertiser* attempted to explain the financial predicament of the colony. The newspaper said that expensive wars on the frontier, extravagant public buildings, impolitic restrictions on trade and general bad management had reduced the colony to "the lowest point of depression". However, the newspaper did acknowledge that drought, bad harvests, the depreciation of the currency and the inability of Cape wines to compete on the London market had contributed to economic distress.[2] Criticism of Somerset's administration of the Cape has been questioned by recent historians,[3] but an unfavourable balance of trade over a series of years bears witness to the fact that the colony had been living beyond its means.[4]

The timing of Sir Lowry Cole's arrival in the Cape ensured that he was not personally associated with the social reforms. He came to the Cape from Mauritius with the reputation of a popular governor who had steered his colony towards prosperity. Since his salary of £7 000 per annum exceeded that of the president of the United States of America by a thousand pounds the *South African Commercial Advertiser* claimed that colonists were entitled "to the most active attention to their interests, both here and in England from a governor possessing abilities, experience, and political influence to support sound views of them".[5] Cole was fortunate, moreover, in that his arrival coincided with a swing in the economic fortunes of the colony. Schumann has shown that the period 1826–1849 taken as a whole was a period of rapid advance, but a more detailed analysis indicated moderate prosperity from 1827 to 1830 followed by recession and moderate depression from 1830 to 1834.[6] So far as the colonial government was concerned, the period 1828–1833 inclusive produced an excess of revenue over expenditure of £11 572.7.7½d., but in 1829 and in 1831 the annual accounts showed a deficit.[7] These dificits alarmed officials in the Colonial Department in London, because they suggested that measures taken on the advice of the commissioners of inquiry to balance the colonial budget were inadequate. The rise and fall of the economic tide forms the background of the political scene of Cole's administration.

The Cape was a difficult colony to govern, not least because of its immense size and the very low density of population.[8] The judicial and administrative reforms and the policy of ameliorating the condition of slaves had added to the expense of government. Certainly the collection of taxes had been improved by increased staff but the amount collected did not yield the sum anticipated.[9] It was unfortunate that the analogy was drawn between the governor and the president of the United States for their powers were in no ways similar. Cole had only marginal powers of discretion and his initiative was crippled by financial stringency.

In Britain, interest on the national debt was still a major item in national accounting. The abolition of income tax in 1816 had meant that the chief reliance for revenue must be placed on the land tax and on customs and excise duties. Even Huskisson could do little except re-adjust the customs pattern. Free trade in any real sense was not practicable until the re-introduction of income tax in 1842. Although Great Britain was growing increasingly rich in the period 1815–1848, government expenditure was carefully scrutinized. Briggs says "the pressure on the Treasury sprang simply from the demand for 'retrenchment' which country gentlemen and urban radicals shared".[10]

Closely associated with financial stringency in London, was the pressure of new administrative patterns. Greater Treasury controls meant closer budgeting by departments of state. A Colonial Audit Office was established in 1814. Its powers were increased during the twenties and although it merged with the Audit Office of the United Kingdom in 1832[11] this did not mean that colonial accounts were less carefully checked. The official attitude was that colonies should live of their own: they should be solvent enough to pay even the salaries of officials appointed by Britain. Until a colony was solvent its governor could not venture into constructive planning.

It is the financial difficulties of the British Government, seen in relation to the inadequate financial resources of the Cape government which explains the Colonial Department's attitude to government expenditure in the colony. Without investment and planned development the Cape could not prosper; until it prospered at least to the minimum point of solvency it could not go forward with the provision of public utilities. This dilemma it is proposed to illustrate from the fate of two projects: the one, the construction of a new pass over the Hottentots Holland Mountains, the other, the construction of a pier in Cape Town harbour.

Cole appreciated that if his government's financial position was to be improved, the economy of the colony had to be developed. In his opinion the first requirement was to develop the lines of communication. Bad roads inhibited internal trade and hindered administration, both civil and judicial. As long as the colony was without good roads, Cole argued, it would remain poor and semi-barbarous.[12] Wagon tracks, sometimes impassable, had to circumvent mountain ranges and often added days to a journey with corresponding expense to the traveller. It was with the object of reducing the cost of transport to Cape Town from Caledon, Swellendam and other districts even further east, that Cole gave directions for the construction of a new pass over the Hottentots Holland range.

News of the project soon reached the Colonial Department in London from outside sources. The governor himself forgot to report the venture to the secretary of state. An inquiry from the under-secretary in the Colonial Department,[13] and advice of his neglect from the colonial auditor-general, must have reached Cole about the same time.[14] So confident was he of the utility of the project that his apology for his oversight carried with it assumption of approval by the secretary of state. The pass was expected to cost £2 672.8.6d. to build and about half that sum had been spent when the governor officially reported the project. He assured Sir George Murray that the construction of the road was very popular with the colonists because it would make land carriage to the markets of Cape Town shorter and therefore cheaper. It encouraged production in the hinterland. Cole commented with some satisfaction that more grain was sown in the districts of George and Swellendam "than for many years".[15]

The secretary of state was clearly puzzled by the necessity for the road. Hay had admitted to Cole that the Colonial Department was deficient in geographical knowledge of the colony.[16] This probably explains why the secretary of state thought Cole's new project seemed unnecessary[17] because a pass had already been built over the same range at Fransch Hoek. Cole explained that the advantages anticipated by the Fransch Hoek Pass had not materialised: the farmers in the rich grain area beyond the Hottentots Holland Mountains preferred the shorter but precarious passage through the kloof, where the new pass was being built, when they brought their produce to Cape Town for sale.[18] Utility was insufficient explanation in a colony where there was a deficit in the revenue. The secretary of state instructed Cole to suspend work on the project immediately, and for the future told him that he had to get permission from England for any project which exceeded £200 in value. Moreover, the secretary of state warned Cole that unless he obeyed financial instructions he might bring considerable embarrassment upon himself.[19]

On receipt of these instructions Cole suspended work on the road. Merchants in Cape Town responded swiftly. They engaged to subscribe £900 towards the cost of completion of the pass. Backed by the security of public support, Cole authorized the resumption of work on the road.[20] Goderich, who had succeeded Murray as secretary of state, was irritated by Cole's persistence with the project despite orders to desist. He argued it would be unfair to call for public aid at a late stage in building the pass, nor did he regard it as consistent with Cole's position as governor to owe his immunity from a heavy surcharge to the liberality of the colonists. In the circumstances he approved the further expenditure of £900 to complete the work, but forbade the governor to consider any future projects.[21]

The pass was named Sir Lowry's Pass in honour of the governor and still carries the main highway from Cape Town to the east. Cole's foresight in building the pass was soon rewarded. Lease of a toll, allowing for maintenance, brought the colonial treasury £490 in two years.[22] This was part of a general increase in revenue from tolls, town taxes and wharf dues.[23] Figures spoke louder than words. In the case of the pass they were "well calculated to reconcile His Majesty's Government to the expense which it occasioned".[24] The secretary of state invited the governor to submit specific proposals for future public works.[25] Cole seems to have been reluctant to take the initiative again because his requests for money for public works were confined to repairs or improvements to roads, bridges or government buildings. Goderich, however, proved to be more responsive to public demand, if somewhat rash.

A violent gale in July 1831 wrecked six vessels anchored in Table Bay and destroyed the greater part of their cargoes. The port captain of Cape Town reported that had there been a jetty "at the north end of the town" adequate assistance could have been given to the ships.[26] Cape Town businessmen were quick to see that the disaster would reflect adversely on trade, because ships would avoid the port for want of adequate security. In the heat of the moment general accusations were made at a public meeting in Cape Town about the irresponsible expenditure of public money, and allegations were made that the government had refused permission to build a stone pier to protect shipping in Table Bay. The meeting resolved to ask the government to publish the Revenue and Expenditure Accounts so that the public could scrutinize them, and proposed to erect a jetty at their own expense, or supplement government funds to carry on and complete the work. It was suggested that wharfage dues should be appropriated to pay for the new jetty.[27]

Cole challenged particular individuals to substantiate their complaints about government expenditure. He proved they were directed either against previous administrations or were unfounded.[28] This correspondence, and a newspaper report of the meeting,[29] Cole sent to the secretary of state. The governor's conscience was clear. He supported the colonists' request for the publication of the annual accounts. Goderich authorised Cole to publish them without hesitation and sympathised with the colonists' desire for a new pier. He agreed that Cole had acted properly in asking for advice, but asserted that the proposed pier was of such importance to the colony that the government should build it without calling upon individuals disposed to subscribe money for it. He regretted that Cole had not sent him an estimate of the cost, nor any plans so that he might consider the merits of maintaining the old wooden structure as well. Despite his ignorance of particulars, he directed Cole to ensure work was begun at once, and adopted the colonists' suggestion of using the wharfage dues to pay for it.[30]

After his previous experience with the road through the pass, and well aware of the financial difficulties of the colony, Cole was surprised by these commands. But the African trade was Britain's most rapidly expanding market. From 1816 to 1842 British exports to Africa increased by £1,3 million (325%) which amounted to 12½% of the net gain of £10,2 million in the value of all British exports.[31] At this time Cape Town was the most important port of entry in Africa for British goods.

It was almost eighteen months before Cole could submit details of the pier project, but he did order preliminary tasks to be carried out. A building to house a forge was built, equipment purchased, and a quarry opened. He explained that the quarrying of the stone was likely to take longest, so that in fact there was no delay. The total cost of the project was estimated at £16 804.2.1d. But Cole opposed allotting revenue from a single source to one purpose. He suggested instead that the work should be paid for by a re-issue of paper money recently returned to the colonial treasury for loans repaid.[32]

By the time Cole's despatch reached England, however, Goderich had been replaced at the Colonial Department by Lord Stanley. Stanley went through the same patterns of reaction as Goderich had previously done on the question of the pass. He was alarmed by the expense of the project and ordered the suspension of work on the pier while the British Government considered the matter.[33] £2 316 had been spent on the pier by the time this despatch arrived in Cape Town. Cole's interim successor, Wade,[34] authorized a further very small sum to secure the work already done.[35]

Naturally the Cape Town merchants were perturbed. They begged that work be resumed on the pier, or alternatively they sought permission to complete it themselves.[36] Meanwhile the Admiralty had been consulted. The officer commanding the Cape station supported the utility of the work,[37] but Stanley stood his ground and held that it would be inexpedient to complete it until the finances of the colony improved.[38] The subject was not raised again till 1843. In that year a committee appointed to investigate the practicability of making Table Bay a safe harbour, recommended a project estimated at £700 000 (sic). Some preliminary work was done in the forties but it was not till 1855 that a loan was secured from the British Government to complete the job.[39]

The return of Cape finances for 1829 revealed a deficit of over £17 000.[40] The British Parliament was not prepared to vote any grant-in-aid[41] because of the precarious state of British finances. The huge national debt which had accumulated during the wars with France (1793–1815) placed a heavy burden on the finances of the British Government.[42] In 1830, the income paid into the exchequer was over £50 million, but almost £30 million went to pay interest on the public debt.[43] Thus the British Government was in no position to come to the financial aid of a colony that was unable to pay its debts. The Cape therefore had to find its own solution to its financial problems: expenditure had to be pruned to the level of its resources.

Suspension of public works was an obvious economy, but not necessarily wise policy. It certainly made an immediate reduction in expenditure but, as the examples of the pass over the Hottentots Holland Mountains and the Cape Town pier show, the reductions retarded economic development, and therefore held back ways of increasing the revenue of the colonial government in the long term. In any case money saved by cuts in government expenditure on public works was not by itself sufficient to bring expenditure down to the level of income. Other remedies also had to be found.

In an effort to cut expenditure, Goderich, while secretary of state, ordered the reduction of salaries and the consolidation of some offices in the government service at the Cape. He proposed, for example, to consolidate the offices of civil commissioner and resident magistrate and revive the office of heemraden[44] to assist the holder of the combined office. Moreover, he decided to raise additional income by imposing a tax of 5 shillings per head on all slaves between the ages of ten and sixty years and instructed the governor accordingly. He estimated this would yield £6 000 per annum and go a long way to establishing a favourable balance of revenue and expenditure. To soften the blow of additional taxation he suggested relief by the repeal of a tax on carts and wagons used in agriculture "and some other dues which although trifling in amount are said to be particularly burdensome to the poorer farmers".[45]

Cole was put out by these instructions. He commented that after a three-year residence in the colony he could be considered to have some estimate of the interests, habits and prejudices of the colonists and pointed out that several of the reductions of staff and salary were neither feasible nor judicious. In particular he criticised Goderich's instruction to consolidate the offices of civil commissioner and resident magistrate. Cole thought that such a move would throw an intolerable burden on one man and harm the public service. Furthermore, he dismissed as impracticable Goderich's suggestion that heemraden be restored as advisers to the civil commissioners. Cole wrote,

> "As a Collector of Taxes he (the civil commissioner) cannot stand in need of it, and in inspecting and valuing lands their interference would be anything but advantageous; if they be restored in their former judicial functions, the objections to a sort of standing jury appointed by Government will be revived and the Slave Laws will most certainly become abortive".[46]

Later Cole criticised the expediency of imposing a per capita tax on slaves. It was a tax which had been considered before and abandoned. The majority of the predial slaves were employed by the wine farmers. There had been a steady depreciation in the price of wine for some years and in March 1832 the price had fallen to half that of the previous year. Cole argued that it was impossible for the wine farmers to bear any additional taxation. As it was, they faced ruin because of the necessity to maintain their slaves though there was no profitable employment for them. A tax on slaves, he said, would exasperate the wine farmers "to a degree that would be actually dangerous to the well-being of the Colony". Nor did he think that the wine farmers would derive real benefit from any repeal of duties paid on wine brought to market. In Cole's view the corn farmers could sustain further taxation and would be prepared to pay more tax if the roads were further improved.[47]

Goderich countered most of Cole's objections[48] concerning the consolidation of offices. Cole accepted the opinion of his superior though he considered some of the measures inexpedient. He again protested against the order to restore the heemraden and recommended instead that colonists who lived in towns and villages should be empowered to elect local boards to manage local concerns and to raise local taxes for that purpose, subject to the approval of the Governor in Council. This proposal was approved and was the genesis of the Local Government Ordinance (No. 9 of 1836).[49] This measure relieved the colonial government of expenses in matters of purely local concern. When Cole returned to England in 1833, on his retirement from the governorship of the Cape, the secretary of state consulted him on other measures to reduce expenditure. Cole repeated his belief that the best way to improve the Cape's finances permanently was to re-appraise the burden of taxation. He commented on the distribution of work among officials and made practical suggestions to reduce the cost of administration. These comments and suggestions were forwarded to his successor along with a new schedule of the colonial establishment.[50]

Meanwhile in August 1833 a statement of the revenue and expenditure for 1832 was published in the colony. These accounts revealed an income of over £130 000 and expenditure of over £126 000, and therefore an excess of revenue over expenditure of £4 000. The largest single item of expenditure was not the civil government as might have been expected, but the Judicial Department. Salaries and contingencies in this department accounted for £33 478.11.0$\frac{1}{8}$d. To this sum should be added £2 138.0.10$\frac{3}{4}$d. for the expenses of witnesses and summoning jurors. Thus total expenditure on the judiciary amounted to £35 616.11.10$\frac{7}{8}$d. – or more than a quarter of the entirere venue. The *Graham's Town Journal* observed that this figure was "about £15 000 more than the expense of the Judicial Department of the *penal* Colony of New South Wales, although the revenue of that settlement is not far short of ours".[51]

The accounts also revealed how little was spent on education. This must seriously have hampered instruction of the English language and inhibited the anglicization of the colonists. Furthermore, it suggests that the amount spent on the education of the slaves must have been very limited. Similarly the amounts spent on the roads, bridges and ferries, and on the erection and repairs of public works and buildings was very small for a colony the size of the Cape.

One item which seemed to be excessive was the amount paid out in pensions for retired civil and military servants. The *Graham's Town Journal* commented that colonists were not disposed "to carp at a fair remuneration to old and useful servants of the Government".[52] There was reason to doubt whether all the pensioners had given a life time of service to the Cape. The *Graham's Town Journal* singled out Sir Richard Plaskett by way of example.

He was a former secretary to the colonial government who had only three years employment at the Cape, yet received a pension of £500. If the pension he was granted was for services rendered elsewhere than at the Cape, then the *Graham's Town Journal* argued that it was not right for the colony to carry the entire burden of the pension.[53]

The income of the colony was dependent upon indirect taxation. This was widely distributed so that no single source carried too great a burden. The Customs Department rendered a sum of over £15 000 made up from duties, store rent and wharfage. Stamp dues, and interest earned by the Lombard Bank[54] each rendered about the same figure. The *Graham's Town Journal* singled out the *Transfer Dues* for criticism. The editor thought it was inexplicable that a heavy duty of 4 per cent should be charged on the purchase of landed property any more than on the purchase of any other commodity. He thought the tax was unreasonable in principle, and "unequal in its pressure" because it fell exclusively on the landowners.[55] But it would seem from an examination of the accounts that the one source which did not contribute as much as it might have done to the colonial revenue was that derived from land.

In 1813 Sir John Cradock had abolished the Dutch practice of alienating land by the grant of loan farms.[56] These farms were of approximately 6 000 acres and were leased annually from the government. Continuity of lease meant that in practice the lessee was assured of permanent occupation. This tenure was replaced by grants of land made in perpetual quitrent. Each grant had to be properly surveyed and the holder issued with a title-deed. In making grants emphasis was placed on the encouragement of agriculture. Pastoral farming was thought to encourage laziness and hinder the process of civilization and common defence. The quitrent grants were expected to give greater security to the holder of the title, restrict dispersion of the population into the interior, draw the Dutch colonists closer to the British Government and increase the revenue of the colonial government.[57]

Cradock's reforms were unrealistic. Even as he prepared them, the judges on circuit in the eastern districts reported: "There is in fact no other way or prospect for the Young People, than the easy livelihood of breeding cattle".[58] Moreover, land grants were badly administered. In December 1830, it was discovered that more than 4 500 applications for grants made between 1813 and 1828 had not been acted upon.[59] In 1832 the surveyor-general reported delays of more than twenty years in the issue of title-deeds although all expenses had been paid by the applicants.[60] In theory applicants were not able to take up occupation of land until a grant had been made. In the face of administrative lethargy, men improvised. They devised an ad hoc remedy which they described as "request" tenure: so named because a formal request for the land had been made to the government, and was even recognized by the local officials. "Request" farms were bought and sold as if their tenure were legal. The only loser was the government which collected no rent until the grant was made.[61] In any case there were a number of farmers who did not want to own land. They had no motive to do so, because "a farm on wheels" was less troublesome to manage than a loan farm.[62]

The commissioners of inquiry were critical of the policy and operation of Cradock's land proclamation. They recognized the need to encourage pastoral farming and proposed a general assessment on all occupied land whether or not it was held by legal title. As a temporary measure they recommended that leases of 7 to 10 years would be granted where full title was not held. The lessee would avoid the expense of an application and survey costs as leases would only be made on an estimation of the size of the land. They recommended that the revenue due to the government for such a lease should be a small levy both on the value of the livestock that could be grazed on the land, and on all arable land on the holding.[63]

On the advice of the commissioners of inquiry a Land Board was created and a surveyor-general appointed in 1828. The Board was composed of the treasurer, the auditor-general and the surveyor-general.[64] This body made recommendations to the governor. Usually he accepted its advice, but not invariably so.[65] The Board ignored the backlog of neglected applications for land and concentrated on new assessments for lands where titles had been issued. The result of their inquiry was not an increase, but a decrease in rents due. Their action in good faith and equity further reduced colonial income from taxes on land.[66] The Board rejected the commissioners' recommendation to offer long-term leases because it would discourage colonists from applying for a quitrent grant, and would lead to disputes over assessed rents when a quitrent grant was made.[67] Thus the principle of perpetual quitrent remained the basis for the alienation of Crown land. The Board did, however, accept the commissioners' recommendation to establish a standard scale for rents. One was drawn up but proved unworkable. Consequently the Board was given authority to deviate from it.[68] But rents assessed on grants made in 1830 were queried by the secretary of state because they only amounted to a fraction of a farthing per acre.[69]

Meanwhile, the British Government had decided to apply to the Cape principles controlling the alienation of land initially developed in the context of British North America and Australia. These principles aimed to prevent unlimited expansion and the wasteful dispersal of the population, through the encouragement of agriculture. All Crown lands were to be sold by auction at a minimum upset price. A proportion of the revenue was to be applied to the encouragement of immigration. In part the policy was motivated by the ideas of Wakefield and in part it was in the process of formulation even before Wakefield published his ideas in *A Letter from Sydney* in 1829.[70] Goderich explained to the governor of New South Wales that the British Government wanted to avoid "the formation of a race of men wandering with their Cattle over the extensive Regions of the Interior, and losing, like the descendants of the Spaniards in the Pampas of South America, almost all traces of their original civilization".[71] These words could equally have been applied to the Cape. Copies of the regulations in operation in British North America and Australia were sent to Cole, but his pencil comments on the secretary of state's despatch suggest he did not understand the principles behind the required change of policy. "It will seem from this", he wrote, "that the Government of the Cape is not obliged to follow either of the enclosed regulations, but merely to get the highest prices for land".[72]

Burroughs has shown in a recent study that the attempts to fashion the Australian economy and to control the progress of settlement in terms of Goderich's recommendations were administratively unfeasable and economically unsound.[73] Even in Canada they did not work: wholesale disposal of public lands in the past rendered almost hopeless the introduction of any new system, and there was not the same need for an immigration fund comparable with Australia.[74] This might also have proved to be the case at the Cape, but Goderich's recommendations were not given a chance. A Government Notice in May 1832 did proclaim that in future Crown lands would be sold by public auction to the highest bidder but that applications for quitrent grants made before Goderich's despatch was received at the Cape on the 9th January that year would still be honoured.[75] Thus the Land Board continued to apply the principles of quitrent tenure until 1843.[76] In June that year a committee was formed under John Montagu, the secretary to the colonial government who had had experience in New South Wales, to supervise the sale in freehold of unappropriated Crown land by public auction at the upset price of 2 shillings per acre. In the first full year of its operation, 1844, land sales totalled £8 080.[77]

Easier sources of revenue to collect and administer than the tax on land, were those imposed on imports and exports. Even farmers did not escape these taxes. Neumark has argued that all farmers were linked in trade with the ports of the colony.[78] He contends that the supply of fresh meat and vegetables to passing ships was the staple of the colonial economy.[79] His thesis has been questioned by Hancock who holds that the ever extending frontier was populated by less affluent trekkers whose contacts with the markets receded with the horizon.[80] Certainly Cole did not regard the supply of ships as the staple of the colony. He considered wine the colonial staple[81] and this explains his concern to promote the interests of the wine industry at the Cape.

Official encouragement had been given to the wine industry in 1811. Cradock observed in a proclamation that the Cape was the only area in all the British dominions which produced wine and that colonists at the Cape would be well advised to take advantage of the situation and plan accordingly. He said that it was folly to produce inferior wine in order to make a quick profit and that if markets for Cape wine were to be assured it was necessary for the quality of the wine to be improved. He promised the government's constant support and patronage of the wine industry of the colony and offered rewards for the production of the best wine for export.[82]

Cradock's proclamation stimulated investment in the wine industry. A net capital of 21 000 000 rixdollars was invested in it over a period of years. There were over a thousand vineyards and thirty million vines and about one-third of the population of the colony was employed in the wine industry.[83] Cape wine, however, was generally of inferior quality and could not compete on an open market with wine of European production. Reciprocity treaties in terms of Huskisson's Trade Act of 1825[84] considerably reduced the margin of protection. Nevertheless wine exports continued to grow and in 1829 reached a maximum of £149 073, a little over half (50,16%) of the total exports of the colony.[85] But when the British Government proposed to reduce the preference still further by an additional import duty of 6d a gallon on Cape wine, there was genuine concern in the colony for the future of the industry.

Cole explained to the secretary of state that a leaguer (152 gallons) of Cape wine fetched from £3 to £3.15.0d. on the British market and that the increased duty would effectively double the price of wine or, more probably, reduce the sum paid to the Cape producer to so low a figure that he faced ruin. Cole claimed that there had been some improvement in the quality of wine which he hoped would raise it in estimation and price but begged for the removal of every impediment to the advance of the industry.[86]

The British Government responded with a decision to delay the increase in duty for three years so that stocks could be reduced.[87] This concession offered breathing space but was no real solution to the problem. Bourke, the former lieutenant-governor of the colony, added his voice to the protagonists. In a memorandum to the Colonial Department he asserted that British manufactures were chiefly bought in exchange for Cape wine. If, by raising the price to the consumer, there was less demand for Cape wine in Great Britain, he argued that there would be a corresponding decrease in the quantity of British manufactures exported to the Cape.[88]

The validity of Bourke's view was borne out by a marked recession in the retail trade as a result of the steep decline in the price of wine in Britain. It was customary for farmers to spend 100 000 to 150 000 rixdollars a month from October to January inclusive in the shops of Cape Town. Their purchases were usually British manufactures. But in October 1831 it was estimated that less than 20 000 rixdollars was spent. Retailers were unable to settle their accounts with wholesalers so that both were financially embarrassed. This was a factor which, in the opinion of the *South African Commercial Advertiser*, would persuade the British Government to desist from enforcing the additional duty on Cape wine.[89]

The prospect for the wine industry was dismal. Over-production threatened the industry even in France itself. Market prices in France were so low that an empty cask was popularly reckoned to sell for more than a full one and some workers faced unemployment.[90] It was therefore with considerable alarm that the Cape wine farmers received the news that the British chancellor of the exchequer had proposed to abandon such protection as remained and had introduced a Bill into the British Parliament to equalize the duty on wines imported into the United Kingdom.[91] Quality aside, the cost of transport alone would have given European producers considerable advantage over Cape producers. The real intention of the Bill was to stop the long established preference in favour of Portuguese wines rather than to favour France or prejudice the Cape wine industry. The Bill was amended to secure a preferential duty for Cape wine. The Act[92] prescribed a duty of 2s.9d. on Cape wine – an increase of 4d a gallon – but wines from other countries had to pay 5s.6d which effectively reduced the duty on French wine by 1s.9d.[93]

In an effort to assist the Cape wine industry the British Government attempted to secure preferential duty for Cape wine imported into the United States of America, but was unsuccessful.[94] However, more life was injected into the economy of the colony, especially the wine industry, by an Order in Council of the 22nd February 1832.[95] Generally a 3% import duty was to be charged on goods made in Britain and a 10% duty on goods of foreign manufacture, but casks and barrels, or material to make them, were exempt from duty altogether. Foreign ships which belonged to countries in amity with Great Britain were entitled to carry to the Cape goods made in their respective countries, and carry away Cape produce "to any country whatever". A further boon granted by the Order was the proclamation of Cape Town, Simonstown and Port Elizabeth as free ports. By way of encouragement to entrepôt trade, Cape Town and Simonstown were given the additional advantage of being proclaimed free warehousing ports.

Government action certainly gave some impetus to the trade of the Cape. Schumann has shown that the period 1834–38 was one of revival and marked prosperity.[96] Wine sales improved and earned approximately £90 000 in foreign trade each year from 1833 to 1839.[97]

But wine was not the only beneficiary of the new arrangements. Grain farmers had already learned to appreciate the British connection. In 1827 more than 50 000 muids of grain were exported to Britain. In the opinion of the *South African Commercial Advertiser* wheat sold on the British market was always sure to command a remunerating price for South African farmers.[98] Soon wool began to be an important export. In 1830 only £222 worth was exported, in 1832 £935 worth was exported.[99] By 1866 the value of wool exported from the eastern districts of the Cape alone amounted to £1 735 298.[100] Trans-frontier trade also contributed to colonial exports. Wagons penetrated the South African hinterland laden with goods of British manufacture which were exchanged for hides, skins, horns, and ivory. Indeed import and export figures for 1830–1834 show that only in the eastern districts was there a favourable balance of trade.[101] Not surprisingly then, the *Graham's Town Journal* claimed that it was the traders who were responsible for the "flourishing state of the frontier" and who had raised the eastern districts "to a level with the Western, and had saved the new settlement[102] from utter ruin and dispersion".[103] Boastful though this statement may be, it illustrates that profits could be made at the Cape by men of enterprise.

With the significant exception of trans-frontier commerce, the economy of the Cape was essentially rural. Goods for export always had to sustain a long journey and were at the mercy of oversea markets governed by the laws of supply and demand in a much more sophisticated economy. Association with Britain brought the Cape into the network of British trade. The colony's principal trade was with Great Britain, but Mauritius, St. Helena, New South Wales, South America and the West Indies figure prominently in trade returns.[104] The Order in Council of 1832 shows that Britain was concerned to expand the commerce of the colony.

In Britain the current of opinion was towards freer trade and freer enterprise. But successive chancellors of the exchequer were themselves hard put to balance their budgets. Consequently, though Britain was prepared to lend her manpower, the British Government insisted that each colony was financially self-supporting and solvent. Both Cole and Goderich, each in his own way, appreciated the utility of government investment and promoted expensive projects only to discover they had to be delayed because of an insufficiency of cash on hand. Cole at least had the satisfaction of observing financial returns from the construction of the pass over the Hottentots Holland Mountains, which even to-day carries the main highway from Cape Town to the east. The success of the scheme points to the probable success of more lavish investment similar to the success of Montagu's financial reform in the forties.[105] Cole was too pessimistic when he wrote, ". . . it is a very miserable poor colony and will always be so, I fear",[106] but to a governor faced with the necessity of raising enough money to meet the current expenses of administration and also to finance projects to develop the colony the difficulties must have seemed insoluble.

The accounts published in 1832 indicate that there was some imprudent expenditure not all of it the fault of the colonial government. For example, the amount paid in pensions was very high. Cole admitted this. In a letter to Hay he commented that some pensions, including the one granted to Sir Richard Plaskett who was secretary to the colonial government for three years, were unjustified but, on the whole, he did not think it wise to tamper with them. He observed that many of the pensioners were old and could not, therefore, be a charge on the colony for any length of time.[107] A schedule of reductions in the establishment sent to Cole's successor, D'Urban, reduced the amount paid in pensions by only £300. This saving was effected by a reduction by that amount of the pension paid to Sir Richard Plaskett by the Cape government. The charge was transferred to the government of Malta where Plaskett had served for a much longer period.[108]

Savings in excess of £10 000 were anticipated by a reduction in the establishments and of salaries. The governor's salary was reduced to £5 000, and one judge who received a salary of £1 500 was transferred to New South Wales and not replaced.[109] These measures were practicable, but others were not necessarily so. The consolidation of the offices of civil commissioner and resident magistrate, for example, placed a very heavy burden on the officials who held that combined office.[110] The extent of the colony rendered necessary the employment of a civil and judicial establishment out of proportion to its scanty population and poor resources. This was an evil which, Cole said, could not be remedied.[111]

Careful pruning of administrative costs, however, could not alone remedy the financial embarrassment of the colonial government. More cash had to be raised. Land provided an obvious source of income, but administrative inefficiency and some misunderstanding on the part of the governor delayed adequate returns from this source. Consequently the colonial government had to lean on indirect taxes most of which were raised on imports and exports, and therefore fluctuated with the varying fortunes of colonial trade. The colony was unfortunate that in Cole's period at the Cape the wine industry was passing through a period of acute depression. However, too much emphasis on the importance of the wine trade to the colonial economy must be avoided. The expansion of the trans-frontier trade and the beginnings of sheep farming were pointers to future prosperity. Cole himself had observed that the grain farmers could sustain higher taxation, and his recommendation that there should be a re-appraisal of the burden of taxation[112] indicates that he was aware that the colonial government was not tapping the most lucrative sources of wealth.

The financial plight to the colonial government was a source of concern to colonists. Trade, and therefore their pockets, suffered through lack of facilities. The fact that they were prepared to pay for the completion of the Hottentots Holland pass and the Cape Town pier suggests that money was available in the colony for investment. Loans could have been raised to finance public utilities and would have had the additional advantage of injecting cash into the economy, thus providing additional stimulus to trade. The suspension of public works which were obviously beneficial to the colony caused considerable dissatisfaction and led to complaints about the mismanagement of the colonial finances. Whether or not the allegation was justified, it made a convenient platform for those who favoured constitutional reform at the Cape.

FOOTNOTES

1. 6 Geo. IV, c. 114. See Chapter III, pp. 49–50.
2. *S.A.C.A.*, 28 January 1829.
3. See Chapter V. p. 94, fn. 92.
4. P.P. 1829 (300). Report of the Commissioners of Enquiry upon the trade of the Cape of Good Hope, 3 October 1829.
5. *S.A.C.A.*, 21 March 1829.
6. C. G. W. Schumann, *Structural Changes and Business Cycles in South Africa* (1806–1936), p. 71, fn. 1.
7. The deficit in 1829 was £6 761.17.5d. and in 1831 it was £4 934.13.5⅛d.

8. Murray in a debate in the House of Commons said, "Its extent was nearly equal to that of the United Kingdom – about 600 miles long and 300 wide. The colonists amounted to only 119,966 souls of whom the slaves amounted to 31,000 the free blacks to 35,000 and whites to 53,966". See *Parliamentary Debates*, published under the superintendence of T. C. Hansard, New Series, Vol. XXIV, c. 1007–8, 24 May 1830. This debate is printed in G. W. Eybers, *Select Constitutional Documents Illustrating South African History, 1795–1910*, pp. 30–38. Compare figures given Chapter V, p. 92, fn. 42.
9. C.A., G.H. 1/17, Goderich to Cole, 27 May 1831.
10. A. Briggs, *The Age of Improvement*, p. 361.
11. D. M. Young, *The Colonial Office in the early Nineteenth Century*, pp. 185–186.
12. C.A., G.H. 23/9, Cole to Murray, 10 February 1831.
13. C.A., G.H. 1/16, Hay to Cole (Private), 27 August 1829.
14. C.A., G.H. 23/9, Cole to Murray, 8 February 1830.
15. *Ibid.*
16. C.A., G.H. 1/16, Hay to Cole (Private), 27 August 1829.
17. C.A., G.H. 1/16, Murray to Cole, 3 May 1830.
18. C.A., G.H. 23/9, Cole to Murray, 8 February 1830.
19. C.A., G.H. 1/16, Murray to Cole, 3 May 1830.
20. C.A., G.H. 23/9, Cole to Murray, 10 February 1831.
21. C.A., G.H. 1/17, Goderich to Cole, 24 May 1831.
22. C.A., G.H. 23/9, Cole to Goderich, 24 August 1831.
23. C.A., G.H. 1/18, Goderich to Cole, 13 January 1832.
24. C.A., G.H. 1/18, Goderich to Cole, 26 November 1831.
25. C.A., G.H. 1/18, Goderich to Cole, 13 January 1832.
26. C.O. 48/143, The port captain (J. Bance) to the secretary to government (J. Bell) 19 July 1831, enclosed in Cole to Hay, 6 August 1831.
27. C.A., G.H. 23/9, Cole to Goderich, 2 August 1831.
28. *Ibid.*
29. *S.A.C.A.*, 20 July 1831.
30. C.O. 49/25, Goderich to Cole, 23 October 1831.
31. A. H. Imlah, *Economic Elements in the Pax Brittanica*, pp. 129–130.
32. C.A., G.H. 23/10, Cole to Goderich, 8 March 1833.
33. C.A., G.H. 1/20, Stanley to Cole, 27 May 1833.
34. Acting governor of the Cape of Good Hope 10 August 1833 to 16 January 1834.
35. C.A., G.H. 23/10, Wade to Stanley, 24 October 1833.
36. C.A., G.H. 23/10, Wade to Stanley, 9 December 1833.
37. C.O. 48/152, Report of Rear Admiral Warren, enclosed in Barrow to Hay, 23 December 1833.
38. C.O. 49/26, Stanley to D'Urban, 3 April 1834.
39. J. J. Breitenbach, "The Development of the Secretaryship to the Government at the Cape of Good Hope under John Montagu, 1845–1852", *Archives Year Book for South African History*, 1959. Vol. II, pp. 218–221.
40. C.A., G.H. 1/17, Goderich to Cole, 27 May 1831. Goderich arrived at this figure by adding to the deficit of £6 761.17.5d shown in the accounts of the Cape Government additional charges "including advances from His Majesty's Treasury to the Colonial Agent" and "the charge for the Maintenance of the Cape Corps."
41. C.A., G.H. 1/17, Goderich to Cole, 27 May 1831.
42. G. R. Porter, *The Progress of the Nation* (revised edition by F. W. Hirst), p. 615.
43. Porter, p. 617.
44. The office of *heemraden* was created in 1685. A minimum of four and a maximum of eight heemraden were nominated in each district from among the leading citizens of the district to assist the landdrost. The powers of the Board of Landdrost and Heemraden were many and varied and included both judicial and administrative functions. The office was abolished on 1 January 1828 when the inferior courts of the colony were reformed. See K. S. Hunt, "The Development of Municipal Government in the Eastern Province of the Cape of Good Hope, with special reference to Grahamstown, 1827–1862", *Archives Year Book for South African History*, 1961, p. 138.
45. C.A., G.H. 1/17, Goderich to Cole, 27 May 1831.

46. C.A., G.H. 23/9, Cole to Goderich, 10 October 1831.
47. C.A. G.H. 23/10, Cole to Goderich, 4 March 1832.
48. C.A., G.H. 1/18, Goderich to Cole, 28 March 1832.
49. Hunt, p. 143.
50. C.A., G.H. 1/20, Cole to Hay (undated), enclosed in Stanley to D'Urban, 31 December 1833.
51. *G.T.J.*, 8 August 1833.
52. *Ibid.*
53. *Ibid.*
54. The Bank was established by the Dutch East India Company in March 1793 and was subsequently maintained by the Government. It issued short loans at low rates of interest.
55. *G.T.J.*, 8 August 1833.
56. L. C. Duly, *British Land Policy at the Cape*, 1795–1844, p. 48.
57. *Ibid.*, pp. 45–49.
58. C.O. 48/13, Report of the commission of circuit to Cradock, 28 February 1812, enclosed in Cradock to Liverpool, 21 May 1812, quoted by Duly, p. 48.
59. Duly, p. 104.
60. *Ibid.*, p. 113.
61. *Ibid.*, pp. 77–78.
62. W. K. Hancock, "Trek", *Economic History Review*, 2nd series, Vol. X, (1957–58), p. 333.
63. Duly, pp. 98–99.
64. *Ibid.*, p. 100.
65. *Ibid.*, p. 104.
66. *Ibid.*, pp. 109–110.
67. *Ibid*, pp. 104–105.
68. *Ibid.*
69. C.A., G.H. 1/18, Goderich to Cole, 25 November 1831.
70. P. Burroughs, *Britain and Australia*, 1831–1855, pp. 36–37.
71. C.O. 202/25, Goderich to Darling, 23 March 1831. Quoted by Burroughs, p. 54.
72. C.A., G.H. 1/17, Marginalia on Goderich to Cole, 5 August 1831.
73. Burroughs, pp. 58–59.
74. H. E. Egerton, *A Short History of British Colonial Policy*, (9th edition), pp. 244–245.
75. Cape of Good Hope *Government Gazette*, 18 May 1832.
76. Duly, p. 117.
77. Breitenbach, p. 214, fn. 123, says "Montagu took as his model the Crown land Sales Act passed in 1842 (*C.H.B.E.*, Vol. VII, p. 167); the regulations, laid down for the disposal of Crown land at the Cape, reflect the spirit of the above act, point by point".
78. S. D. Neumark, *The South African Frontier: Economic Influences, 1652–1836*, p. 137.
79. *Ibid.*, p. 175.
80. Hancock, pp. 331–339.
81. C.A., G.H. 23/9, Cole to Goderich, 2 April 1831.
82. Theal, *R.C.C.*, Vol. VIII, pp. 214–5, Proclamation by Cradock, 19 December 1811.
83. B. J. T. Leverton, "Government Finance and Political Development in the Cape, 1806–1834", *Archives Year Book for South African History*, 1961, p. 303.
84. 6 Geo. IV, c. 114.
85. Schumann, p. 73.
86. C.A., G.H. 23/9, Cole to Murray, 20 February 1829. See pp. 130–1 his rejection of a per capita tax on slaves for the same reason.
87. C.A., G.H. 1/16, Murray to Cole, 21 July 1829. See also *S.A.C.A.*, 30 April 1831.
88. C.O. 48/131, Memorandum by R. Bourke, 28 February 1831.

89. *S.A.C.A.*, 26 October, 1831.
90. *S.A.C.A.*, 9 March 1831.
91. *S.A.C.A.*, 30 April 1831.
92. 1 & 2 Will. IV, c. 30.
93. *Parliamentary Debates*, published under the superintendence of T. C. Hansard, 3rd series, Vol. VI, c. 442–445, 22 August 1831.
94. C.A., G.H. 1/20, Stanley to officer administering the government, 31 August 1833.
95. *The London Gazette*, 3 April 1832.
96. Schumann, p. 71.
97. *Ibid.*
98. *S.A.C.A.*, 29 November 1828.
99. *G.T.J.*, 7 March 1833.
100. A. Wilmot and J. C. Chase, *A History of the Colony of the Cape of Good Hope from its Discovery to the year 1819, and from 1820 to 1868*, p. 301.
101. A. Wilmot and J. C. Chase, appendix IV.

	Western Districts	*Eastern Districts*
Imports	£1 748 325	£134 119
Exports	955 548	207 382

102. The Albany Settlement of 1820.
103. *G.T.J.*, 4 July 1833.
104. *The South African Almanac and Directory for 1830*, p. 130, gives these figures for the value of colonial produce exported from Table Bay in 1828:

To Great Britain	£132 300
St. Helena	12 071
Mauritius	38 312
East Indies	4 249
South America & West Indies	17 411
New South Wales	20 833
Netherlands	860
Bourbon	300
Java	2 858
Hamburgh	4 653
Total	£233 847

105. Breitenbach, Chapter II.
106. Scottish Record Office, G.D. 45, 5/23, Cole to Dalhousie, 1 November 1830.
107. C.A., G.H. 1/20, Cole to Hay, undated, enclosed in Stanley to D'Urban, 31 December 1833.
108. C.A., G.H. 1/20, Stanley to D'Urban, 31 December 1833.
109. See Chapter X, p. 162.
110. Hunt, p. 151.
111. C.A., G.H. 1/20, Cole to Hay, undated, enclosed in Stanley to D'Urban, 31 December 1833.
112. C.A., G.H. 23/10, Cole to Goderich, 4 March 1832, and repeated in C.A., G.H. 1/20 Cole to Hay, undated, enclosed in Stanley to D'Urban, 31 December 1833.

CHAPTER IX

CONSTITUTIONAL DEVELOPMENTS AT THE CAPE

Controls on the autocratic powers of the governor of the Cape of Good Hope first appeared when a Council of Advice was established in 1825. On the same day that additional instructions were issued to Cole to create a council in Mauritius[1] a similar document was forwarded to Lord Charles Somerset,[2] then governor of the Cape. These two councils were almost identical in composition and the authority given to them, and resembled a pattern of conciliar government found in several British colonies. The earliest example of a colonial council with purely advisory functions seems to have been that which existed in Virginia from 1612 to 1618,[3] but councils did not really develop as an instrument of colonial government until the second half of the eighteenth century. The decision of Murray in 1763 to exercise his discretion to govern Quebec with only the help of an advisory council marked the inauguration of an institution which became the predominant form of colonial council in the government of conquered colonies in the nineteenth century.[4]

Britain's short occupation of San Domingo (1794-1798) is of special interest because it established some characteristics later included in instructions for governors of many colonies conquered from France, Spain and the Netherlands during the Revolutionary and Napoleonic Wars, 1793-1814. All executive power, both civil and military, was vested in the governor, but provision was made for him to choose a committee of six from among the landed proprietors to assist him "in all details of administration and police". The governor was not bound to accept the advice of the committee. If he thought the occasion warranted it he was authorised to act contrary to their opinion, leaving members of council free to record their opinion. In such cases the governor had to make an explanatory statement to the secretary of state and send him the opinions of those who dissented from him.[5]

The precedent of San Domingo established that such a council was not expected to do any more than advise the governor. It had no means of coercion except to record its dissent and the reasons thereof. It could only act as a brake on the arbitrary action of a governor insofar as its record of dissent was heeded by the British Government.[6]

The conciliar form of government established in San Domingo was not reproduced exactly whenever it was desired to introduce a council of advice. The particular conditions and past experience of colonies were always taken into account. In Demerara and Essequibo, for example, the Dutch had created advisory bodies which consisted of official members and members who were elected by an electoral college. These advisory bodies were retained by the British.[7] In San Domingo and other conquered colonies where advisory councils were introduced,[8] the members of council were usually officials though sometimes provision was made to nominate colonists too. The same procedure was introduced into Sierra Leone in 1811 and New South Wales in 1823 by act of parliament. In Malta yet one further innovation was made: when a council was created there in 1813 the governor was expressly told that only he had the right to initiate matters for discussion.[9] An examination of the advisory councils established in Mauritius[10] and the Cape in 1825 shows evidence of Britain's past experience in conciliar government.

At the Cape the presidency of the Council of Advice was vested in the governor and membership made up of the chief justice, the officer next in command of the forces to the governor, and three senior colonial civil servants. They were Lieutenant-Colonel J. Bell, (the deputy quartermaster-general), W. Bentink (the auditor-general), and J. W. Stoll (the treasurer), each of whom was personally named in the instructions. A secretary, entitled "Clerk of the Council" was required to be present at all meetings. He had to take full minutes – a copy of which had to be forwarded twice a year to the Crown through the secretary of state.

Only the governor, or the officer administering the government for the time being, could summon a meeting of the Council. If it was not possible for him to attend the most senior member present was to take the chair. A quorum was fixed at three members but, if there were insufficient councillors on the spot to form a quorum, the governor was authorised by a warrant of commission under "the Seal of the Settlement"[11] to appoint a maximum of six persons members of council. Whenever vacancies occurred the governor was required to inform the Crown without delay and submit the names of his appointees for the King's confirmation or disallowance. Until the King's decision was known these temporary members were entitled to all the powers and privileges of councillors. The governor could also suspend members of council. In such cases he had to record in the minutes his reason for so doing, and any reply which might be made by the suspended councillor. However, if the governor felt strongly that his reasons for suspending a councillor should not be recorded in the minutes he was excused from this obligation. In any event a full explanation had to be made immediately to the secretary of state.

The governor alone had the power to initiate discussion in the Council. If a member wished to raise a question he could make his request known to the governor in writing. This application, and the governor's reply, could be recorded in the minutes by the member concerned. Though the governor could decline to raise any subject he was nevertheless bound to consult the Council in all matters executed in terms of his commission and instructions. Only in cases of emergency could he act alone. When he did so he was obliged to submit his emergency measures to the Council for revision or sanction at the first opportunity. Once a subject was before the Council, members were free to express opinions and vote according to their own dictates. They were also entitled to have their opinions recorded in the minutes. In the event of the governor dissenting from a majority decision of the Council, he could carry out the terms of his commission and instructions in opposition to their opinion provided he immediately sent a full explanation to the Crown through the secretary of state.

Legislative enactments of the governor and Council were styled "ordinances". The form of these had to be modelled on acts of the Parliament of Westminster with a preamble, division into sections and short marginal abbreviations. Preparation of draft ordinances was entrusted to the fiscal (after 1827, the attorney-general). Before a draft was submitted to the Council it had to be sent to the chief justice for his opinion as to whether or not it was in harmony with the fundamental laws of the colony[12] and that part of the law of the United Kingdom applicable to the colony. If the chief justice thought it was, the draft was ready to go to the Council. If discussion in council resulted in material amendment the draft had to be returned to the fiscal and chief justice.

When a measure was finally approved by the Governor in Council it had to be signed by the governor, sealed with the seal of his government,[13] and countersigned by the secretary to government and by the clerk of the council. The instrument thus attested had then to be sent to the fiscal who took it to the chief justice or, if he was absent, one of the other judges for registration in the High Court of Justice. Simultaneously, the governor had to send printed copies of the legislation to the heads of departments and publish it in the *Government Gazette*. The operation of all ordinances was suspended until the King's pleasure was known unless the governor considered that the public interest would suffer by such delay.[14]

The Council of Advice at the Cape has been dismissed by several historians as an inconsequential body which had little power to frustrate the instructions of the secretary of state or check the autocracy of the governor.[15] Bathurst had been careful to point out to Somerset that legislation passed by the governor with the advice of the Council was subordinate to that of the King in Parliament or the King in Council.[16] It is true that sometimes the governor and Council of Advice had merely to spell out details of policy determined upon by the British Government[17] and on one occasion the governor used his power to legislate without the concurrence of the Council,[18] but by and large the records of the Council do not reveal a subservient body existing only to rubber-stamp the actions of its superiors. On the contrary, the records of the Council show that it was frequently consulted by the governor and that its members did not hesitate to express opinions opposed to either the secretary of state or the governor, both of whom respected their views.

The power of the Council was put to the test in 1828. The occasion was the rejection of tax proposals recommended by the commissioners of inquiry and submitted to the Council by Bourke on the secretary of state's instructions. The Council made counter-proposals which they considered would raise more money for the colonial exchequer and distribute the tax burden more equitably.[19] Hay, the under-secretary at the Colonial Department admitted that the Council's proposals were "more palatable and more productive" and the governor was instructed to carry them out. Thereby, in Hay's view, the independence of the Council was "satisfactorily manifested" though the recommendations of the commissioners were "set at nought, and their labours to a certain extent declared useless".[20]

Four points were raised in the course of debate on the tax proposals, the clarification of which also shed light on the constitutional powers of the Council. First it was asked whether members of council were bound to vote for laws recommended by the secretary of state even though they deemed them highly impolitic. Secondly, doubt was cast on the governor's power to promulgate legislation in his own name without the Council's advice because the 33rd Article of the Charter of Justice issued subsequent to the Council's creation directed the Supreme Court to apply, judge and determine local legislation made by the governor of the colony "with the advice of the Council of Government thereof". The third point was raised as the result of an assertion by the chief justice that ordinances of the Governor in Council could only be set aside by the King in Council and not merely by notification through the secretary of state. The final point was also raised by the chief justice. He asserted that every member of council was entitled to initiate discussion and take the Council's opinion upon it. These problems were submitted to James Stephen whose opinion[21] formed the basis of subsequent communications with the governor.[22]

On the first point, Stephen stated that council members were not only free but were bound to vote and act according to their own judgment even in the case of laws recommended by the British Government. In Stephen's opinion they could not "consistently with the terms of their oath,[23] vote for any law which they might conscientiously deem it unwise to pass". He explained that the governor and the Council were frequently called upon to promulgate laws which could be passed by the King in Council, but because local authorities were better placed to estimate the wisdom of legislation, implementation was left to them. If local authorities were merely intended to consider the details without any examination of the principle, then reference to them by the British Government was unnecessary and improper because it would throw on them a responsibility which only the British Government ought to bear. Thus the power of the Council of Advice to question legislation submitted to it was beyond doubt.

The second point raised suggested some conflict between the Charter of Justice and the governor's commission and instructions. The latter empowered the governor in an emergency to publish a proclamation in his own name and on his own responsibility although in opposition to the Council. This was valid until the King's pleasure was known. However, the 33rd Article of the Charter of Justice directed the Supreme Court to apply, judge and determine all laws in existence when the Charter was promulgated and all other laws made by the King in Parliament, or the King in Council, or by the governor of the colony "*with the advice of the Council of Government*". Consequently, the legality of a proclamation of the governor in opposition to the Council was questionable. Stephen held that the governor could lawfully promulgate an ordinance made by "*the Governor with the advice of his Council*" even though every member of council had voted against it, because the words "*with their advice*" meant nothing more than "*having received or taken their advice*". The governor did not need the concurrence of the Council. The style and form of legislation had to be invariable. Hence, Stephen declared that for legal purposes all legislation, including ordinances made by the governor in opposition to the Council, should be promulgated in the same style.[24]

Stephen was surprised that the third point could have been raised by a lawyer. The chief justice claimed that disallowance of colonial ordinances could not be conveyed in a despatch from the secretary of state because a passage in Lord Bathurst's instructions to Lord Charles Somerset stated that the legislative power of the Governor in Council was subordinate to that of the King in Council or the King in Parliament. Stephen thought the chief justice should have known that the reservation of the legislative powers of the Privy Council and Parliament was necessary because of the decision in the case of *Campbell v Hall* in 1774.[25] The reserved legislative powers of the Privy Council and Parliament certainly had no reference to the manner of signifying the King's confirmation or rejection of ordinances passed in the colony. Stephen asserted that the whole government of the colony, the Council itself included, had no other foundation than the King's commission to the governor under the Great Seal. This required the governor not only to do particular acts it prescribed and execute the powers it gave, but to do all other acts and execute all other powers prescribed in one of three ways: by instructions issued under the Signet and Sign Manual, by intructions issued in Council, or by instructions issued through one of the principal secretaries of state. The King's instructions conveyed through a secretary of state consequently claimed obedience in the colony on the same authority as instructions issued with the advice of the Privy Council. Stephen remarked that it was invariable practice with respect to the legislative acts of the conquered colonies to signify the King's pleasure through the secretary of state. He observed that in the case of New South Wales, Parliament itself had pointed out this procedure as the proper method of signifying allowance or disallowance. Consequently he said that he could see no reason why the Cape should be an exception to the general rule.

The final point, the assertion of the chief justice that all members of council were entitled to initiate discussions, Stephen promptly dismissed. Since the chief justice did not give reasons for his opinion Stephen could not controvert them, but he considered the assertion was as much at variance with the letter as with the spirit of the governor's instructions.

While the resolution of the problems raised in council settled the legal constitutional issues, the part played by the chief justice raised grave doubts of the wisdom of his inclusion in the Council. Sir John Wylde,[26] the chief justice, had been a difficult member of the Council ever since he joined it in January 1828.[27] Several pages of the minute book are taken up with his remonstrances. Francis Leveson Gower considered that he had "traveled out of his province" and "to have started with setting himself at the head of the Colonist party". This suggested to Leveson Gower that he should be put out of the Council or kept from meddling in anything but legal matters.[28] Stephen wrote to Leveson Gower that he had "the best reason to know" that the chief justice was named a member of council contrary to the advice of the commissioners of inquiry "upon a full understanding that he was not to interfere in the business of the Council upon any political subject, but merely for the amendment of the general laws respecting property, and the prevention and punishment of crime." Wylde had clearly exceeded these limitations. Stephen thought that because the chief justice had such considerable judicial power his assumption of political authority could not be "too much deprecated".

Besides, Wylde had an axe to grind. He attributed (Stephen said with justice) the loss of his former office in New South Wales to Bigge as commissioner in that colony. Thus Stephen considered it was "barely possible" that Wylde could be impartial in assessing Bigge's recommendations to improve administration in the Cape. Stephen drew attention to a suggestion of Bourke that the attorney-general should serve on the Council "either together with or to the exclusion of the Chief Justice".[29]

In the circumstances the Colonial Department decided to drop the chief justice from the Council. The attorney-general was not appointed in his place. Hay, in a private and confidential letter to Cole, said he thought it would be better not to have a permanent legal councillor. Instead he suggested that the judges should be called to the Council when their legal opinion was required, like "the twelve judges . . . occasionally called upon to appear in the House of Lords".[30] The example of the Lords was further drawn upon in determining the place of the chief justice and the puisne judges when they attended Council meetings. Hay explained that in the House of Lords strangers were only admitted below the bar. However, when the judges were summoned by the House they sat around the lord chancellor on the Woolsack. Thus, he suggested, when the judges attended the Council, the chief justice should be assigned a seat to the right of the governor and the puisne judges given seats on his left. In the last resort Cole was left to make his own arrangements to accommodate the judges provided it did not "derogate from the entire independence of the council".[31]

The revised relationship of the judiciary with the governor and Council did not prevent the judiciary from questioning constitutional procedure whenever they saw fit. On the occasion of the promulgation of the Consolidated Slave Order in Council of the 2nd February 1830,[32] for example, the judges questioned the right of the governor to legislate by proclamation without discussion in Council. They claimed that the governor had no legislative power except that which he was required to exercise with the advice of the Council.[33] Cole passed the problem over to the secretary of state. Goderich thought it raised "little or no theoretical difficulty". If an act of parliament or legislative Order in Council were remitted to the governor individually and not the Governor in Council the duty of issuing proclamations to execute, explain, or qualify any of the Council's enactments, then those proclamations drew their legal authority from the original legislation and not from the governor's general powers. Goderich pointed out parallel situations in Great Britain. Proclamations by the King, Order of the Lords of the Council, and even rules made by the justices in their sessions had the precise authority of an act of parliament because they were promulgated in the strict exercise of the powers which Parliament had given them.[34]

Further revision of the constitutional position of the chief justice emerged out of controversy over the extra-territorial extension of jurisdiction of the Cape courts.[35] The controversy drew the attention of the secretary of state to the instruction which required the submission of all proposed ordinances to the chief justice for his report that they were not inconsistent with the fundamental laws of the colony, or those of the laws of England applicable to the Cape. Goderich thought this instruction needed modification. In the first place, he did not think that reference should be made solely to the chief justice, but to all the judges who were not absent on circuit. Secondly, he thought that the question put to the judges needed amendment. "Nothing can be more vague than the phrase *fundamental laws*," he wrote. Instead, he said that the enquiry should be "whether, if a law were passed in the terms of the Draft transmitted to the Judges there would be any legal impediment to its execution by the colonial tribunals; and if so, by what means if any, that impediment might be most conveniently surmounted". A reference of this nature, Goderich thought, would obviate the danger of any collision between the legislative and judicial authorities in the colony. This, he submitted, was the main reason, if not the only advantage, of a previous communication with the judges.[36] When a revised Charter of Justice was sent to the Cape in 1832[37] and the chief justice obliged to take his turn on circuit, Cole was instructed to follow this amended procedure.[38]

Correspondence on the constitutional controversies at the Cape throws light on another aspect of colonial policy. There was a movement within the Colonial Department to introduce some constitutional uniformity in the governments of the conquered colonies or, as they were now called, crown colonies.[39] Stephen's comments to Leveson Gower in May 1828 indicate that for a year officials in the Colonial Department had had it in mind to place "all the Councils of all the Crown colonies upon one footing – a measure of the greatest importance in itself, and which would be attended with the utmost convenience in the despatch of public business in the Department". The implementation of this policy was delayed by the law officers of the crown because of the question of admissibility of Roman Catholics into the colonial councils.[40] The Catholic Emancipation Act of April 1829[41] cleared the way for further constitutional progress in the crown colonies. New forms for colonial government occupied the attention of officials in the Colonial Department the following year.[42]

Constitutions which provided for a separate executive council and legislative council were granted to Trinidad in 1831, St. Lucia and Mauritius in 1832, Ceylon in 1833, and the Cape in 1834.[43] Though the Cape was last in this sequence, plans to extend the representation of colonists in the colonial legislature were certainly contemplated as early as October 1831, and Cole was instructed to make this known in the colony. He was also directed to gather information to enable him to discuss constitutional change with the British Government on his return to Britain.[44] The form of the new constitution was obviously already in the mind of the officials of the Colonial Department because the terms "Executive Council" and "Legislative Council" appeared in documents as early as 1832. For example, an Order in Council of the 6th February 1832,[45] directed the governor to issue a proclamation "with the advice of the Executive Council". The revised Charter of Justice, dated at Westminister on the 4th May 1832,[46] also assigned powers to the governor *with the advice of the Executive Council*, and empowered the Supreme Court to apply, judge and determine all laws in existence when the Charter was promulgated and all other laws made by the King in Parliament, the King in Council, and by the governor *with the advice of the Legislative Council of Government*.

In the opinion of the majority of the judges and the attorney-general of the Cape, the Council of Advice was not "deemed or taken, either in law or in fact, to be the Legislative Council of Government". Cole doubted his competence to declare the Council of Advice the Legislative Council contemplated by the British Government. To do so, he thought, would give colonists a false impression of the constitutional changes planned. And this, he wrote, "would not be effaced by any subsequent explanations were it even possible to make any such with propriety".[47] Had he published the Charter, the legislative power of the governor and Council of Advice would have been hamstrung. Consequently he postponed publication with the result that the Charter was not promulgated until 1st March 1834 after the constitutional changes had been made.

The governor was obliged to move cautiously. White colonists at the Cape disliked the colony's constitution and would gladly have made political capital out of any constitutional error he made. Even though Sir John Truter and Andries Stokenstrom were added to the Council in 1827 to represent colonial opinion it had no elected members.[48] Furthermore, debates in council were conducted behind closed doors. Colonial government, therefore, was shrouded in an air of secrecy and mystery. The stand the Council sometimes took on behalf of white colonists was unknown to them.[49] Thus public criticism of the system of government was inevitable. The editor of the *South African Commercial Advertiser*, for example, complained of the confined nature of government:

> "Closetted with a little Council of Civil Servants, who may or may not know just about as much of Colonial affairs as himself, he (the Governor) receives the reports of other Civil Servants, to which after chewing the cud of solitary reflection, a reply is sent in a sealed letter, or a reference is made to the Colonial Office in London, for authority to proceed to action on the official information thus obtained. The people in the meantime, whose fate is thus bandied about, know as much of the matter as the world before the Flood."[50]

A few weeks later, he wrote:

> "We maintain that the present Form of Government is opposed to reason and common sense – that it neither does nor can work favorably to the Colony – that

> Free Institutions are essential not only to our well-being, but to our very existence."[51]

Colonists lost no opportunity to make their views known to the British Government. In a petition presented to the House of Commons on the 24th May 1830, the British settlers and others of Albany[52] requested the introduction of the "Representative System" at the Cape. They claimed that the Council of Advice was an inadequate check on the autocracy of the governor. Two-thirds of the members of council, they said, were without local knowledge "or any paramount interest whatever, in the soil, commerce, or general welfare of the Colony". The petitioners complained that they had no control over the imposition of taxes or the expenditure of revenue. They drew attention to a recommendation of the commissioners of inquiry that a legislative assembly should be created in the colony as soon as "the native inhabitants" had a better grasp of the English language. They reckoned that since the government had opened schools in the more important towns and villages in 1822, English was generally better understood.[53] But, in any case, the petitioners pointed to the precedent of Canada "where the existence of two languages did not appear a sufficient reason to the British Government to withhold from them the inherent right of having a voice in the administration of their own affairs".[54]

In a debate on the petition in the House of Commons, Sir George Murray stated that it was inexpedient to introduce a representative legislature in a country where slavery existed. He reminded the House of the difficulty Parliament always experienced in its attempts to ameliorate the condition of slaves wherever a colonial legislature existed. Another obstacle he raised was the problem of the small ratio of population to the size of the colony. This factor posed the possibility that "power would speedily centre in the hands of those who resided in and near Cape Town".[55]

The problem of geography the colonists could not answer, but in a subsequent petition to the King they stated that they were prepared to co-operate with the British Government to remove obstacles to constitutional reform. The reform of the House of Commons in Britain encouraged colonial optimism and they begged the King to commit the government of the colony "to a Governor appointed by the Crown, an Executive Council chosen by him under the sanctions of the Crown, and a Legislative Assembly composed entirely of Representatives freely elected by the inhabitants".[56] A pencil comment on the petition shows that officials in the Colonial Department had made up their minds not to take any action until Cole returned to Britain. Fortunately his opinion on the extent to which elected representatives of colonists should be admitted to the councils of government in the colony has not been lost in the limbo of verbal discussion for his attitude emerges very clearly from his correspondence.

In a private letter to Hay, Cole pointed out that trial by jury had been of questionable benefit to the colony,[57] and he feared that an assembly dominated by white colonists would discriminate against people of colour. On another occasion he wrote that if a representative assembly could be granted to a colony

> "where slavery exists and where almost the whole of the Slave Proprietors resent the interference of the British Government for the protection of the Slaves, where the old inhabitants, the mass of whom are of a different nation, and speak a different language from the mother country, and many of whom possess great influence, ascribe, whether truly or not, their real or pretended ruin and that of the Colony

> to the depreciation of the currency occasioned by acts of the British Government,[58] and where the great majority of the people clamour for the removal of the ancient restrictions on the native tribes,[59] then may a legislative assembly . . . be granted to the Cape of Good Hope without hesitation."[60]

He was convinced that a legislative council composed chiefly of colonists would "generally be found in opposition to the Supreme as well as the Local Government."[61]

Cole was obviously opposed to any diminution of the power of the British Government. He did not think that the Council of Advice was out of touch with the problems of the colony. Four of the six members[62] were men "intimately acquainted with the people and as closely connected with them as any four persons that could be named." Indeed he thought members of council had all the qualifications necessary to represent the colonial point of view. However, he supported the colonists disapproval of the secrecy which surrounded council business. An oath of secrecy which bound members of council created an unhealthy mystery about the Council's proceedings. Thus he thought that

> "if the Council were partially opened; if two or three persons unconnected with the Local Government and independent of it were added, and if the Account of Revenue and Expenditure were published in the Colony . . . the great majority of well-informed colonists of all classes would be perfectly content."[63]

Cole suggested that some concession to popular government could be made at the municipal level. He disliked a suggestion of the secretary of state to revive the office of heemraden as assistants to the civil commissioner cum resident magistrate when the two latter offices were consolidated as an austerity measure.[64] As an alternative, he suggested local government institutions should be established in the several towns and villages. Such local government institutions, he asserted, would reduce the pressure on district officials yet not interfere with the collection of revenue for the colonial exchequer, preserve the professionalism of the courts, and gradually accustom the colonists "to the management of their common concerns" so that in due course an assembly could be granted "with a fairer promise of success than at present."[65]

Cole's proposal for the election of municipal boards was adopted by the Colonial Department and proved highly successful.[66] Authority was given for the annual publication of the colonial accounts.[67] And the constitutional arrangements introduced at the Cape in 1834[68] reflected Cole's recommendations. The Executive Council was composed of four officials and the Legislative Council composed of the same officials, the attorney-general, and from five to seven nominated colonists. The latter were to be chosen from "the Chief Landed Proprietors and Principal Merchants" who had lived in the colony for at least two years. The governor retained the right to initiate legislation but the consent of the Legislative Council was required for all legislation. Ordinances could only be set aside if the King in Council refused assent or failed to approve them in two years. A check was placed on any discrimination on grounds of colour by a positive instruction to the governor not to assent to any legislation which so discriminated. Meetings of the Legislative Council were soon thrown open to the public. Debates and decisions were reported in the colonial press and subjected to public scrutiny. Political life at the Cape had taken a new turn. There were still no elected representatives of the colonists, but at least the public were able to see the legislature at work.

FOOTNOTES

1. C.O. 168/8, Additional instructions to Cole, 9 February 1825, enclosed in Bathurst to Cole, 9 February 1825.
2. C.O. 49/16, Additional instructions to Lord Charles Somerset, 9 February 1825, enclosed in Bathurst to Somerset, 9 February 1825. This document is printed in Theal, *R.C.C.*, Vol. XX, pp. 7–11, and Harlow and Madden, *British Constitutional Developments, 1774–1834*, pp. 111–114.
3. A. B. Keith, *The First British Empire*, p. 24.
4. M. Wright, *The Development of the Legislative Council, 1606–1945*, Vol. I, p. 36.
5. Harlow and Madden, p. 83.
6. M. Donaldson, Ph.D. thesis in the course of preparation at Rhodes University on the minutes and appendices of the Council of Advice at the Cape of Good Hope with special reference to the Eastern Cape 1825–1834.
7. See D. J. Murray, *The West Indies and the Development of Colonial Government, 1801–1834*, pp. 59–62.
8. For example, Ceylon and Trinidad in 1801, Malta and the Ionian Islands in 1813 and St. Lucia in 1817.
9. *C.H.B.E.*, Vol. II, pp. 180–181.
10. See Chapter II, pp. 39–40.
11. Term used in the governor's instructions.
12. See p. 146.
13. Words used in the original document are ". . . sealed with the seal of your Government."
14. C.O. 49/16, Bathurst to Somerset, 9 February 1825.
15. *C.H.B.E.*, Vol. VIII, (2nd edition), p. 257, and Walker, p. 166.
16. C.O. 49/16, Bathurst to Somerset, 9 February 1825.
17. For example, see Chapter VII, pp. 115–116.
18. Chapter VII, pp. 119–120.
19. C.O. 48/124, Bourke to Huskisson, 7 March 1828, Private and Confidential.
20. C.A., G.H. 1/15, Hay to Cole, 19 June 1828, Private and Confidential.
21. C.O. 48/126, J. Stephen to Lord F. Leveson Gower, 22 May 1828.
22. C.A., G.H. 1/15, Hay to Cole, 19 June 1828, Private and Confidential and Murray to Cole, 12 July 1828.
23. C.O. 49/16. In terms of the additional instructions to Lord Charles Somerset, 9 February 1825, members of council had to take the oath of loyalty to the Crown "and also the usual oaths for the due execution of their places and trust respectively". Somerset added on his own initiative an oath of secrecy, see Chapter II, p. 41.
24. This question was also raised in connection with the Council's rejection of Cole's measure to amend Ordinance 19 of 1826. See Chapter VII, p. 114.
25. See Chapter I, p. 19.
26. See Chapter X, p. 165, fn. 34.
27. R. Kilpin, *The Romance of a Colonial Parliament*, Part II, pp. 45–46.
28. C.O. 48/124, Undated minute bound with Bourke to Huskisson, 7 March 1828, inscribed with the initials F. L. G. –probably the under-secretary, Lord Francis Leveson Gower.
29. C.O. 48/126, Stephen to Lord F. Leveson Gower, 22 May 1828.
30. C.A., G.H. 1/15, Hay to Cole, 19 June 1828, Private and Confidential.
31. *Ibid.*
32. See Chapter VII, pp. 114–115.
33. C.A., G.H. 23/9, Cole to Goderich, 1 June 1831.
34. C.A., G.H. 1/18, Goderich to Cole, 3 December 1831.
35. See Chapter X, pp. 162–163.
36. C.A., G.H. 1/18, Goderich to Cole, 3 December 1831.
37. See Chapter X, p. 161.
38. C.A., G.H. 1/19, Goderich to Cole, 16 June 1832.
39. Murray, p. 158.
40. C.O. 48/126, Stephen to Leveson Gower, 22 May 1828.

41. 10 Geo. IV, c. 7.
42. Harlow and Madden, pp. 104–107, Stephen to Twiss, 25 August 1830. See also H. T. Manning, "The Colonial Policy of the Whig Ministers 1830–7", *Canadian Historical Review*, Vol. XXXIII (1952), Part I, pp. 203–236, and Part II, pp. 341–368; and H. T. Manning, "Colonial Crises before the Cabinet 1829–35", *Bulletin of the Institute of Historical Research*, Vol. XXX, (1957), pp. 41–61.
43. M. Wright, Vol. I, pp. 59, 128–129.
44. C.A., G.H. 1/18, Goderich to Cole, 14 October 1831.
45. See Chapter VII, p. 120.
46. C.O. 49/25, See Chapter X, pp. 320–321.
47. C.A., G.H. 23/10, Cole to Goderich, 8 February 1833.
48. C.O. 49/19, Goderich to Bourke, 14 June 1827. Some slight amendment was made to the composition of the Council. The secretary to the colonial government and auditor-general ceased to have ex-officio membership, and two colonists were added. This made little difference to the nature of the Council because Lieutenant-Colonel Bell, named a member of council, soon became secretary to the colonial government, and of the two colonists added, Stockenstrom was commissioner general for the eastern districts and former landdrost of Graaff-Reinet and therefore an official in the employ of the colonial government, and Truter, the former chief justice of the colony, was a pensioner.
49. See Chapter VII, p. 114.
50. *S.A.C.A.*, 16 March 1831.
51. *S.A.C.A.*, 4 May 1831.
52. The white inhabitants of Albany at this time were the British settlers of 1820, other British settlers who came to Albany before and after the main settlement, and some colonists of Dutch descent.
53. C.O. 48/146, Cole to Goderich, 31 December 1832 has enclosed a list of the schools in the colony supported by the colonial government at the time. Often they were run by the clerk of the *Dutch Church* either on Bell's or the Lancastrian system. No record has survived of the number of children who attended these schools. E. G. Malherbe, *Education in South Africa, 1652–1922*, p. 58 fn. 11, says that in 1828 there were 675 pupils in the government schools in Cape Town, but after the Dutch language was excluded from the syllabus in that year attendance declined in a few years to below 300. In the more conservative country districts it is probable that proportionately the decline was even greater. The colonists' assertion is therefore suspect.
54. Petition of the British settlers and others of the District of Albany, which was ordered by the House of Commons to be printed on 24 May 1830. See *Commons Journal*, Vol. LXXXV, pp. 466–467. Canada was divided into two provinces – Upper Canada and Lower Canada – each with a governor (or lieutenant-governor), executive council, legislative council and assembly. See F. Madden, *Imperial Constitutional Documents, 1765–1965, a supplement*, pp. 12–18.
55. *Parliamentary Debates*, published under the superintendence of T. C. Hansard, New Series, Vol. XXIV, c. 1007–8, 24 May 1830. This debate is printed in G. W. Eybers, *Select Constitutional Documents illustrating South African History, 1795–1910*, pp. 30–38.
56. C.O. 48/146, Memorial to the King in Council enclosed in Cole to Goderich, 6 January 1832, from "the undersigned inhabitants of the Cape of Good Hope." Unfortunately the signatures were cut off, presumably either before transmission to Great Britain, or when the document was filed.
57. C.A., G.H. 23/9, Cole to Hay, 18 April 1831, Private and Confidential. See Chapter X, p. 161.
58. i.e. reference to the conversion of the colonial currency from rixdollars to sterling in 1825.
59. The ancient restriction on the native tribes would appear to refer to legislation which prohibited contact between the colonists and the tribes beyond the frontiers. Ordinance 49 of 1828 admitted them to the colony to work on contract for colonists. Cole suspended the Ordinance because it posed a threat to the security of the colony. See Chapter VI, pp. 101–102.
60. C.O. 48/146, Cole to Goderich, 6 January 1832.
61. C.A., G.H. 23/10, Cole to Goderich, 8 February 1833.
62. Sir J. Truter, A. Stockenstrom, P. G. Brink and J. W. Stoll.
63. C.O. 48/146, Cole to Goderich, 6 January 1832.
64. See Chapter VIII, p. 130.
65. C.O. 48/146, Cole to Goderich, 6 January 1832.

66. See K. S. Hunt, "The Development of Municipal Government in the Eastern Province of the Cape of Good Hope with special reference to Grahamstown, 1827–1862", *Archives Year Book for South African History*, 1961.
67. C.A., G.H. 1/19, Goderich to Cole, 29 March 1832, enclosing a circular dated 8 December 1831, sent to governors of colonies where there were no legislative assemblies but where there were legislative councils.
68. C.O. 49/25, Instructions to Sir Benjamin D'Urban, 8 November 1833. Letters Patent dated 23 October 1833.

CHAPTER X

JUDICIAL DEVELOPMENTS AT THE CAPE

When the British Government considered alterations to the judiciary of the Cape of Good Hope in the third decade of the nineteenth century, it was natural for these changes to reflect developments in other parts of the Empire. Experience in Canada had taught the British Government that less muddle and tension was created if an established legal system was retained in a colony ceded to Britain by another sovereign power.[1] The policy was continued in Trinidad after its cession to Britain by Spain in the Treaty of Amiens, 1802. Spanish law, moreover, offered greater security to people of colour than was customary in the older British colonies of the West Indies.[2]

A growing awareness in Britain of the situation of coloured people in the colonies is evident from a request made by the House of Commons to the Crown in 1797. The Crown was asked to secure to negroes throughout the British West Indian Islands "the certain, immediate and active protection of the law".[3] Hence the Spanish legal system in Trinidad was in closer harmony with the objectives of British policy than was generally the case in the older established British colonies in the Carribean. An attempt by a small but active faction of English settlers to establish in Trinidad the pattern of government in the older colonies was firmly rejected by the British Government in 1810.[4] Although Liverpool expressed his indecision as to the future of the legal system, Spanish law was retained in Trinidad where English became the language of the courts in January 1814.[5] Recognition of the established law of a colony was a cardinal feature of the treaties of cession of 1814. They were superseded only by British statutes generally applicable to all British territory.[6]

At the Cape, the professed basis of regulation was "the Roman Law with as much of the modern alteration introduced by the States of Holland as was found applicable to the circumstances of the colony".[7] This was augmented in 1715 by the addition of the "Statutes of India" which were not repugnant to the proclamations and resolutions of the government of the Cape. These "Statutes" were a series of regulations governing the conduct and property of people subject to the control of the Dutch East India Company and made by Company officials in Batavia. The greater part of those "Statutes" adopted in the colony concerned the treatment and punishment of slaves. Derived themselves from Roman Law they re-inforced many of the harsh distinctions in the initial legal system of the Cape applicable to slaves who transgressed.[8]

When the Cape was administered by the Dutch East India Company the courts of justice developed in the hands of amateurs under the control of the local government.[9] The temporary nature of the first British occupation of the Cape (1795–1803) explains the limited changes then made: the number of judges was reduced from thirteen to eight, and these exchanged fees for fixed salaries.[10] More radical reform was undertaken by officials of the Batavian Republic[11] during the three years of their administration of the Cape (1803–1806). In the first place the High Court was made independent of the executive. Secondly, the amateur judges were replaced by men who, if they did not have professional training, at least had had experience with the administration of justice. Furthermore, an attorney-general was appointed with responsibilities as public prosecutor.[12] After the

British reconquered the Cape in 1806, the temporary administration of justice and the police was put into the hands of the governor. The earl of Caledon was instructed to exercise his judicial powers in conformity with the "Laws and Institutions" that subsisted under "The Ancient Government of the Settlement" subject to changes made during the previous British occupation.[13] Fortunately he was authorized to depart from his instructions to make "such expedient and useful alterations . . . either absolutely necessary and unavoidable or evidently beneficial and desirable".[14] He must have availed himself of this permission because the innovations introduced under the Batavian Republic were in fact continued. Otherwise the power of amendment rested entirely with the British Government.

Appellate jurisdiction was put in the hands of the governor in terms of Caledon's commission, consequently the link between the executive and the judiciary established in the seventeenth century was continued into the nineteenth century.[15] For practical purposes, however, the High Court of Justice was the more important court in the colony. It exercised original jurisdiction in all cases, though minor cases were usually heard by the district courts.

Minor jurisdiction was exercised in Cape Town by the Burgher Senate and in the country districts by the Courts of Landdrost and Heemraden. The landdrost was a paid official of the colonial government. He was assisted by a minimum of four and a maximum of eight heemraden nominated by the colonial government from the leading citizens of the district. The powers of these institutions were many and varied and included both judicial and administrative functions. They were responsible for settling disputes involving land boundaries, water rights, roads and bridges. They could try all civil cases in which the sum at issue did not exceed £10; in cases where the amount involved did not exceed £2.1.8d. they were a court of final jurisdiction.[16] In 1817 they were given jurisdiction in minor criminal cases.[17] Appeals against decisions of the Court of Landdrost and Heemraden were made to the High Court.

From the beginning of the British occupation of the Cape in 1806, British officials and merchants had resented the maintenance of Roman-Dutch law and the constitution and procedures of the courts, particularly the conduct of proceedings in camera and the absence of a jury.[18] But until the colony was formally ceded to Britain, and while the possibility remained that the colony might be restored to the Dutch, there was no question of any innovation being made in the judiciary except that an attempt was made to make the courts more accessible to colonists.

A proclamation of 1811 provided for two judges of the High Court to go on circuit at least once a year or more often if the need arose. These judges were instructed, moreover, to see that Caledon's proclamation of November 1809 for the treatment of Khoikhoi[19] was strictly applied, and to examine the records of punishments inflicted on slaves by the landdrosts in order to check that slaves were not too severely chastised. So far as it was possible they also had to look into the question of the domestic punishment of slaves and bring to justice slave-owners who had inflicted improper punishments on their slaves. Indeed the judges were directed to investigate the most trivial complaints concerning "the morality and good Government of the Country Districts" and report them to the governor.[20] This proclamation was welcomed by missionaries and others concerned with the welfare of Khoikhoi and slaves, and in 1812 several cases of alleged ill-treatment were brought before the circuit court but many of them could not be substantiated.[21]

It would appear that in cases which involved whites and non-whites, the judicial system favoured the white man.[22] Concern for bias in the judiciary caused Sir John Cradock to bring several cases of miscarriage of justice to slaves to the attention of the secretary of state in 1814.[23] Seven years later, in 1821, the necessity for some reform of the courts was the substance of a memorandum by H. Ellis, the deputy secretary to the colony. He drew attention to the fact that of the members of the Court of Justice at the Cape only the chief justice had had proper legal training and that most of the judges were not fully conversant in English. Dutch was used in all cases brought before the court including cases involving British shipping and commerce. Ellis submitted that a court composed of amateur judges who did not have a good command of English was incompetent to try cases requiring a knowledge of English acts of parliament.[24]

The arrival of a substantial number of British settlers in 1820, and their initial setbacks, complaints and litigation focussed attention on the need for legal reform at the Cape. But even before formal settler pressure was put on the secretary of state in a petition dated 10th March 1823, the British Government had decided to appoint a commission to inquire into Cape affairs.[25] The secretary of state accepted the validity of assertions of the anti-slavery leaders that ameliorative measures were ineffective without a sure administration of the law.[26]

As a result of their investigations the commissioners of inquiry advised the British Government to introduce radical changes in the colonial administration and judiciary.[27] They recommended that the colony should be divided into two provinces and that each province should have its own seat of government and professional judiciary. Bigge, in his report on the courts of justice at the Cape, recommended that English law and procedures should replace the Roman-Dutch ones in both provinces in due course. It was in the spirit of this general recommendation that he proposed that trial by jury should be introduced at the Cape for the trial of criminal offences and in civil cases if both the plaintiff and defendant agreed. He specifically ruled out trial by jury in cases involving the freedom, civil rights, or the property of slaves. And, although he admitted that "neither the habits of the people, nor their feelings of indifference upon all public questions" were favourable to the introduction of trial by jury, he nevertheless recommended its introduction because it would convince the colonists that no attempt against their rights or property could be successful so long as they conscientiously discharged their function as jurors. He thought that the impartiality of a jury would be ensured if jurors were chosen "without any reference to origin or to colour". Because he envisaged it would be difficult to assemble a sufficient number of jurors conversant in English outside of Cape Town or the district of Albany, he suggested that trial by jury should be limited to those two districts for the first five years of its operation. Furthermore, he recommended that a jury should be composed of nine persons, and that questions submitted to them should be decided by a majority of at least two-thirds[28] and not by unanimous agreement as in Britain.

The commissioners, in their report on the administration of the Cape, said that their investigations into the Courts of Landdrost and Heemraden convinced them that it would be wise to abolish those courts. They stated that all those who held the office of either landdrost or heemraden had been prepared to admit "their inability to do justice to the various duties that were thrown upon them".[29] The commissioners found that in cases which involved coloured people the impartiality and justice of the heemraden "were much perverted by the prejudices and habits that have become hereditary amongst them".[30] If justice was to be done to all, irrespective of colour, the judicial powers of the Courts of Landdrost and Heemraden had to be transferred to impartial authority. Thus they recommended that the judicial and magisterial duties of the landdrost and heemraden should be entrusted to officers of the Crown titled "Judges of the County Court" and such other magistrates as might be found competent to discharge the duties of Justices of the Peace. They recommended that these courts should have greater jurisdiction than that possessed by the Courts of Landdrost and Heemraden. They suggested that these courts should be authorized to try slaves and prize negroes[31] for petty larceny and criminal offences, and pass sentence of a maximum of imprisonment with hard labour for one year, or a limited number of lashes.

A Charter of Justice was signed at Windsor on the 6th August 1827.[32] The British Government did not accept all Bigge's recommendations. Pragmatic considerations led to the modification of some suggestions. The colony was not divided into two provinces thus two courts were not established. Moreover, the British Government rejected Bigge's recommendation for the introduction of English law. The secretary of state recognized the importance and necessity of "a gradual approximation of the Law of all Foreign Settlements of the Crown to the Law of England". He thought that the modification of the fundamental laws of foreign colonies was inevitable with the passage of time. Meanwhile, he considered that Roman-Dutch law provided adequately "for the ordinary exigencies of life in every form of Society". The British Government did agree, though, to introduce a professional court and court procedures modelled on the English system and for proceedings to be conducted in the English language.[33]

The Charter of Justice named as the highest court in the colony the Supreme Court of the Cape of Good Hope with its seat in Cape Town. It was made a Court of Record and staffed by a chief justice and three puisne judges all of whom were required by the Charter to have specific professional qualifications. They had to be barristers in England or Ireland of not less than three years standing, or advocates admitted to practice in the Court of Session in Scotland for the same period. Sir John Wylde[34] was named the first chief justice by the Charter, and William Menzies,[35] William Westbrooke Burton,[36] and George Kekewich[37] were named puisne judges. They held office during good behaviour and received fixed salaries. Emoluments derived from fees, perquisites, or places of profit were specifically denied them.

In civil cases in which the sum involved was £1 000 or more, the Charter provided for appeals to be made to the King in Privy Council. The Crown, moreover, reserved the right to receive petitions from persons aggrieved by any judgment of the Supreme Court, and admit an appeal subject to such terms and limitations as were thought fit, and to reverse, correct or vary that judgment. The governor was relieved of appellate jurisdiction, a step which rendered the judiciary independent of executive control.

In order to facilitate justice, Circuit Courts, armed with much of the authority of the Supreme Court, had to be held bi-annually in all the districts of the colony. These courts were presided over by one of the puisne judges in rotation. The Circuit Courts had final jurisdiction in criminal cases, but appeals could be made to the Supreme Court in Cape Town in civil suits in excess of £100. If a judge considered that an action or suit could be more conveniently heard in the Supreme Court or another Circuit Court, he was authorised to transfer the case to the court of his choice.

The Charter provided for all criminal cases brought before the Supreme Court or Circuit Courts to be tried by one or more judges and a jury of nine men. If nine jurors could not be assembled in a country district, six jurors was deemed sufficient. Contrary to Bigge's advice the Charter required jurors to concur in every verdict.

All public prosecutions were entrusted to an attorney-general because in all the West Indian colonies where the English form of trial by grand and petit jury was maintained it had been found expedient to entrust this official with that duty. The secretary of state appreciated that it could be impossible to convene a grand jury outside of Cape Town, and even in Cape Town he thought it would be found necessary to reduce the number below those required in England.[38] If the institution of grand jury was introduced at all, he thought that it should be limited to the case of offenders who were to be tried in Cape Town.[39] Since the grand jury was relieved of the task of prosecution it was only expected to determine whether or not there was a true bill of indictment on the evidence presented by the attorney-general.

The qualification of jurors was left to the colonial government to define, though the secretary of state suggested that "the Office of Juror should be confided to such of the inhabitants as from their education, property and condition in life would be best qualified to understand and perform correctly this important duty".[40]

Ordinance 41 of 1828 laid down that all men between the ages of twenty-one and sixty years who lived and possessed land in the colony on perpetual quitrent, or on loan for a minimum annual rent of £1.17.6d., or freehold land of the same annual value, or paid a minimum tax in Cape Town or district of 20 shillings, or 15 shillings in any other part of the colony, were qualified and liable to serve on juries in criminal cases tried in the district to which the juror belonged.[41] A grand jury was composed of 9 to 17 persons. They had to have higher property qualifications than petit jurors. They had to possess property in land or houses in the vicinity of Cape Town or district of the value of £2 000. Judges, advocates and other court officials, clergymen and church clerks, medical doctors, jailors, and officers of the army and navy on full pay were excluded from jury service.

Effectively service on juries was limited to the very people from whom the heemraden had previously been drawn and whose judicial impartiality and been questioned by the commissioners in their report of the 6th September 1826. The British Government were aware of the commissioners' criticism of the Courts of Landdrost and Heemraden, and the Charter empowered the governor and the Council of Advice to reform the lower courts. Ordinance 33 of 1827 abolished the offices of landdrost and heemraden and transferred their judicial powers to resident magistrates, and their civil powers to civil commissioners. The secretary of state obviously did not appreciate that some of the commissioners' criticism of landdrosts and heemraden could be equally applicable to jurors.

This might not have been the case had the secretary of state been in possession of a later report from the commissioners upon criminal law and jurisprudence at the Cape which was signed by them on the 18th August 1827 in Mauritius[42] twelve days after the Charter of Justice had been signed. It is clear from the internal evidence of Goderich's despatch to Bourke of the 5th August 1827 transmitting a copy of the Charter that he was unaware that the commissioners were going to submit a second report on the Cape's judiciary.[43] The improvement of the courts at the Cape was felt to be urgent[44] thus no time had been lost in preparing the Charter after the receipt of Bigge's report. This meant that the officials who framed the Charter were ignorant of the fuller consideration of the commissioners on the subject of trial by jury for criminal offences.

In the later report the commissioners recommended that exceptions to the general principle of trial by jury should be made for the trial of San, prize negroes during the term of their indentures,[45] and individuals belonging to the chiefdoms beyond the frontier who were working in the colony under contract.[46] They also proposed that the trial of slaves for criminal offences should be excluded from trial by jury. They recommended these exceptions because of "the peculiar relation in which all these classes stand towards the great body of inhabitants from which the juries for the present must necessarily be taken".[47] Though the commissioners recommended that all free people irrespective of colour who were twenty-one years of age and householders or occupiers of houses on lease for at least three years should be liable for jury service, they appreciated that, for a while at least, the majority of people who would qualify as jurors would be the white colonists.[48] A master-servant relationship existed between the white colonists and the classes whom the commissioners proposed to except from the principle of trial by jury. In a case in which the defendant was of the servile class and the jurors were masters or vice versa, there could be doubt about the impartiality of the verdict of the jury.

The commissioners did not exclude the Khoikhoi and people of mixed blood from the right of trial by jury although the relationship between them and the whites was similar to that between those excluded and the whites. They considered that to do so would hinder progress towards removing distinctions between the Khoikhoi and people of mixed blood and the whites. Meanwhile, they suggested that in order to protect the former from juries that might be prejudiced against them for reasons of race, they be allowed an option of being tried by two judges.[49]

Unfortunately, as the practice of trial by jury at the Cape was to show,[50] the Charter did not provide for any of the reservations made by the commissioners in their report of the 18th August 1827 to protect people of colour from juries that might be prejudiced against them. Meanwhile, at the Cape in the case of the *King v Jan de Villiers*, the Bench added a further qualification to be a juryman which it would appear the commissioners had in mind, namely the ability to understand English.[51]

The case opened before the Circuit Court in Worcester in May 1828. The judge objected to one of the six jurors because he did not understand English. He therefore removed the case to Cape Town where the trial was conducted before the Supreme Court. The Court first gave attention to the question of a language qualification for jurors. The chief justice reasoned that while comprehension of English was not prescribed, it was implied because of the British judicial qualifications required of the judges and other court officials, and the practice of the jury system in Great Britain. The Court was an English court, and the chief justice maintained it was indispensable that judge and jury should be able to understand the language of the court; therefore, only those who had sufficient knowledge of the English language were entitled to be empanelled as jurors. The senior puisne judge concurred, but the other two puisne judges dissented. In the circumstances the most junior puisne judge declined to record his judgment so that the issue was determined by a majority decision of the court.[52] The decision of the Supreme Court, however, did not bind the Circuit Courts. Hence on circuit each judge made his own decision on the subject.[53]

Lieutenant-governor Bourke had been most concerned about the repercussions of the procedure and decision of the judges. He raised two points with Huskisson, the secretary of state. In the first place he objected to the disqualification of jurors on grounds of language. Since the majority of witnesses spoke only Dutch, he thought that the jurors who used that language would have the advantage of receiving evidence without an interpreter. Secondly, he disapproved of the right of a judge to remove a case to Cape Town whenever it was impossible to assemble enough jurors. He thought it was intolerable that a person could be sent to be tried – perhaps for his life – "at a place about 600 miles distant from that in which he had made preparation for his defence". A journey of that distance could take from fifteen to twenty days and considerably add to the cost of litigation. "The practice will be most harrassing, vexatious and expensive to the subject, and the charge upon the Treasury for criminal prosecution will be quite enormous," he wrote. He thought that in England an insufficiency of jurors merely led to the postponement of the trial till the next session, and hoped that it would be possible to introduce that practice at the Cape. Thus he suggested that if the law officers of the Crown confirmed that the judges did have the right to transfer cases to Cape Town, the Charter should be amended to bring colonial procedure into line with British practice.[54]

It was at this point that Sir Lowry Cole entered upon his governorship of the Cape. Meanwhile Sir George Murray had succeeded Huskisson as secretary of state. Thus it is a despatch from Murray to Cole which conveys the opinion of the British Government on the questions raised. Murray was not prepared to deny the abstract right of the judges to remove a case from one part of the country to another if they thought it was in the best interests of justice. They were entrusted with this authority in the expectation that they would use it moderately and wisely. If they abused their trust, the British Government would take steps to narrow the extent of their trust. On the question of an English language qualification for jurors, Murray was more emphatic. "Whatever views the judges may take of the legal effect of the Charter, in this respect," he wrote, "it is at least clear that their construction is totally at variance with the real intentions of His Majesty's Government in framing that Instrument". If the judges persisted in excluding the Dutch colonists from acting as jurors, then Murray agreed that the Charter would have to be amended, however reluctant he was to do this.[55] He therefore referred the problem to James Stephen.

Stephen's reply is interesting because, while yet only legal counsellor at the Colonial Department, he did not confine himself solely to the legal issue. He disagreed with the decision of the Cape bench and thought the two junior puisne judges were right. But he did not think that the question of law, important though it was in the judge's debates, need occupy the time of the secretary of state. The decision of the Cape bench could only be set aside either by a contrary advice of the Privy Council if an appeal was brought to them and they decided the colonial judges were wrong, or by direct legislation. Since the British Government had the power to alter the law, Stephen thought that the more material question was what the law ought to be. He set out the arguments for and against the admission of jurors non-conversant with English, and suggested that the wisest course would be "to acquiese in the inconvenience of excluding from juries all persons ignorant of the English language; looking forward to a period not very remote, when the general diffusion of our language through the Colony will so far diminish the difficulty as to render it nearly insignificant".[56]

Stephen's view was certainly optimistic and not without some foundation. In Trinidad, for example, the chief justice told the commissioners of legal inquiry that he was unaware of any difficulties which had arisen from conducting courts proceedings in English.[57] But the composition of the population in Trinidad was rather different from that at the Cape. The majority of the population in Trinidad was slave, and the small European community was divided between Spanish, French and English. Hence English provided a satisfactory lingua franca.[58] At the Cape the Dutch colonists were in the majority. An official inquiry revealed that in the districts of Worcester, Clan William, Swellendam, George, Beaufort and Somerset there was an average of only 8 men who lived in the principal town of the district, or within six hours riding distance of it, who understood English sufficiently well to serve on juries: an average of 74 others were qualified on every other score. If the net was cast wider – to those who lived more than six hours riding distance from the district town – an average of 5 more jurors could be added who understood English, and an average of 283 others disqualified only because they did not understand the language.[59] Effectively in some districts of the colony the language barrier created a situation in which a small group of people could become a semi-permanent panel of jurymen.

Meanwhile, considerable inconvenience was felt by people who were summoned by the high sheriff of the colony to attend the Supreme Court or Circuit Courts as jurors in terms of the qualifications laid down by ordinance, only to discover, when their names were called over in the court, that they could not be empanelled because they did not know enough English. Cole attempted to resolve the problem by amendment to the law. He proposed to write into legislation the exclusion from jury service of those non-conversant with English. He was supported by the majority of the Council, but Stockenstrom recorded his dissent. Stockenstrom reckoned trial by jury was granted as a boon to colonists and that uniformity of practice in the courts should be restored by an approach to the King for an Order to enforce the original intention of the Charter.[60]

When the draft ordinance was submitted to the chief justice for his certification that it was not opposed to the fundamental laws of the colony or the laws of England,[61] he declined to give it on the grounds that sections of the draft were inconsistent with the Charter as they implied that in terms of the Charter itself, those incompetent in English were entitled to serve as jurors. Moreover, he objected to a reference in the draft ordinance to his judgment in the Supreme Court. Ignorance of English, he said was not a "*disqualification*" as stated in the draft, but a "*disability*" in terms of the Charter. However, he agreed that uniformity of practice in the Court was desirable and recommended the governor to refer the problem to the secretary of state.[62] The Council of Advice agreed with the chief justice's opinion, and resolved that no alteration should be made in the jury laws with respect to the "competency or incompetency, ability or disability, qualification or disqualification of persons ignorant of the English language to serve on Grand and Petit Juries".[63] The matter was therefore left for the governor to take up with the secretary of state.

The secretary of state agreed that the contradictory practice of the different judges was undesirable and proposed to set the question "at rest" in a revision of the Charter of Justice then in preparation.[64] This document, signed by the King in May 1832 but not promulgated at the Cape until February 1834,[65] left the matter in no doubt. It declared that no person otherwise competent to serve on a jury should be "taken to be incompetent to serve on such jury by reason of his ignorance or supposed ignorance of the English language".[66]

The colonists liked trial by jury. The procedure gave them some control over the administration of justice. They looked forward to the extension of the privilege to civil cases.[67] Though this had been envisaged in 1827,[68] it was not brought into operation in the revised Charter. In part this may be explained by verdicts returned by jurymen in the period 1827–1832.[69] The discrepancy between sentences passed on white colonists and those passed on coloured ones did not escape the attention of the governor. On occasion he used his prerogative of mercy to commute death sentences on coloureds to transportation to New South Wales or Van Dieman's Land.[70] His policy must have been approved by the British Government because Royal Orders to give effect to the Governor's decision were sent to the Cape.[71] Furthermore, in April 1831, Cole wrote in confidence to Hay,

> "The result of some recent trials in cases of maltreatment of slaves where the prisoners were acquitted in the teeth of the clearest evidence against them, makes it very questionable if the trial by jury in criminal cases has been a benefit to the colony – but whatever difference of opinion there may be as it respects the Criminal Law, I believe that few persons who are not carried away by the popular feeling of Englishmen upon the subject, would consider the extension of it to civil cases as a blessing or likely to establish a purer system of justice here."[72]

In view of the governor's criticism, it may seem surprising that trial by jury was continued in the revised Charter at all. It was probably expected that the problem would resolve itself. The abolition of slavery was already contemplated in 1832, and Ordinance 50 of 1828 had guaranteed the legal equality of all free persons of colour. Thus it would be reasonable to anticipate that coloured people, even ex-slaves, would be called as jurors as soon as they fulfilled the legal qualifications.

Other amendments made by the revised Charter of Justice were not of great significance. It referred to the powers of the governor "*with the advice of the Executive Council*", and with the "*consent of the Legislative Council*" – terms which delayed its publication until a new constitution was promulgated.[73] Judicial appointments ceased to be made under the Great Seal of the United Kingdom and were henceforth made under the Public Seal of the colony in pursuance of warrants under the King's Sign Manual. Reference to the professional qualifications of judges was omitted in the revised Charter because it was considered superfluous to restrict the choice of the Crown. Goderich explained to the governor that it was occasionally possible that men eminently qualified for judicial preferment in the colonies would not be barristers in England or Ireland, or advocates in Scotland. Such appointments, however, were intended as an exception rather than a rule. ". . . It may be readily allowed", wrote Goderich, "that an admission to the Bar, followed by an actual attendance in our Domestic Tribunals, for some years is . . . the best criterion by which the pretensions of candidates for such preferment can be tried".[74] The revised Charter reduced the number of puisne judges from three to two, made technical changes to provide for this reduction, and provided for the chief justice to take a turn on circuit.

The reduction in the size of the bench was dictated by economy and redundancy. When the Court was established in 1827 arrears of judicial business, long delays and uncertainty in the administration of justice had been the substance of repeated complaints. The reformed tribunal not only disposed of arrears, but dealt with cases so promptly that unnecessary litigation was discouraged and the judges were left with insufficient employment. In view of the financial circumstances of the colony, it could not afford the luxury of unnecessary officials. Hence one judge was transferred to New South Wales.[75]

The infusion of professionalism into the courts, the speeding up of the judicial process, and the consequent opportunity to reduce the size of the bench and save expenditure pleased the secretary of state. In a despatch to Cole, Goderich wrote,

> "I cannot but regard with high satisfaction, the success of the remedial measures which I recommended to his late Majesty, and for the zeal with which they have been carried into effect my best acknowledgements are due to the Judges collectively and individually."[76]

It would appear that he did not consider that the problems raised by the introduction of trial by jury detracted from the overall benefit to the colonial judiciary from the reforms he instituted.

Unquestionably the Charter of Justice of 1827 laid the foundations of professional jurisprudence at the Cape. It established colonial courts limited in their jurisdiction to the boundaries of the colony. Since, however, these boundaries were frequently transgressed by colonists, the question of an extension of its jurisdiction beyond the limit of British sovereignty was one of major importance.

English common law did not provide for the trial of British subjects in English courts for offences committed outside the King's dominion except in cases of crime committed in military lines abroad or at sea.[77] The British Government had been forced to make good this omission by statute. In 1817, for example, legislation was passed in an effort to control the scandalous behaviour by British seamen and others who for one reason or another had left their ship to live at the Bay of Honduras – a territory protected but not possessed by the British Crown. This act[78] authorized any court in the King's dominion to punish murder or manslaughter committed in any territory not subject to the sovereignty of Britain, nor any European state, nor the United States of America, by any person sailing in or belonging to a British ship, or who had sailed in, or belonged to, and had quitted any ship to live in that territory. In terms of other British statutes[79] these cases had to be heard after the common course of the Laws of England used for treasons, felonies, murder, robberies and "confederacies of the same".[80] But conditions in southern Africa did not answer to the particulars of the law. British citizens who trespassed beyond the frontiers of the colony were usually colonists, not sailors who had forsaken their ship for the land. Moreover, the difference between the judicial systems of England and the Cape made it unfeasable for Cape courts to hear such suits.

The question of extra-territorial jurisdiction of the Cape courts was raised by a murder committed beyond the boundary of the colony. Both the murderer and the victim were British subjects. The unreformed High Court of Justice had found the murderer guilty and sentenced him to death. Before the sentence could be carried into effect, the Charter of Justice of 1827 had been promulgated. The attorney-general appointed in terms of the new Charter challenged the validity of the sentence on the grounds of the incompetency of the court to judge the case. The question was brought before the judges of the Supreme Court and the opinion of the attorney-general was upheld. The judges pointed out that at no time had colonial courts had extra-territorial jurisdiction beyond the strict terms of the Act of 1817, and that the Charter of Justice of 1827 had not given them any additional authority. They therefore recommended to the governor the expediency of a request to the British Government to extend the jurisdiction of the colonial court on the principle recognized by the 1817 Act, to meet the circumstances of southern Africa.[81] Cole commended the judges' suggestion to the secretary of state, and added that he feared "murders and other atrocities" were frequently committed with impunity beyond the frontier "by those who pass the boundary in pursuit of stolen cattle".[82] These people escaped punishment because of the confined jurisdiction of the court.

Evidently Sir George Murray did not realise the full significance of the authority required to extend the jurisdiction of the Cape judiciary. He instructed Cole to propose an ordinance to the Council of Advice to give colonial courts "jurisdiction over offences committed beyond the limits of your Government by persons usually residing within those limits".[83] In a pencil comment on this despatch, John Bell, the secretary to government at the Cape, observed, "This cannot be done by an Ordinance in Council – a Commission under the Great Seal alone can do it". However an ordinance was prepared. When it was submitted to the chief justice, he declared the draft was not only inconsistent with the fundamental laws of the colony, but that the Charter of Justice itself precluded the colonial government from extending the jurisdiction of the court.[84]

Cole disputed the chief justice's ruling. He explained that in terms of his instructions he did have the power to pass the ordinance because it was prepared in compliance with directions from the secretary of state, and that there was nothing in the Charter itself which deprived him of that power.[85] Cole eventually accepted a proposal of the chief justice to put the problem before all the judges.[86] Their opinion weighed the relative importance of the legislative instruments applicable to the Cape, and concluded that the extended jurisdiction sought for the Cape courts could only be granted by an act of parliament.[87]

When Goderich, who had succeeded Murray at the Colonial Department in November 1830, received the opinion of the judges at the Cape, he readily agreed that the instructions issued by Murray involved a question of considerable doubt and difficulty. The necessity of applying English law had raised similar difficulties in other colonies. In Malta, for example, the ordinary course of criminal justice had no analogy whatever with the English system, thus conformity was impossible. The law officers of the Crown, however, were of the opinion that Parliament had to be understood to have required "only that degree of adherence to the course of the common law of England, of which the Colonial Judicatures were susceptible, regard being had to the peculiar circumstances of different colonies". It was presumed Parliament would not require that which was evidently impossible. Unless that interpretation was put upon the Act of 1817,[88] it was appreciated it would become a dead letter on the statute book. The British Government therefore accepted the opinion of the colonial judges, reserved the question for further consideration, and acknowledged that if any error had been committed, the fault lay not with the governor but the Colonial Department.[89]

The issue lay dormant for another four years. In December 1835 Glenelg told D'Urban that he proposed to submit a bill to Parliament to give the Cape courts extra-territorial jurisdiction in order to enforce the terms of the peace settlement he advocated following the Frontier War of 1834–35.[90]

The Cape of Good Hope Punishment Act of 1836[91] extended the jurisdiction of the Cape courts to cover any territory adjacent to the colony, southward of the twenty-fifth degree of south latitude, though it specifically repudiated sovereignty over this territory.

The Charter of Justice of 1827, the revised Charter of 1832, and the extension of the jurisdiction of the Cape courts in 1836, each mark a positive step forward in the extension of the rule of law in southern Africa. The impartiality of the courts in criminal procedure which involved the question of racial discrimination and trial by jury is open to doubt. But its professionalism ensured greater impartiality than could be expected from the older amateur courts. If the rule of law be reckoned a cardinal feature of western civilization, then the developments in the judiciary in southern Africa in the period under review indicate further progress in its extension on the sub-continent.

FOOTNOTES

1. *C.H.B.E.*, Vol. VI, Chapter 6.
2. L. M. Fraser, *History of Trinidad*, Vol. I, p. 305.
3. G. R. Mellor, *British Imperial Trusteeship*, p. 60.
4. C.O. 296/4, Liverpool to Hislop, 27 November 1810. See also D. J. Murray, *The West Indies and the Development of Colonial Government*, p. 80.
5. C. Reis, *The Government of Trinidad*, (1st edition) p. 27.
6. *Ibid.*, p. 26.
7. Theal, *R.C.C.*, Vol. XXXIII, p. 4, Report of the commissioners of inquiry upon criminal law and jurisprudence, 18 August 1827.
8. *Ibid.*, pp. 1–3.
9. *C.H.B.E.*, Vol. VIII, (2nd edition), pp. 862–863.
10. Walker, p. 126.
11. The name by which the United Provinces of the Netherlands were known at this time.
12. Walker, p. 134, and Theal, *R.C.C.*, Vol. XXVIII, pp. 3–4, Report of the commissioners of inquiry on the courts of justice at the Cape, 6 September 1826.
13. C.O., 49/9, Instructions to the earl of Caledon, 1 August 1806.
14. *Ibid.*
15. See Chapter V, p. 88.
16. K. S. Hunt, "The Development of Municipal Government in the Eastern Province of the Cape of Good Hope with special reference to Grahamstown", *Archives Year Book for South African History*, 1961, p. 138.
17. Walker, p. 141.
18. *C.H.B.E.*, Vol. VIII, (2nd edition), p. 202.
19. See Theal, *R.C.C.*, Vol. VII, pp. 211–216. This proclamation declared that Khoikhoi must have a fixed place of abode. They could not remove themselves from one district to another without written authority from the landdrost. Khoikhoi taken into service by colonists for longer periods than a month had to have a written contract signed in triplicate before the landdrost or field cornet. They had to be paid wages, and an allowance of liquor was specifically excluded as part payment.
20. Theal, *R.C.C.*, Vol. XXIV, pp. 451–463, Proclamation by Caledon, 16 May 1811.
21. *C.H.B.E.*, Vol. VIII, (2nd edition), pp. 290–291.
22. Theal, *R.C.C.*, Vol. XXXIII pp. 6–9, Report of the commissioners of inquiry, 18 August 1827.
23. Theal, *R.C.C.*, Vol. X, pp. 1–60, Cradock to Bathurst, 15 April 1814.
24. Theal, *R.C.C.*, Vol. XIV, pp. 183–187.

25. *C.H.B.E.*, Vol. VIII, (2nd edition), p. 250. Wilmot Horton, under-secretary of state for War and the Colonial Department, moved an address asking for a commission of inquiry into Cape affairs on 25 July 1822.
26. Murray, p. 142.
27. Theal, *R.C.C.*, Vol. XXXIII, pp. 1–130, Report of the commissioners of inquiry upon criminal law and jurisprudence, 18 August 1827.
P.P. 1826–7, XXI (282) Report of the commissioners of inquiry on (i) the Administration of the Cape of Good Hope; and (ii) the Finances of the Cape of Good Hope, 6 September 1826; and Theal, *R.C.C.*, Vol. XXVIII, pp. 1–111, Report of J. T. Bigge on the courts of justice at the Cape, 6 September 1826.
28. Theal, *R.C.C.*, Vol. XXVIII, pp. 24–25, Report of J. T. Bigge upon the courts of justice, 6 September 1826.
29. P.P. 1826–7, XXI (282), Report of the commissioners of inquiry on (i) the Administration of the Cape of Good Hope; and (ii) the Finances of the Cape of Good Hope, 6 September 1826, p. 19.
30. *Ibid.*
31. See fn. 45 below.
32. C.O. 49/21, contains the copy of the Charter kept by the Colonial Department.
33. C.O. 49/21, Goderich to Bourke, 5 August 1827.
34. Sir John Wylde (1781–1869) was called to the Bar at the Middle Temple in 1805. He served as judge-advocate of New South Wales from 1815 to 1825 when he returned to England. In 1827 he received the degree of Doctor of Laws of the University of Cambridge, and was appointed chief justice at the Cape in the same year. He remained in office until 1855.
35. William Menzies (1795–1850) was admitted to the Faculty of Advocates in Scotland in 1816. He was appointed to the Cape bench in 1827, and became an authority on Roman-Dutch law. According to H. R. Hahlo and E. Kahn, *South Africa, the Development of its Laws and Constitutions*, p. 206, he protected Roman-Dutch legal principles "from invasion of English law". The first set of Cape Law Reports was published from his manuscripts thirty years after his death.
36. Sir William Westbrooke Burton (1794–1888) became a student at the Inner Temple after a short career in the navy. He was called to the Bar in 1824, and was recorder of Daventry, 1826–1827. After his appointment to the Cape bench in 1827, he went to Holland for six months to study Dutch and Roman-Dutch law. In 1829 Burton published a text-book entitled *Observations on the insolvent law of the Colony of the Cape of Good Hope with an appendix of forms applicable to the colonial ordinance No. 64.* He was subsequently appointed to the bench in New South Wales (1832–1844) (See p. 162), and Madras (1844–1857). He returned to New South Wales in 1857 and was president of the Legislative Council of New South Wales (1858–1862).
37. George Kekewich (1778–1862) was called to the Bar at Lincoln's Inn and came to the Cape in 1808. Two years later he was appointed assessor in civil and criminal cases of the Court of Appeals, and in 1811, judge of the Vice-Admiralty Court, a post he held till he was transferred to the Cape bench. He retired in 1843. According to Hahlo and Kahn, p. 206, fn. 49, he was "utterly undistinguished".
38. An English grand jury was composed of twenty-three men "of substantial position". A grand jury was summoned in all cases brought for trial before an Assize Court or the Court of Quarter Sessions. After being addressed by the judge, bills of indictment, i.e., formal written accusations against persons, were put before them. They deliberated in secret, heard as much of the evidence for the prosecution as they wished to hear, and decided whether or not the accused ought to be tried. See R. M. Jackson, *The Machinery of Justice in England* (4th edition), pp. 93–94.
39. C.O. 49/21, Goderich to Bourke, 5 August 1827.
40. *Ibid.*
41. Ordinances 83 and 84 amended these figures because errors of calculation were made when they were fixed. Petit jurors had to possess either quitrent land for which they paid a minimum annual rent of £1.10.0d., or at least a quarter share in a loan place, or possess a freehold or loan freehold place, or if resident in Cape Town, paid a minimum annual tax of £1.10.0d or paid at least £2 in quitrent and taxes; people who lived outside Cape Town were qualified if they paid a minimum annual tax of £1, or £1.10.0d in quitrent and tax. The sons of people who had the requisite property and/or tax qualifications were also liable for jury service.
42. Theal, *R.C.C.*, Vol. XXXIII, pp. 1–130, Report of the commissioners of inquiry upon criminal law and jurisprudence, 18 August 1827.
43. C.O. 49/21, Goderich to Bourke, 5 August 1827, the former wrote:

> "The subject of the administration of criminal justice is passed over by the Commissioners in their report without any particular remark. I presume it to have been their intention to dispose of this question by their general advice respecting the introduction of the Law of England to which I have already adverted."

The second report actually dealt with the subject in detail.

44. Theal, *R.C.C.*, Vol. XXXI, pp. 402–4, Goderich to the attorney and solicitor-general, 25 May 1827.
45. Prize negroes were people (usually Africans) taken from on board slave-ships which had been captured at sea by British cruisers. They could be apprenticed for fourteen years under terms which were intended to prepare them for free citizenship. Between 1808 and 1816, 2 000 prize negroes were landed at the Cape.
46. See Chapter VI, p. 99.
47. Theal, *R.C.C.*, Vol. XXXIII, p. 112, Report of the commissioners of inquiry, 18 August 1827.
48. *Ibid.*, p. 114.
49. *Ibid.* p. 113.
50. See p. 161.
51. See p. 155.
52. C.A., G.H. 23/9, Cole to Murray, 6 June 1829.
53. C.A., A.C. 24 February 1831.
54. C.O. 48/125, Bourke to Huskisson, 11 August 1828.
55. C.A., G.H. 1/15, Murray to Cole, 22 February 1829.
56. C.O. 48/130, Stephen to Hay, 24 August 1829.
57. C.O. 318/69, Report of commissioners of legal inquiry into the West Indian colonies, p. 67.
58. *Ibid.*
59. C.A., A.C. 24 February 1831.
60. *Ibid.*
61. See Chapter IX, p. 142.
62. C.A., A.C. 31 March 1831.
63. *Ibid.*
64. C.A., G.H. 1/18, Goderich to Cole, 3 December 1831.
65. See Chapter IX, p. 147.
66. Clause 34.
67. C.O. 48/142, "Petition to the King by the inhabitants of the Cape Colony", sent through Cole by the Committee of the Commercial Exchange and enclosed in Cole to Goderich, 18 April 1831. The signatures have been cut off, thus there is no indication how many people signed it.
68. C.O. 49/21, Goderich to Bourke, 5 August 1827.
69. Rev. W. Wright, *Slavery at the Cape of Good Hope*, pp. 39–53 and pp. 79–104 lists several cases which suggest there was some miscarriage of justice.
70. C.A., G.H. 23/9, Cole to Goderich, 10 December 1831.
71. C.A., G.H. 1/19, Goderich to Cole, 10 May 1832.
72. C.A., G.H. 23/9, Cole to Hay, 18 April 1831, Private and Confidential.
73. See Chapter IX, p. 149.
74. C.A., G.H. 1/19, Goderich to Cole, 16 June 1832.
75. C.A., G.H. 1/19, Goderich to Cole, 29 March 1832. Notice was given in this despatch that the judiciary would be reduced and Burton transferred to New South Wales. This was confirmed in Goderich to Cole, 16 June, 1832, C.A., G.H. 1/19. Burton left the Cape for New South Wales on the 14 October 1832, see C.A., G.H. 23/10, Cole to Goderich, 24 November 1832.
76. C.A., G.H. 1/19, Goderich to Cole, 16 June 1832.
77. H. Jenkyns, *British Rule and Jurisdiction beyond the Sea*, pp. 127–129.
78. 57 Geo. III, c. 53.
79. 57 Geo. III, c. 53 taken in conjunction with 40 Geo. III, c. 54, and 28 Hen. VIII, c. 15.
80. i.e. accomplices.
81. C.O. 48/131, Statement made in the Supreme Court by the chief judge and three puisne judges on 30 July 1829, enclosed in Cole to Murray, 1 August 1829.
82. C.A., G.H. 23/9, Cole to Murray, 1 August 1829.
83. C.A., G.H. 1/16, Murray to Cole, 29 November 1829.

84. C.A., G.H. 23/9, Cole to Goderich, 1 June 1831.
85. *Ibid.*
86. *Ibid.*
87. C.O. 48/143, Judicial opinion enclosed in Cole to Goderich, 1 June 1831
88. 57 Geo. III, c. 53.
89. C.A., G.H. 1/18, Goderich to Cole, 3 December 1831.
90. P.P. 1836, XXXIX (279), Glenelg to D'Urban, 26 December 1835.
91. 6 & 7 Will. IV, c. 57.

EPILOGUE

Sir Lowry Cole's domestic affairs had long made him anxious to return to Britain. He was granted leave of absence in October 1831, shortly before the publication of the Order in Council of the 2nd November 1831[1] which caused unrest at the Cape. Under the circumstances he declined the offer because he considered that conditions in the colony warranted his personal supervision.[2] Apparently the colonists were pleased with his decision to remain at his post. *De Zuid-Afrikaan* published the news that he could go on leave, and even proceeded to name a successor should he resign the governorship. It added, "We need hardly say that on public grounds we hope this event (that is, Cole's resignation) may be long delayed."[3] Yet when Cole did leave the Cape sixteen months later, *De Zuid-Afrikaan* had completely altered its opinion of him. The change is observable from the publication in June 1832 of the ordinance to prohibit meetings without special authority, and Cole's proclamation which threatened banishment from the colony for disturbers of the peace.[4] The discontent caused by these measures uncovered the hostility of many of the colonists of Dutch descent towards British administration in general.

After Cole had left the Cape in August 1833, *De Zuid-Afrikaan* attacked his administration. The newspaper's criticism focussed on three points: Cole was alleged to have neglected the roads; failed to have enacted an ordinance to prevent vagrancy among the Khoikhoi; and failed to withdraw regulations to ameliorate the condition of slaves in the face of alleged authority to do so from the secretary of state. In presenting its case the newspaper distorted the facts and appealed to the prejudices of its readers.

De Zuid-Afrikaan observed that Cole's censure and threatened surcharge to cover the cost of the pass over the Hottentots Holland Mountains[5] had indelibly associated him in the minds of the colonists with road-making. It pointed out that valedictory addresses laboured the fact that Cole was responsible for improving roads in the colony but, it continued, there was no reason to thank the governor for any improvement to roads, for example, in the neighbourhood of Paarl, because these had only been carried out by the assessed labour of the colonists. Besides, *De Zuid-Afrikaan* argued, the Hottentots Holland Pass incident had cured Cole's "disease for road-making", and that generally there had been some deterioration in the conditions of roads and some passes in particular while Cole was governor.[6]

But the restriction placed on the governor's authority by the secretary of state, forbidding him to spend more than £200 on any public project without the secretary of state's prior approval,[7] clearly inhibited his initiative with respect to all public works, roads included. The construction and repair of roads and mountain passes was expensive because distances were colossal and the terrain was difficult to cross. Confined, as Cole was, to a very limited budget there may well have been some decline in the standards of road maintenance. But the financial success of the toll over the Hottentots Holland Pass[8] suggests that this venture at least was a boon to the colony.

De Zuid-Afrikaan's attack on Cole for his failure to enact a vagrancy ordinance is an indicator of the racial bias of the newspaper. The question had agitated the minds of the white colonists ever since Ordinance 50 had been passed in July 1828. The freedom of movement it gave Khoikhoi and other free persons of colour must have caused some dislocation of the labour force. It was only human nature for those Khoikhoi who had had harsh masters to seek employment elsewhere or find a retreat in a mission station. Bourke had intended to couple Ordinance 50 with a vagrancy ordinance but when Cole became governor, soon after Ordinance 50 had been passed, he elected to give that ordinance "full scope to work unfettered by any restraints". He had hoped vagrancy would decrease with the passage of time and, in January 1831, he told the Council of Advice that he did not think he had been disappointed. However, he did think it was probably necessary to legislate to prevent vagrancy.[9]

According to *De Zuid-Afrikaan* a vagrancy ordinance was prepared, but Cole had not carried out the measure because he feared the influence of the *South African Commercial Advertiser* and "the Saints".[10]

There is no doubt that the humanitarians in Britain exercised considerable influence on colonial policy in the early thirties, and Fairbairn, the editor of the *South African Commercial Advertiser*, was associated with them because his newspaper had championed the Khoikhoi and supported British slave policy. Certainly Cole would have appreciated that any move he might make which appeared to place restrictions on the free non-white colonists would be severely criticised in Britain. It was arguable that a vagrancy ordinance would infringe on their liberty, was therefore a contradiction of Ordinance 50, and thus ultra vires. This may explain why Cole did not introduce the measure he had mentioned to the Council. Shortly after he left the Cape a draft ordinance was passed by a narrow majority in the Legislative Council, but it was disallowed by the Crown.[11]

De Zuid-Afrikaan's criticism of Cole for not suspending all, or part, of the Order in Council of November 1831 for the amelioration of the condition of the slaves in terms of the Order in Council of February 1832[12] suggests at best that the editor lacked commonsense or, more probably, sought to make political capital out of a distortion of the facts. Stanley, while secretary of state for War and the Colonial Department, was reported to have said that the later Order in Council gave to the governor and Council of Advice "the power to suspend the operation of the former Order."[13] But an examination of the Order shows that the governor was given discretionary power only in matters of detail.[14] There was never any intention of destroying the aims and spirit of British slave policy. *De Zuid-Afrikaan* therefore erroneously concluded that Cole's failure to exercise his discretion entirely in favour of the white colonists was "culpable neglect" of colonial interests.[15]

Neither of the two other newspapers at the Cape indulged in malicious criticism when Cole left the Cape though they did not disguise their dislike of the form of colonial government which then existed in the colony. The *Graham's Town Journal* described the period of Cole's administration as one of a "peculiar, critical, and delicate nature," and complimented Cole on his ability to avoid difficulties. "No Governor of the Cape," it said, "ever quitted this Colony who stood less chargeable with radical errors of government."[16] The *South African Commercial Advertiser* was only a shade less complimentary. It considered that it would be unfair to Cole "to review too rigidly" the acts and consequences of his government because his power and influence were so circumscribed by successive secretaries of state. But it did add that the Cape would be fortunate if subsequent governors had Cole's personal qualities of "simple honesty of heart, and sterling integrity of purpose".[17]

Clearly there was a fair measure of respect for Cole as governor and as an individual, but there was general criticism of some of the measures which he was called upon to introduce on behalf of the British Government. This led to criticism of the form of government and demands for a legislature more representative of colonial opinion. But the actual rôle played by Cole must have been impossible for any colonists to assess with accuracy. He was always strictly correct in his dealings with the public. He always aimed to interpret the intentions of the Colonial Department. Any criticism he had of measures proposed by the British Government were made only to those who were privileged to receive it, such as the secretary of state or the under-secretary in the Colonial Department, or to the Council of Advice. In any such cases his opinion would not be known to colonists. He was essentially a disinterested party who stood aloof from the problems which confronted him, yet tackled those problems with vigour to the best advantage of the colony he governed.

By 1823 reaction to the wars with Napoleon had given way to a new spirit of reform and reconstruction. British industry was so far in advance of the rest of the world that it was secure from the fear of foreign competition. Nevertheless, new markets and new sources of raw materials were vital if progress and expansion were to be maintained. Industrialists therefore welcomed as practical any solutions offered by the economic theory of Adam Smith. Artificial barriers in the form of fiscal protection were condemned as uneconomic. Businessmen anxious for profits sought to buy their raw materials on the lowest market and sell their finished product at the best possible price. There was not, however, any dramatic shift from protection to free trade. The process was evolutionary rather than revolutionary. And in the period under review the British Government moved forward to reduce discriminatory duties and to enlarge the area of trade open to British manufactures by negotiating treaties with foreign powers for reciprocal privileges of trade. This policy naturally had repercussions in the colonies which, though individual units themselves, were an integral part of British economic life.

The attack on economic protection struck a blow at the roots of privilege. New notions of the equality of man, discredited at first by the excesses of the French Revolution, had found a different philosophical basis and were given a new cloak of respectability by the teaching and philosophy of Jeremy Bentham. Bentham's maxim – it is the greatest happiness for the greatest number that is the measure of right and wrong – fitted well into the concept of British parliamentary government at that time, and provided an impetus to social reform both at home and abroad.

Industrialization was bringing greater fluidity into the structure of British society. Privilege was challenged. It did not give way gracefully, though it accepted the need to meet altered circumstances. This attitude is shown, for example, in the reform of the House of Commons itself in 1832. There was no call for revolution but an appeal to challenge outmoded principles. Thus a gradual change in British society was generated from within.

The experience of the colonies was very different from that of the metropolitan power. In the early nineteenth century the majority of the population in Mauritius and the Cape lived either directly or indirectly off the land. Much of the land was owned by white colonists while their labourers were slaves or free persons of colour. Thus the divisions of colonial society were made all the sharper by differences in culture and skin pigmentation. It was a structure, moreover, which the privileged white landowners had no desire to change and which the labourers were insufficiently powerful to challenge. In Mauritius the rigours of a plantation economy intensified the pattern after 1825 when the duties on Mauritian-grown sugar had been equalized with those from the West Indies when it was sold on the British market. At the Cape it was extended by the northward and eastward migrations of the colonists. And although the British settlers of 1820 were specifically forbidden slave labour they relied for their labour upon free coloured people. Thus the British settlers joined the colonists of Dutch descent in their approach to the question of colour. Indeed there was nothing in the pattern of society in either Mauritius or the Cape which remotely suggested that colonial society was prepared to remould itself to meet the requirements of Great Britain which represented the changing attitude of Europe to the question of colour.

In the third decade of the nineteenth century the British Government began to take measures to introduce into the British colonies principles conceived in Britain. It planned greater freedom of trade for the Empire, and it proposed to ameliorate the condition of slaves to prepare them for emancipation. The former was attractive to colonists because, with some exceptions like that of the wine industry at the Cape, trade increased. The latter, Mauritian colonists resented, not only because it threatened their privileged position, but also because it came at a time when increased economic opportunity put a premium on labour. At the Cape it was resented for the opposite reason. The wine trade was depressed, and legislation to ameliorate the condition of slaves appeared to slave-owners to be yet another threat to their investment of capital. Thus the move for social reform met stiff opposition in both Mauritius and the Cape. The British Government, however, was resolute in the application of its policies though it showed patience and some flexibility in matters of detail.

In the conquered colonies, where the authority of the British Government was unimpeded, it fell to the lot of the governor, armed with some of the powers of the Royal prerogative, to execute British policy. He was bound to obey his instructions from Britain however unpopular they were with a section of the colonists. This sometimes led to criticism that the British Government was out of touch with local conditions. It seems never to have occurred to critical white colonists that, for example, it was they who were out of touch with trends in Great Britain. However, the British Government was alive to colonial criticism, and indeed it was in response to complaints of the British settlers at the Cape about the governor[18] and the colonial government that the Cape was added to Mauritius and Ceylon in the terms of reference of the commissioners of eastern inquiry. The commissioners' investigations were conducted over several years and dealt with a wide range of topics of general concern for colonial government as well as inconsequential minutiae. Their reports which were submitted to the secretary of state for War and the Colonial Department are a mine of information. These gave officials both in the Colonial Department and in the colony detailed background knowledge of local conditions. Their recommendations for reform were treated with great respect although the secretary of state was obliged to modify or reject some. And even among those introduced, practice at the Cape showed that the reforms created new problems or could not be sustained on grounds of expense. Cole's work in Mauritius where he executed several changes unaided by the commissioners of inquiry, and the work he did at the Cape to resolve problems created through changes made on their recommendation, suggests that their contribution to policy making should not be exaggerated. They established facts which enabled the authorities responsible for government to take action. Policy decisions were taken by the British Government and the general spirit behind them was the introduction of British principles so far as this was compatible with the general interests of the whole community in the colony irrespective of colour, race, or creed.

Judicial reforms at the Cape, although they pleased the secretary of state, did not necessarily have the results anticipated. Some professionalism was infused into legal proceedings, but the introduction of the British system of trial by jury in criminal cases inhibited progress towards judicial impartiality for all freemen irrespective of colour. The qualifications for jurymen placed legal authority in criminal cases into the hands of the very people whose social and economic position was threatened by the broader application of British policy. But it could be argued that, given freedom to develop, free coloureds would in time qualify for jury service. The establishment of the principle of trial by jury, however, was an indication of the direction of British policy. It naturally pleased the privileged white colonists to discover that (by accident) they possessed a power which they could use to protect themselves from the full impact of social change. Moreover, the publication of a French translation of the Cape Charter of Justice of 1827 in the Mauritius *Government Gazette* in April 1828[19] would seem to have been intended as an indication to colonists in Mauritius of the principles behind the revision of their Charter then in progress.

The British Government required social change:[20] slaves were gradually to be prepared for emancipation and free people of colour made equal in law with those of pure European descent. But it seemed to privileged white colonists as if the British Government was intent on their ruin. Unrest was general in slave owning colonies. At the Cape, where the pattern and organization of slavery was totally at variance with the other colonial communities, the Consolidated Slave Order in Council of November 1831 suggested to slave-owners that the British Government had no real knowledge of local circumstances. The appeal of the governor for modification of the Order did bring a satisfactory response from the British Government but it came too late to eradicate from the minds of slave-owners convictions of the oppression of a foreign government whose social policies they abhorred. Not surprisingly, therefore, they sought to put a brake on the authority of the British Government by seeking a representative assembly. But, concerned as it was for the community as a whole, and determined to secure the improvement of the condition of the slaves and free coloured people, the British Government would have been irresponsible to have acquiesced in such demands. It therefore kept government in its own hands and those of its nominees. Meanwhile, at the Cape, towns and villages were empowered to elect boards of municipal commissioners to ease the pressure of work on local officials, give the inhabitants of these town and villages some control over purely local matters, and provide colonists with some experience of representative institutions.

A tremendous responsibility rested upon the shoulders of a colonial governor in the conquered colonies. He was the executor of policies which required changes in the structure of a society which left to itself would not have reformed. This caused antagonism and resentment and called for both tact and tenacity. The governor was fortunate to be aided by the improved economic opportunities offered by the changes in British trade regulations, as witness the development of the sugar industry in Mauritius. As stated, the Cape proved an exception to the rule. The removal of tariff protection for Cape wine sold in Britain could have seriously handicapped the Cape wine industry. Thus the governor persuaded the British Government to continue tariff protection for Cape wine in contradistinction to the general movement of British policy. But in addition to harmonizing policy in the colony with major policy decisions in Britain, a colonial governor had to contend with purely local problems. At the Cape, frontier conditions required constant vigilance, just as in Mauritius the distance of the dependencies from the main island called for special care in the suppression of the slave trade. Hurricanes, drought, administrative and financial problems all occupied the attention of the governor.

It was an exacting task for one man and it is not surprising that the British Government, which in any case disliked government by a single individual, created a council of officials with whom the governor could share responsibility. The governor's power remained considerable for he alone could initiate discussion, and there was no question but that the council was subordinate to the British Government in the last resort. But the council did put a brake on gubernatorial authority, especially as the governor was obliged to explain in detail to the secretary of state for War and the Colonial Department any action he took contrary to its advice. Moreover, successive secretaries of state encouraged the independence of thought of members of the council, and, on occasion, accepted policy amendments they recommended on the grounds that people on the spot should know best.

The constitutional and judicial changes at Mauritius and the Cape during Cole's governorships reflect the same pattern of government which Professor Harlow finds in the case of Quebec in 1774.[21] Former alien colonies had to be anglicized before constitutional advance could be made there. The question therefore arises, what did the British Government understand by anglicization? The term was a vague one and was never defined. It may have meant little more than the legal use of English for administration. But it seems to have meant more than a superficial acceptance of the English language and English political and judicial forms: it involved also – and perhaps unwittingly – an acceptance of principles of liberty and respect for the rule of law which had evolved within the homogeneous Anglo-Saxon community of Great Britain. In fact anglicization would seem to be an assimilation to British traditions and standards of values. As a policy it failed to make Englishmen out of French Canadians – and in Canada the question of colour was of no importance. In Mauritius and the Cape where there was not only the question of colonists of alien European descent but also a colour bar which divided master from servant in a conservative, mainly rural, community it was impossible to expect a fusion of racial groups even for political and judicial purposes. The formation of an integrated community was frustrated, and the spirit of freedom and legal equality logically inherent in anglicization was doomed.

Since the governor of a conquered colony was the servant of the Crown and therefore the executor of the British Government, it would seem at first sight that his was the rôle of little more than a mere administrator. But an examination of Cole's work in Mauritius and the Cape suggests that this was not the case. He played a vital part in the translation of policy into action. His skill lay in his ability to convert decisions taken in Britain into practical measures in the colony committed to his charge. Sometimes this was impossible. As the master of the colony then, it was the governor's duty to plead in mitigation for the colonists.

The serious attention given to his opinion by successive secretaries of state indicates the importance which the British Government put upon his advice. He was the man on the spot and was expected to be thoroughly conversant with local problems. Thus the success or failure of colonial policy depended considerably upon the rapport between the governor and the secretary of state.

On the whole, Cole was a successful governor. He was not given to personal flights of fancy and took a practical line in all matters that came before him. He never hesitated to draw the attention of the secretary of state to the problems of the colony he governed, and beg on behalf of colonists for a change of policy if he believed it to be in their best interest. Equally, he was firm in his determination to execute the King's government. He had great strength of character and superior administrative ability. Judge Burton in a private letter to General Bourke described Cole as "candid, open, warm-hearted, and a little passionate," but he did not think that he "had the art of making others work or the capacity for an application to work" that Bourke had.[22] This may have been so: it was the judgment of one close to the centre of power in the Cape. But the evidence suggests that Cole's work was done thoroughly, his administration was efficient, and the relationship between the governor and his principal officers almost always amicable. Hence his management of government was sound. When, on the one occasion in his ten years of office, civil disobedience seemed a probability he did not flinch from his duty. He was prepared to wield the iron hand of discipline without regard for personal popularity. It would be easy to criticise autocratic measures such as those Cole enforced in 1832 when civil disobedience threatened to disrupt the execution of unpopular slave legislation, but it did prevent any serious disturbance by slave-owners who bitterly resented government interference with their labour. The Consolidated Slave Order in Council of November 1831 was without doubt a blunder in the context of the Cape: that general dissatisfaction did not develop into open revolt must be attributed to Cole's sense of justice and resolute belief that the King's commands must not only be done, but seen to be done. This approach increased in the minds of white colonists at the Cape the conviction that the British Government had no understanding of the local situation. But the British Government, and Cole as its executor first in Mauritius and then at the Cape, was not concerned simply to forward the interest of one section of the population only but with all the King's subjects irrespective of colour, race or creed. Its policy was directed towards achieving the greatest good for the greatest number.

FOOTNOTES

1. See Chapter VII, pp. 119–120.
2. P.R.O. 30/43/95, Cole to Lady Grantham, 14 March 1832.
3. *Z.A.*, 30 March 1832.
4. See Chapter VII, pp. 119–120.
5. See Chapter VIII, p. 128.
6. *Z.A.*, 16 August 1833.
7. See Chapter VIII, p. 128.
8. *Ibid.*

9. C.A., A.C. 6 January 1831.
10. *Z.A.*, 30 August 1833. *The Saints* was the name given to a group of humanitarians in Britain who had led the anti-slavery movement. The group included among others men like Wilberforce, Zachary Macaulay, T. Fowell Buxton and the elder and younger James Stephen.
11. *C.H.B.E.*, Vol. VIII, (2nd edition), pp. 297–298.
12. See Chapter VII, pp. 119–120.
13. *Z.A.*, 29 November 1833.
14. See Chapter VII, p. 120.
15. *Z.A.*, 29 November 1833.
16. *G.T.J.*, 15 August 1833.
17. *S.A.C.A.*, 14 August 1833.
18. Lord Charles Somerset, see Chapter V, p. 94, fn. 92.
19. C.O. 171/3, Mauritius *Government Gazette*, 12, 19 and 26 April 1828.
20. See Chapter I, p. 21.
21. V. T. Harlow, *The Founding of the Second British Empire*, Vol. II, p. 713.
22. Rhodes House, Oxford, Mss t $\frac{7}{8}$, Bourke Papers, Burton to Bourke, 27 February 1831

APPENDIX A

POLITICAL OFFICIALS AT THE COLONIAL DEPARTMENT, 1812–1834

Period of Office	Secretary of State	Period of Office	Under-secretary
11.6.1812 to 29.4.1827	Earl Bathurst	11.6.1810 to 4.8.1812	R. Peel
		5.8.1812 to 11.12.1821	H. Goulburn
30.4.1827 to 16.8.1827	Viscount Goderich	12.12.1821 to 5.1.1828	R. J. Wilmot Horton[1]
17.8.1827 to 29.5.1828	W. Huskisson	15.10.1827 to 5.2.1828	Hon. E. G. Stanley[2]
		6.2.1828 to 30.5.1828	Lord Francis Leveson Gower
30.5.1828 to 21.11.1830	Sir George Murray	31.5.1828 to 21.11.1830	H. Twiss
22.11.1830 to 2.4.1833	Viscount Goderich	22.11.1830 to 2.4.1833	Viscount Howick
3.4.1833 to 4.6.1834	Viscount Stanley	3.4.1833 to 4.6.1834	J. G. Shaw-Lefevre

1. R. J. Wilmot Horton was first known as R. J. Wilmot. He added the name Horton by royal license on 8 May 1823.
2. Did not draw an official salary until 6 January 1828. R. W. Hay was appointed permanent under-secretary, 5 June 1825 and held office until 1836.

APPENDIX B

The number of slave-owners in each of the districts of the Cape of Good Hope is listed under four categories:

A. = Those with more than 8 slaves.

B. = Those with 8 slaves.

C. = Those with fewer than 8 slaves.

D. = Total

District	A	B	C	D
Cape Town & District	338	52	1 454	1 844
Stellenbosch	372	38	770	1 180
Worcester	122	28	422	572
Swellendam	104	29	595	728
George	117	17	278	412
Uitenhage	36	5	252	293
Albany	6	–	35	41
Somerset	50	18	339	407
Graaff-Reinet	73	27	430	530
Clan William	49	5	173	227
Beaufort	9	2	140	151
Totals	1 276	221	4 888	6 385

These figures are compiled from enclosures in C.O. 48/142, Cole to Goderich, 21 April 1831.

BIBLIOGRAPHY

I. MANUSCRIPT SOURCES

A. *Official*

There is necessarily duplication of material in the official records in London and Port Louis, and London and Cape Town. Copies of despatches were always kept but enclosures were not. These have to be found in the centre where the despatch was received. Moreover, departmental memoranda and pencil marginalia bound with despatches make examination of despatches in both centres worthwhile.

(1) *Colonial Office Records* deposited in the Public Record Office, Chancery Lane, London, W.C. 2.

(*a*) *General*

C.O. 323/144–165 – Private letters to R. W. Hay.
C.O. 324/73–74 – Private letters from earl Bathurst.
C.O. 324/75 – Minutes by earl Bathurst.
C.O. 324/76–78 – Private letters from R. W. Hay.
C.O. 324/94 – Private and unofficial letters from R. W. Hay.
C.O. 324/95–100 – Private letters from R. Wilmot Horton (1825–1827).
C.O. 324/101–102 – Private letters from viscount Goderich and W. Huskisson.
C.O. 324/105–6 – Circulars to governors.

(*b*) *Mauritius*

C.O. 167 – Original correspondence to the secretary of state. Special attention was paid to Volumes 3, 4, 5, 7, 66–101, and 103–4 which include despatches from the governor, and 126 which contains correspondence from the commissioners of eastern inquiry.
C.O. 168 – Colonial Department copies of correspondence from the secretary of state. Special attention was paid to Volumes 1, 2, and 6–14.
C.O. 170/1 – Minutes of governor's advisory council.
C.O. 172/39–42 – Manuscript copy of *Statisque de l'Ile Maurice* by d'Unienville.
C.O. 172/43–52 – Blue books of statistical information.

(*c*) *The Cape of Good Hope*

C.O. 48 – Original correspondence to the secretary of state. Special attention was paid to Volumes 124–151 which include some correspondence from the commissioners of eastern inquiry and despatches from the governor.
C.O. 49 – Colonial Department copies of correspondence from the secretary of state. Special attention was paid to Volumes 16, 19, 21–25, and 124.
C.O. 50/1 – Ordinances of the Cape of Good Hope, 1825–1843. (Several ordinances passed during the period of Sir Lowry Cole's administration of the Cape are missing from this volume).
C.O. 52/64–70 – Blue books of statistical information.
C.O. 414/1–18 – Records of the commissioners of eastern inquiry concerning the Cape of Good Hope.

(*d*) *West Indies*

C.O. 112/5 – Despatches to governor of Demerara and Essequibo, 11 January 1817 to 19 April 1824 re amelioration of the condition of the slaves.
C.O. 296/4 – The secretary of state to the governor of Trinidad, 1810.
C.O. 318/69 – Report of the commissioners of legal inquiry into the West Indies.

(2) *Admiralty Records* deposited in the Public Record Office, Chancery Lane, London, W.C. 2.
Adm 1/69–70 – Despatches from the commodore, Cape of Good Hope Station concerning the slave trade in Mauritius.

(3) *War Office Records* deposited in the Public Record Office, Chancery Lane, London, W.C. 2.
W.O. 1/342 – in which is bound the Articles of Capitulation signed by the Dutch authorities at the Cape in 1806.

(4) *Mauritian Colonial Government Records* deposited in the Mauritius Archives, Sir William Newton Street, Port Louis, Mauritius.
S.A. Volumes 6–13 – Original correspondence of the secretary of state to the governor.

S.D. Volumes 7–10 – Copies of correspondence from the governor to the secretary of state.
R.A. Volumes 247–385 – Minutes of governor's advisory council and the governor's minutes.

(5) *Cape of Good Hope Colonial Government Records* deposited in the Cape Archives, Queen Victoria Street, Cape Town.
G.H. 1/15–20 – Original correspondence of the secretary of state to the governor.
G.H. 23/9–11 – Copies of correspondence of the governor to the secretary of state.
C.O. 336, 367, 373, 390, 402 – Letters received by officials in the government offices in Cape Town (including the governor) from the commissioner-general for the eastern districts.
C.O. 4899, 4900 and 4903 – Copies of correspondence from the secretary to the colonial government to the commissioner-general for the eastern districts.
C.O. 5302 – Copies of miscellaneous correspondence from the secretary to the colonial government from 15 September 1828 to 5 August 1833.
C.O. 5970–5975 – Blue books of statistical information 1828–1833 inclusive. There is no blue book in the Archives for 1832.
A.C. 1–13 – Minutes of the Council of Advice and appendices. Appendix C to the minutes is missing.

B. *Public Societies*

i) *Anti-Slavery Society* minutes deposited at Rhodes House, Oxford. Volume E2 was of special interest because it includes a statement of the impression of the views of Sir George Murray on the question of slavery gauged by a deputation from the Anti-Slavery Society in an interview, 9 February 1830.
ii) Records of the *London Missionary Society* deposited at the Congregational Council for World Mission, Livingstone House, 11 Carteret Street, London, S.W. 1.

(*a*) *Mauritius*
Box 1, Folders 1–4 were examined. These folders contain letters from various people (among them the governor and J. le Brun, a missionary belonging to the London Missionary Society) from 1813 to 1836.

(*b*) *The Cape of Good Hope*
Boxes 10, 11, 12 and 13 were examined. These boxes contain letters from several missionaries (including Dr. J. Philip) working at the Cape and beyond the colonial frontier to the secretary of the London Missionary Society in London from 1826 to 1833.

C. *Private Papers*

Bathurst Papers – deposited in the British Museum. Bloomsbury, London, W.C. 1. Special attention was paid to Loan 57, Volumes 14–17, 23, 55–58 and 64.
Bourke Papers – deposited at Rhodes House, Oxford. Special attention was paid to Volumes Mss. Afr. $\frac{7}{8}$.
Cole Papers – deposited in the Public Record Office, Chancery Lane, London, W.C. 2. The entire series classified at P.R.O. 30/43 were used.
Dalhousie Papers – deposited in the National Library of Scotland, Princes Street, Edinburgh, include a couple of letters from Cole.
Goderich Papers – deposited in the Buckinghamshire County Record Office, Aylesbury, but little of interest to the present study was found there.
Huskisson Papers – deposited in the British Museum, Bloomsbury, London, W.C. 1. Special attention was paid to Volumes Add. Mss. 38291, 38298–302.
Philip Papers – (i.e. transcription made by W. M. MacMillan) deposited at Rhodes House, Oxford. Special attention was paid to Mss. Afr. S216, 219A, and 219B.
Ripon Papers – deposited in the British Museum, Bloomsbury, London, W.C. 1. Special attention was paid to Add. Mss. 40862–3, and 40878–80.

II. PRINTED PRIMARY SOURCES

A. *Parliamentary Papers*
Unless indicated by the abbreviations H.L. for House of Lords, or C.P. for Command Paper, the references given below are to House of Commons' Papers.

(*a*) *General*
1820, II (300) – Report from the Select Committee on improving the foreign trade of the country.
1824, XXIII (160) – Colonial acts re treatment of slaves.
1824, H.L., CLXXIV – Papers re amelioration of slavery.
1826, XXVI (332) – Instructions for commissioners of eastern inquiry.

1826, C.P., XXIX – Papers presented to Parliament by His Majesty's Command in explanation of the measures adopted by His Majesty's Government for the amelioration of the condition of the slave population in His Majesty's possessions in the West Indies and on the Continent of South America.
1826–7, XXIII (465) – Slave laws and regulations re labour.
1826–7, XXV, pp. 53 and 347 – Papers re measures of amelioration.
1830–1, XVI (305) – Abstract of slave population in each colony.
1831–2, XLVI (279), (649), (733) – Papers re consolidation of slave laws.
1833, XII (717) – Treasury minute (1831) on the expenditure and revenue of the colonies.

(*b*) *Mauritius*
1826, III (430) – Report from Select Committee on slave trade.
1826–7, VI (90) – Minutes of slave trade committee.
1826–7, XVIII (283), (346) – Papers re sugar exported, 1812–25.
1826–7, XXII (68), (14), (5), (376) – Correspondence with the governor of Mauritius re slave trade.
1828, XXV (206) – Correspondence re slaves at Seychelles.
1829, XXV (292) – Report of commissioners of eastern inquiry on the slave trade in Mauritius.
1830, XXI (212), (352) – Correspondence re finances.
1830, XXVII (354), (393) – Accounts re sugar exported, 1825–30.

(*c*) *The Cape of Good Hope*
1826–7, XXI (202) – Cape Papers re slaves. Proclamations from 1809 to 1823 showing care for the interests of the slaves and restrictions on the powers of their owners.
1826–7, XXI (282), (406) – Cape, Reports of commissioners of eastern inquiry on government and finances, 6 September 1826.
1826–7, XXI (371) – Papers re administration of the Cape of Good Hope, December 1821–April 1826.
1826–7, XXII (129) – Slave trade and slavery at the Cape of Good Hope.
1826–7, XXV (335) – Reports from protectors of slaves including the Cape of Good Hope.
1829, V (300) – Report of the commissioners of eastern inquiry on the trade, harbours, and navigation of the Cape 3 October 1828.
1829, XXV (339) – Orders in Council re natives of South Africa.
1830, XXI (8) – Order in Council re colonial slave laws.
1830, XXI (584) – Report of commissioners of eastern inquiry on native tribes and missionary institutions at the Cape of Good Hope, 28 January 1830.
1830–1, XVI (230) – Papers re slaves at the Cape of Good Hope.
1834, XLIV (617) – Proclamations re aborigines at the Cape of Good Hope.
1835, XXXIX (50), (252) – Papers re aborigines at the Cape of Good Hope.
1836, VII (538) – Report of Select Committee re aborigines in British colonies, August 1836, T. F. Buxton, chairman. (Minutes, appendix and index only).
1836, I (471) – Bill for the punishment of offences within certain territories adjacent to the Cape of Good Hope.
1837, VII (425) – Further report from Select Committee on aborigines, 1830–6, T. F. Buxton chairman.

B. *Acts of Parliament*
1. *The Statutes at Large from Magna Charta to the forty-first year of King George the Third*, by Owen Ruffhead, 18 Volumes, London, 1769–1800.
2. *The Statutes of the United Kingdom of Great Britain and Ireland*, with notes, references and an index by T. E. Tomlins, J. Raithby, H. Simons, C. D. Bevan and G. F. Rickards. 29 Volumes, (From 41 George III to 33 Victoria, 1800–1869), London, 1804–1869.

C. *Parliamentary Debates*
Cobbett's Parliamentary Debates – Volumes I to XXII cover the period from November 1803 to 4 May 1812.
Parliamentary Debates – printed by T. C. Hansard on behalf of several editors, but a continuation of the former series. Volumes XXIII to XLI cover the period 5 May 1812 to 28 February 1820.
Parliamentary Debates – published under the superintendence of T. C. Hansard, second series. Volumes I to XXV cover the period 21 April 1820 to 23 July 1830.
Parliamentary Debates – published under the superintendence of T. C. Hansard, third series. Volumes I to XX cover the period 26 October 1830 to 29 August 1833.

D. *Official Publications*

(*a*) *General*
London Gazette – Set available at the Institute of Historical Research, Senate House, University of London, Malet Street, London, W.C. 1. The volume for 1811 was used.

(*b*) *Mauritius*

Government Gazette 1823–1828 – deposited in the Public Record Office, Chancery Lane, London, W.C. 2, and classified in C.O. 171/1–3.

(*c*) *The Cape of Good Hope*

Government Gazette 1828–1833 – deposited in the Public Record Office, Chancery Lane, London, W.C. 2, and classified in C.O. 52/1–6.

E. *Collections of Documents*

(*a*) *General*

Bathurst Papers – Report on the manuscripts of earl Bathurst, preserved at Cirencester Park, edited by F. Bickley, *Historical Manuscripts Commission* number 76, 1923.

Bell, K. W. and Morrell, W. P. – *Select Documents on British Colonial Policy, 1830–1860*, Oxford 1928.

British and Foreign State Papers 1812 – compiled by the Librarian and Keeper, Foreign Office. London 1832 –

Harlow, V. T. and Madden, A. F. – *British Colonial Developments, 1774–1834*, Oxford, 1953.

Keith, A. B. – *Selected Speeches and Documents on British Colonial Policy, 1763–1917*. 2 Volumes. Oxford, 1918; republished in one Volume 1961.

Madden, A. F. – *Imperial Constitutional Documents, 1765–1965: A Supplement*. Oxford, 1966.

(*b*) *Mauritius*

Napal, D. – *Les constitutions de l'Ile Maurice: documents réunis*. Mauritius archives publication, number 6. Port Louis, 1962.

(*c*) *The Cape of Good Hope*

Eybers, G. W. – *Select Constitutional Documents illustrating South African History (1795–1810)*. London, 1918.

Harding, W. – *The Cape of Good Hope Proclamations from 1806 to 1825, as now in force and unrepealed, and the Ordinances passed in Council from 1825–1839*. 2 Volumes. Cape Town, 1839.

Theal, G. McC. – *Records of the Cape Colony from February 1793 to April 1831*. 35 Volumes. Printed for the government of the Cape Colony. London, 1897 to 1905.

F. *Contemporary Newspapers and Almanacs*

1. *The Graham's Town Journal* published in Grahamstown and retained in the Cory Library, Rhodes University, Grahamstown. The first number was published on 30 December 1831. The British Museum depository at Colindale has copies of the newspaper from 23 March 1832. All issues to December 1833, during which period the paper was published weekly, were consulted.
2. *The South African Commercial Advertiser* published in Cape Town and retained in the South African Public Library, Cape Town. Copies of this paper are available in the British Museum newspaper depository at Colindale. The first number was published on 7 January 1824, but the paper was twice suspended by government order, i.e. 10 May 1824 to 31 August 1825, and from 10 March 1827 to 3 October 1828. All issues from 3 October 1828 to December 1833, during which period the newspaper was published twice weekly, were consulted.
3. *De Zuid-Afrikaan* published in Cape Town and retained in the South African Public Library, Cape Town. Copies of the paper are available in the British Museum newspaper depository at Colindale. The first number of the paper was published on the 9 April 1830. All issues to December 1833, during which period the newspaper was published twice weekly, were consulted.

G. *Contemporary Periodicals*

The Anti-Slavery Monthly Reporter, 1826–1834, published in London by the Anti-Slavery Society and retained in the British Museum, Bloomsbury, London W.C. 1.

H. *Contemporary Books and Memoirs*

(*a*) *General*

Huskisson, W. – *The Speeches of the Rt. Hon. W. Huskisson*. 3 Volumes. London, 1831.

Martin, R. M. – *Statistics of the Colonies of the British Empire*. London, 1839.

Porter, G. R. – *Progress of the Nation in its various Social and Economical Relations*. London, 1847. Subsequently edited by F. W. Hirst, and republished, London, 1912.

(*b*) *Mauritius*

D'Unienville, M. – *Statisque de l'Ile Maurice* (A Manuscript copy of this work is available in the Public Record Office, C.O. 172/39–42). 1838.

Flemyng, F. P. – *Mauritius, or the Isle of France – An account of the Island, its history, geography, products and inhabitants*. London, 1862.

Milbert, M. J. – *Voyage pittoresque a l'Ile de France*. 2 Volumes. Paris, 1812.
North-Coombes, A. – *The Evolution of Sugar Cane Culture in Mauritius*. Port Louis, 1837.
Pridham, C. – *England's Colonial Empire: An Historical, Political and Statistical Account of the Empire, its Colonies and Dependencies:* Volume I, 'The Mauritius and its Dependencies'. London, 1846.
Stirling, E. – *Cursory notes on the Isle of France made in 1827*. Calcutta, 1833.
Telfair, C. – *Some account of the State of Slavery at Mauritius since the British occupation in 1810*. Port Louis, 1830.
Vicars, R. – *Representation of the State of Government Slaves and Apprentices in the Mauritius*. London, 1830.

(c) *The Cape of Good Hope*
Chase, J. C. – *Practical considerations on the exact position of the slave question*. Cape Town, 1831.
Chase, J. C. – *The Cape of Good Hope and Eastern Province of Algoa Bay*. London, 1843, republished Cape Town, 1967.
Hutton, C. W. (ed.) – *The Autobiography of Sir Andries Stockenstrom, Bart*. Cape Town, 1887.
Long, U. (ed.) – *The Chronicle of Jeremiah Goldswain*. Volume I (1819–1836). Van Riebeeck Society Publication, number 27, Cape Town 1946.
Miller, T. – *Consideration of the exact position of the slave question*. Cape Town, 1831.
Moffat, R. – *Missionary Labours and Scenes in Southern Africa*. London, 1842.
Philip, J. – *Researches in South Africa*. 2 Volumes. London, 1828.
Pringle, T. – *Narrative of a Residence in South Africa*. London, 1834, edited by A. M. L. Robinson and republished Cape Town, 1966.
Rose, C. – *Four years in South Africa* – London, 1829.
Wilmot, A. and Chase, J. C. – *A History of the Colony of the Cape of Good Hope from its discovery to the year 1819, and from 1820 to 1868*. Cape Town, 1869.
Wright, W. – *Slavery at the Cape of Good Hope*. London, 1831.

III. SECONDARY SOURCES

(1) *Bibliographies and Guides*
Apart from standard library indexes and catalogues, reference was made to the following bibliographical works. With three notable exceptions this list does not include the bibliographies to be found in the more reputable secondary works, which were nevertheless frequently used.

(a) *General*
Adam, M., Ewing, I., and Munro, J. (ed.) – *Guide to Parliamentary Papers relating to the Dominions*. Edinburgh, 1913.
Ford, P., and G. – *A Guide to Parliamentary Papers*. Oxford, 1955.
Guiseppe, M. S. and others, (ed.) – *Guide to the contents of the Public Record Office* Volume II. London, 1963
Hewitt, A. R. – *Guide to Resources for Commonwealth Studies in London, Oxford and Cambridge: with biographical and other information*. London, 1957.
Institute of Commonwealth Studies – File on theses in progress and completed at universities in the United Kingdom on colonial and commonwealth subjects.
Institute of Historical Research – Bulletin – review on books published, and lists of theses completed in Britain, and current work in progress. London, 1923–
National Register of Archives – Files kept at Quality Court, Chancery Lane, London, W.C. 2.

(b) *Mauritius*
Holland Rose, J., Newton, A. P., and Benians, E. A. (ed.) – *Cambridge History of the British Empire*, Volume II, bibliography. Cambridge, 1940 reprinted 1961.
Toussaint, A. and Adolphe, H. *Bibliography of Mauritius*, 1502–1954. Port Louis, 1956.
—Supplements to the above are published in the *Annual Report of the Mauritius Archives Department 1955–1967*. Port Louis, 1956–1968.

(c) *The Cape of Good Hope*
—*Africana Notes and News*, published by the Africana Society, Africana Museum. Johannesburg, 1943–
—*Bibliography of African Bibliographies*, fourth edition published by The South African Public Library. Cape Town, 1961.
—*Bibliographical Series Consolidated List*, 1941–1966, published by the University of Cape Town Libraries. Cape Town, 1966.
Hinchliff, P. (compiler) – *Calendar of Missionary Correspondence from the Colony of the Cape of Good Hope, compiled from the Archives of the English Missionary Societies*, published by the National Council for Social Research, Pretoria, 1967.

Lewin Robinson, A. M. (compiler) – *Catalogue of Theses and Dissertations accepted for Degrees by South African Universities, 1818–1941.* Cape Town, 1943.
Ferdinand Postma Library, University of Potchefstroom (compilers) – *Union Catalogue of Theses and Dissertations of South African Universities*, Supplements 1–7. Potchefstroom, 1960.
Holland Rose, J., Newton, A. P., and Benians, E. A. (ed.) – *Cambridge History of the British Empire.* Volume VIII, bibliography, 2nd edition, Cambridge, 1963.
Long, U. (compiler) – *An index to authors of unofficial privately owned manuscripts relating to the History of South Africa, 1812–1920.* Cory Library, Rhodes University, Grahamstown, 1941.
Malan, S. I. (compiler) – *Union Catalogue of Theses and Dissertations of South African Universities, 1942–58.* Potchefstroom, 1959.
Mendelssohn, S. – *South African Bibliography.* 2 Volumes. London, 1910.
Muller, C. F. J., van Jaarsveld, F. A. and van Wijk, T. – *A Select Bibliography of South African History*, published by the University of South Africa. Pretoria, 1966.
Register of Current Research in the Humanities in South Africa, published by the Government Printer, Pretoria. Pretoria, 1963–
Union List of South African Newspapers, November 1949, published by the South African Library. Cape Town, 1950.
United Kingdom Publications and Theses on Africa, 1963, 1964 and 1965, compiled by the Standing Conference on Library Materials on Africa, published by W. Heffer and Sons. Cambridge 1966 and 1967.
Theses on Africa accepted by Universities in the United Kingdom and Ireland, compiled by the Standing Conference on Library Materials on Africa, and published by W. Heffer and Sons. Cambridge 1964.
van der Walt, A. J. H., Wiid, J. A., and Geyer, A. L. – *Geskiedenis van Suid-Afrika*, bibliography. 2nd edition, Cape Town, 1965

(2) *Monographs*

(*a*) *General*

Armytage, F. – *The Free Port System in the British West Indies.* London, 1953.
Aspinall, A. – *The Cabinet Council, 1783–1835.* London, 1952.
Aspinall, A. – *Cornwallis in Bengal.* Manchester, 1931.
Bartlett, C. J. – *Great Britain and Sea Power, 1815–1853.* Oxford, 1963.
Bearce, G. D. – *British Attitudes towards India, 1784–1858.* Oxford, 1961.
Bentham, J. (ed. with an introduction by Montague, F. C.) – *A Fragment on Government.* Oxford, 1891.
Binney, J. E. D. – *British Public Finance and Administration, 1774–92.* Oxford, 1958.
Brady, A. – *William Huskisson and Liberal Reform.* London, 1928.
Briggs, A. – *The Age of Improvement.* London, 1959.
Brock, W. R. – *Lord Liverpool and Liberal Toryism, 1820–27.* Cambridge, 1941.
Burn, W. L. – *The British West Indies.* London, 1951.
Burns, A. *History of the British West Indies.* London, 1954.
Burroughs, P. – *Britain and Australia 1831–1855: A Study in Imperial Relations and Crown Lands Administration.* Oxford, 1967.
Burt, A. L. – *Evolution of the British Empire and Commonwealth from the American Revolution.* Boston, 1956.
Carmichael, G. – *The History of the West Indian Islands of Trinidad and Tobago, 1498–1900.* London, 1961.
Chalmers, R. – *A History of Currency in the British Colonies.* London, preface 1893.
Checkland, S. G. – *The Rise of Industrial Society in England, 1815–1855.* London, 1964.
Clapham, J. H. – *The Economic History of Modern Britain; the Early Railway Age, 1820–1850.* London, 1926.
Cohen, E. W. – *The Growth of the British Civil Service, 1789–1939.* London, 1941.
Cole, M. L. and Gwynn, S. – *The Memoirs of Sir Lowry Cole.* London, 1934.
Coupland, R. – *East Africa and its Invaders.* Oxford, 1938.
Coupland, R. – *The British Anti-Slavery Movement.* London, 1933– republished 1964 with new introduction by J. D. Fage.
Coupland, R. – *Wilberforce.* Oxford, 1923.
Cumpston, I. M. – *Indians Overseas in British Territories, 1834–1854.* London, 1953.
Egerton, H. E. – *A Short History of British Colonial Policy.* 9th edition, London, 1928.
Fay, C. R. – *Huskisson and His Age.* London, 1951.
Fieldhouse, D. K. – *The Colonial Empires.* London, 1966.
Foord, A. S. – *His Majesty's Opposition 1714–1830.* Oxford, 1964.
Fraser, L. M. – *History of Trinidad.* 2 Volumes. 1891–1896.
Gash, N. – *Mr. Secretary Peel.* London and Southampton, 1961.
Graham, G. S. – *The Politics of Naval Supremacy.* Cambridge, 1965.
Graham, G. S. – *Great Britain in the Indian Ocean, 1810–1850.* Oxford, 1967.

Grant, F. J. (ed.) – *The Faculty of Advocates in Scotland, 1532–1943*. Edinburgh, 1944.
Hahlo, H. R. and Kahn, E. – *South Africa, the Development of its Laws and Constitutions*. London and Cape Town, 1960.
Harlow, V. T. – *The Founding of the Second British Empire*, 2 Volumes. Volume I, London, 1952. Volume II, London, 1964.
Holland Rose, J., Newton, A. P. and Benians, E. A. (ed.) – *The Cambridge History of The British Empire*, 8 Volumes:
—Volume I, 'The Old Empire from the beginning to 1783'. Cambridge, 1929 reprinted 1960.
—Volume II, 'The New Empire 1783–1870'. Cambridge, 1940 reprinted 1961.
—Volume III, 'The Empire-Commonwealth, 1870–1919'. Cambridge, 1959.
—Volume IV 'British India, 1497–1858'. Cambridge, 1929.
—Volume V, 'The Indian Empire 1858–1918', with chapters on the development of Administration 1818–58. Cambridge, 1932.
—Volume VI. 'Canada and Newfoundland'. Cambridge, 1930.
—Volume VII. part I. 'Australia'. Cambridge, 1933. part II. 'New Zealand' Cambridge, 1933.
—Volume VIII. South Africa. 2nd edition, Cambridge, 1963.
Hoskins, H. L. – *British Routes to India*. London, 1928.
Imlah, A. H. – *Economic Elements in the Pax Britannica*. Cambridge, Mass., 1958.
Jackson, M. V. – *European Powers and South-East Africa*. London, 1942.
Jackson, R. M. – *The Machinery of Justice in England*. 4th edition, Cambridge, 1964.
Jenkyns, H. – *British Rule and Jurisdiction beyond the Seas*. Oxford, 1902.
Jones, W. D. – *Prosperity Robinson: the Life of Viscount Goderich, 1782–1859*. New York, 1967.
Judd, G. P. – *Members of Parliament, 1784–1832*. New Haven and London, 1955.
Keith, A. B. – *Constitutional History of the First British Empire*. Oxford, 1930.
Keir, D. L. – *The Constitutional History of Modern Britain Since 1485*. 9th edition London, 1969.
Knapland, P. – *The British Empire, 1815–1939*. London, 1942.
Knaplund, P. – *James Stephen and the British Colonial System, 1813–1847*. Madison, 1953.
Knorr, K. E. – *British Colonial Theories, 1570–1850*. Toronto, 1944.
Knowles, L. C. A. – *Economic Development of the Overseas Empire*, Volumes I and III. London, 1924.
Kuczinski, R. R. – *Demographic Survey of the British Colonial Empire*, Volume III. Oxford, 1949.
Lovett, R. – *The History of the London Missionary Society, 1795–1895*. London, 1899.
Lloyd, C. – *The Navy and the Slave Trade*. London, 1949.
Madden, A. F., and Robinson, K. (ed.) – *Essays in Imperial Government presented to Margery Perham*. Oxford, 1963.
Majumdar, R. C., Raychaundhuri, H. C. and Datta, K. – *An Advanced History of India*. London, 1963.
Manning, H. T. – *British Colonial Government after the American Revolution*. New Haven, 1933.
Mathieson, W. L. – *British Slavery and its Abolition 1823–1838*. London, 1926.
Melbourne, A. C. V. – *Early Constitutional Development in Australia, New South Wales, 1788-1856*. Oxford, 1935, reprinted Sydney, 1963.
Mellor, G. R. – *British Imperial Trusteeship, 1783–1850*. London, 1951.
Mendis, G. C. *The Colebrooke-Cameron Papers*, 2 Volumes. London, 1956.
Mills, A. – *Colonial Constitutions: An outline of the Constitutional History and Existing Government of the British Dependencies, with schedules of the Orders in Council, Statutes, and Parliamentary Documents relating to each dependency*. London, 1856.
Muir, R. – *The Making of British India, 1756–1858*. Manchester, 1915.
Murray, D. J. – *The West Indies and the Development of Colonial Government*. Oxford, 1965.
Neatby, H. – *Quebec: the Revolutionary Age 1760–1791*. London, 1966.
Parris, H. – *Constitutional Bureaucracy*. London, 1969.
Philips, C. H. – *The East India Company, 1784–1834*. Manchester, 1940.
Platt, D. C. M. – *Finance, Trade and Politics: British Foreign Policy 1815–1914*. Oxford, 1968.
Reis, C. – *The Government of Trinidad, being a brief history of its government and laws under Spanish and British rule*. 1st edition, London, 1915.
Roberts-Wray, K. – *Commonwealth and Colonial Law*. London, 1966.
Schuyler, R. L. – *The Fall of the Old Colonial System, a study in British Free Trade, 1770–1870*. New York, 1945.
Steven Watson, J. – *The Reign of George III, 1760–1815*. Oxford, 1960.
Warner, O. – *William Wilberforce*. London, 1962.
Webster, C. K. – *The Foreign Policy of Castlereagh*. London, 1931.
Wight, M. – *The Development of the Legislative Council 1606–1945*. London, 1945.
Williams, E. – *Capitalism and Slavery*. Chapel Hill, North Carolina, 1944.
Woodward, E. L. – *The Age of Reform 1815–1870*. 2nd edition, Oxford, 1962.
Wrong, H. *The Government of the West Indies*. Oxford, 1923.
Young, D. M. – *The Colonial Office in the early Nineteenth Century*. London, 1961.

(b) Mauritius
Barnwell, P. J. and Toussaint, A. – *A Short History of Mauritius*. London, 1949.
Benedict, B. – *Indians in a Plural Society*. London, 1961.
Benedict, B. – *Mauritius, the problems of a plural society*. London, 1965.
de Burg-Edwards, S. B. – *The History of Mauritius, 1507–1914*. London, 1921.
Pitot, A. – *L'Ile Maurice 1810–1833*. Port Louis, 1910.
Scott, R. – *Limuria: the Lesser Dependencies of Mauritius*. London, 1961.
Toussaint, A. – *History of the Indian Ocean*. London, 1966.
Walter, A. – *The Sugar Industry of Mauritius*. London, 1910.

(c) South Africa, including the Cape of Good Hope
Botha, C. G. – *Administration of the Cape, 1653–1834*. Cape Town, 1926.
Brookes, E. H. – *The History of Native Policy in South Africa from 1830 to the present day*. Cape Town, 1934.
Brookes, E. H. and Webb, C. de B. – *A History of Natal*. Cape Town, 1965.
Cory, G. – *The Rise oj South Africa*. 5 volumes London, 1910–1930. Chapters I to VI of Volume VI were published posthumously in the *Archives Year Book for South African History, 1939*, part I. Cape Town, 1940.
de Kock, M. H. – *Economic History of South Africa*. Cape Town, 1924.
Dracopoli, J. L. – *Sir Andries Stockenström: the origins of the racial conflict in South Africa*. Cape Town, 1969.
Duly, L. – *British Land Policy at the Cape, 1795–1844*. Durham, N.C. 1968.
du Plessis, I. D. – *The Cape Malays*. Cape Town, 1944.
du Plessis, J. – *A History of Christian Mission in South Africa*. London, 1911.
Edwards, I. E. – *The 1820 Settlers in South Africa*. London, 1934.
Edwards, I. E. – *Towards Emancipation: a Study in South African Slavery*. Cardiff, 1942.
Galbraith, J. S. – *Reluctant Empire: British Colonial Policy on the South African Frontier, 1834–1854*. Berkeley and Los Angeles, 1963.
Hofmeyr, J. H. (in collaboration with F. W. Reitz) – *The Life of Jan Hendrik Hofmeyr*. Cape Town, 1913.
Keppel-Jones, A. (in consultation with Heathcote, E. K.) – *Philipps, 1820 Settler*. Pietermaritzburg, 1960.
Kilpin, R. *Romance of a Colonial Parliament*. London, 1930.
Leipoldt, C. F. L. – *Three Hundred Years of Cape Wine*. Cape Town, 1952.
MacMillan, W. M. – *The Cape Colour Question*. London, 1927.
MacMillan, W. M. – *Bantu, Boer, and Briton*. London, 1929.
Majeke, N. – *The Role of the Missionary in Conquest*. Cape Town, no date.
Malherbe, E. G. – *Education in South Africa, 1652–1922*. Cape Town, 1925.
Marais, J. S. – *The Cape Coloured People 1652–1937*. London, 1939, reprinted by University of the Witwatersrand Press 1962.
Marais, J. S. – *Maynier and the First Boer Republic*. Cape Town, 1944.
Miller, A. K. – *Plantagenet in South Africa*. London, 1965.
Neumark, S. D. – *The South African Frontier*. Stanford, 1957.
Omer-Cooper, J. D. – *The Zulu Aftermath*. London, 1966.
Schapera, I. – *The Khoisan Peoples of South Africa*. London, 1930 reprinted 1960.
Schreuder, D. M. – *Gladstone and Kruger*. London and Toronto, 1969.
Schumann, C. G. W. – *Structural Changes and Business Cycles in South Africa*. London, 1938.
Seligman, C. G. – *Races of Africa*. 3rd edition, Oxford, 1957.
Soga, J. H. – *The South-Eastern Bantu*. Johannesburg, 1930.
Theal, G. McC. – *History of South Africa, 1795–1872*, Volumes I to V. Facsimile edition, Cape Town, 1964.
Walker, E. A. – *A History of Southern Africa*. 3rd edition, 1957, re-issued with corrections, 1959, new impression 1965, London.
Williams, D. – *When Races Meet*. Johannesburg, 1961.
Wilson, M. and Thompson, L. (ed.) – *The Oxford History of South Africa*, Volume I. Oxford, 1969.

(3) *Articles in Periodicals*

(a) General
Beaglehole, J. C. – The royal instructions to colonial governors; 1783–1854: a study in British colonial policy. *Bulletin of the Institute of Historical Research* Volume VII, number 21.
Beaglehole, J. C. – 'The Colonial Office 1782–1854. *Historical Studies of Australia and New Zealand* Volume I (1941).
King, A. H. K. – 'Sir Richard Bourke and his two colonial administrations, a comparative study of Cape Colony and New South Wales'. *Royal Australian Historical Society: Journal and Proceedings* Volume 49.
Manning, H. T. – 'The Colonial Policy of the Whig Ministers, 1830–1837'. *Canadian Historical Review* (1952) Volume XXXIII.

Manning, H. T. – 'Colonial Crises before the Cabinet, 1829–1835'. *Bulletin of the Institute of Historical Research* Volume XXX (1957).

(*b*) *Cape of Good Hope*

Gailey, H. A. (Jr.) – 'John Philip's Role in Hottentot Emancipation'. *The Journal of African History*, Volume III, number 3, 1962.

Hammond-Tooke, W. D. – 'Segmentation and Fission in Cape Nguni Political Units'. *Africa*, Volume XXXV, number 2, April 1965.

Hancock, W. K. – 'Trek'. *Economic History Review*, Second Series, Volume X, 1957–58.

Lye, W. F. – 'The Difaqane: the Mfecane in the Southern Sotho area 1822–1824'. *The Journal of African History*, Volume VIII, number 1, 1967.

Oliver, R. – 'The Problem of Bantu Expansion'. *The Journal of African History*, Volume VII, number 3, 1966.

Reyburn, H. A. – 'Studies in Frontier History'. Six articles. *The Critic*, A South African Quarterly Journal, October 1934 to February 1936.

Robertson, H. M. – '150 Years of Economic Contact between Black and White', part I. *The South African Journal of Economics*, Volume II, 1934.

Roberts, M. – 'Lord Charles Somerset and the 'Beaufort Influence'.' *Archives Year Book for South African History*, Volume II, (1951).

van Warmelo, N. J. – 'History of the amaNgwane Tribe'. *Ethnological Publications* Volume VIII, Department of Native Affairs, Union of South Africa, 1938.

(4) *Unpublished Article*

G. E. C. (the initials of Sir George Cory) – 'A Short History of Slavery at the Cape'. Typescript prepared for the *South African Historical Society*, retained in the Cory Library, Rhodes University, Grahamstown.

(5) *Dictionaries*

Dictionary of Australian Biography.
Dictionary of Mauritian Biography Numbers 1–25. Mauritius 1941–1952.
Dictionary of National Biography, 66 Volumes. London 1885–1901.
Dictionary of South African Biography, Volume I. Pretoria 1968.

(6) *Theses*

(*i*) *Published*

The Cape of Good Hope

Breitenbach, J. J. – 'The Development of the Secretaryship to the Government at the Cape of Good Hope under John Montagu, 1845–1852.' *Archives Year Book for South African History, 1959*, part II.

Fryer, A. K. – 'The Government of the Cape of Good Hope, 1825–1854: The Age of Imperial Reform. *Archives Year Book for South African History, 1964*, part I.

Hunt, K. S. – 'The Development of Municipal Government in the Eastern Province of the Cape of Good Hope (1827–1862)'. *Archives Year Book for South African History 1961.*

Leverton B. J. T. – 'Government Finance and Political Development in the Cape (1806–1834)'. *Archives Year Book for South African History, 1961.*

(*ii*) *Unpublished*

(*a*) *General*

Jones, E. G. – Sir R. J. Wilmot Horton, Bart, Politician ad Pamphleteer. Bristol, M.A., 1936.

Madden, A. F. – The attitude of the Evangelicals to the Empire and imperial problems, 1820–1850. Oxford, D. Phil. 1950.

Tucker, H. F. G. – The Press and the Colonies 1802–1833. Bristol, M.A, 1936.

(*b*) *Mauritius*

Field, A. G. – The expedition to Mauritius in 1810 and the establishment of British control. London, M.A., 1931.

Howells, B. M. – Mauritius 1832–1849, a study of a sugar colony. London, Ph.D., 1952.

Jones, M. K. – The Slave Trade at Mauritius. Oxford, B.Litt., 1936.

Lamusse, M. J. R. – The Economic Development of the Mauritius Sugar Industry. Oxford, B.Litt., 1958.

Napal, D. – Constitutional Development of Maurtius, 1810–1948. London, M.A., 1962.

(*c*) *The Cape of Good Hope*

Crankshaw, G. B. – The Diary of C. L. Stretch – a critical edition and appraisal. Rhodes, M.A., 1960.

Hughes, M. C. – Lord Charles Somerset in South Africa: a re-assessment. Liverpool Ph.D., 1964.

Key, G. C. O. – A Critical Study of the Administration of Lord Charles Somerset during the period 1820–1826. Rhodes University College, M.A., 1935.
King, A. H. K. – Aspects of British Colonial Policy 1825–37, with particular reference to the administration of Major General Sir Richard Bourke in the Cape and New South Wales. Oxford, D. Phil., 1960.
Scheepers, U. – The Governorship of Sir Galbraith Lowry Cole. Rhodes University College, M.A., 1940.
Sole, D. B. – The separation movement and the demand for resident government in the Eastern Province (comprising a record of political opinion in the Province during the half century 1828–1878). Rhodes University College, M.A., 1939.
Urie, J. M. – A critical study of the evidence of Andries Stockenström before the Aborigines Committee in 1835 viewed in the light of his statements and policies before 1835. Rhodes, M.A., 1954.
Venter, P. J. – Notes on Cape Administration, 1806–1910. Microfilm 36, Cory Library, Rhodes University, Grahamstown.
Williams, D. – The Missionary as Government Agent on the Eastern Frontier: 1818–1830. Witwatersrand, M.A., 1953.

IV. ATLASES

Boeseken, A. J. in oorleg met Steytler, F. A., du Toit, P. S., Smuts, J. A., en Hiemstra, L. W. – Geskiedenis-Atlas vir Suid-Afrika. 2nd edition Johannesburg, no date.
Walker, E. A. – Historical Atlas of South Africa. Oxford 1922.

Map A.

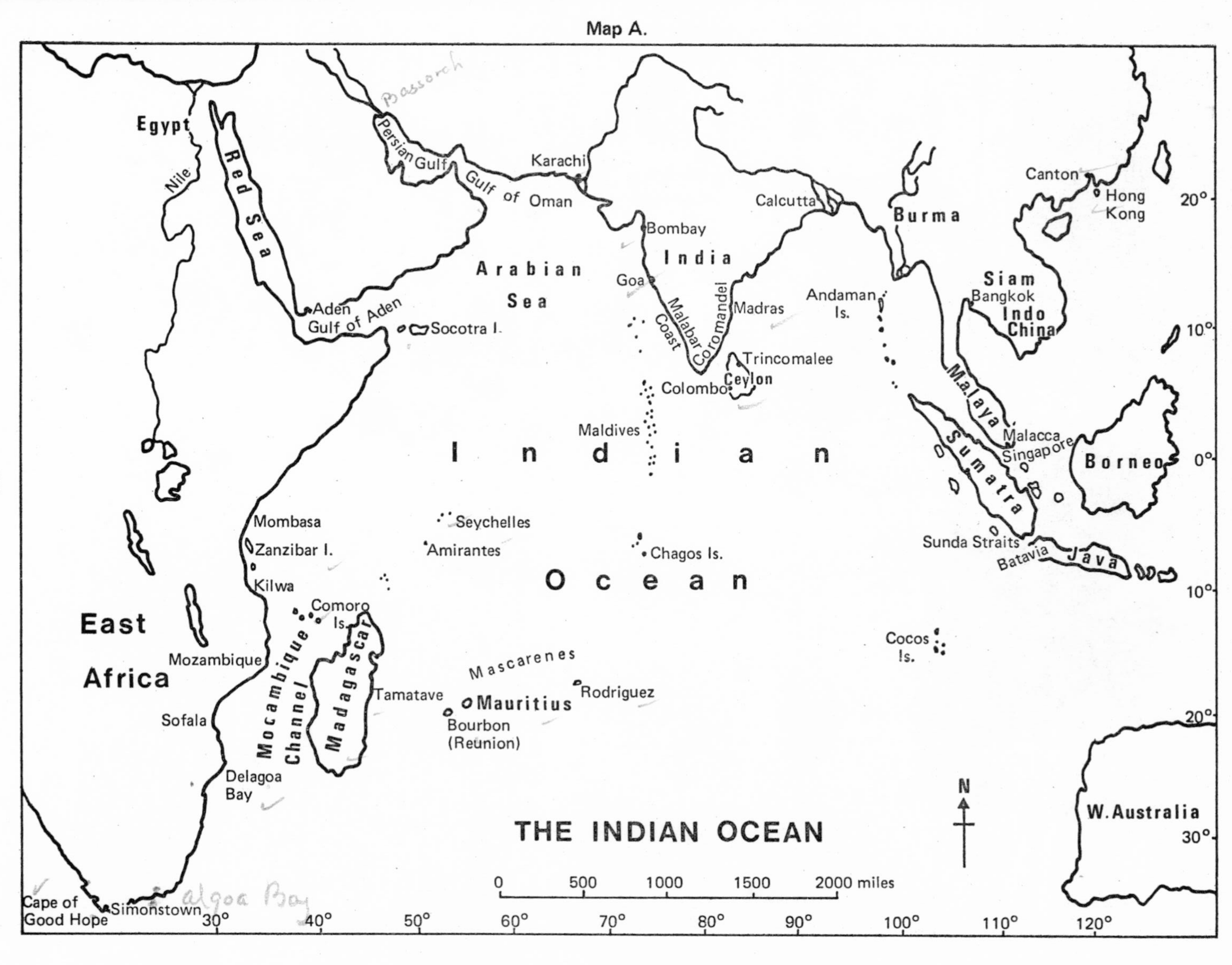
Egypt
Nile
Red Sea
Persian Gulf
Gulf of Oman
Karachi
Aden
Gulf of Aden
Socotra I.
Arabian Sea
Bombay
India
Goa
Malabar Coast
Coromandel
Madras
Calcutta
Trincomalee
Ceylon
Colombo
Maldives
Andaman Is.
Burma
Siam
Bangkok
Indo China
Canton
Hong Kong
Malaya
Malacca
Singapore
Sumatra
Borneo
Sunda Straits
Batavia
Java
Indian Ocean
Mombasa
Zanzibar I.
Kilwa
Seychelles
Amirantes
Chagos Is.
Comoro Is.
East Africa
Mozambique
Mocambique Channel
Madagascar
Tamatave
Mascarenes
Mauritius
Rodriguez
Bourbon (Reunion)
Cocos Is.
Sofala
Delagoa Bay
Cape of Good Hope
Simonstown
THE INDIAN OCEAN
N
0
500
1000
1500
2000 miles
W. Australia
30°
40°
50°
60°
70°
80°
90°
100°
110°
120°
20°
10°
0°
10°
20°
30°

Map B.

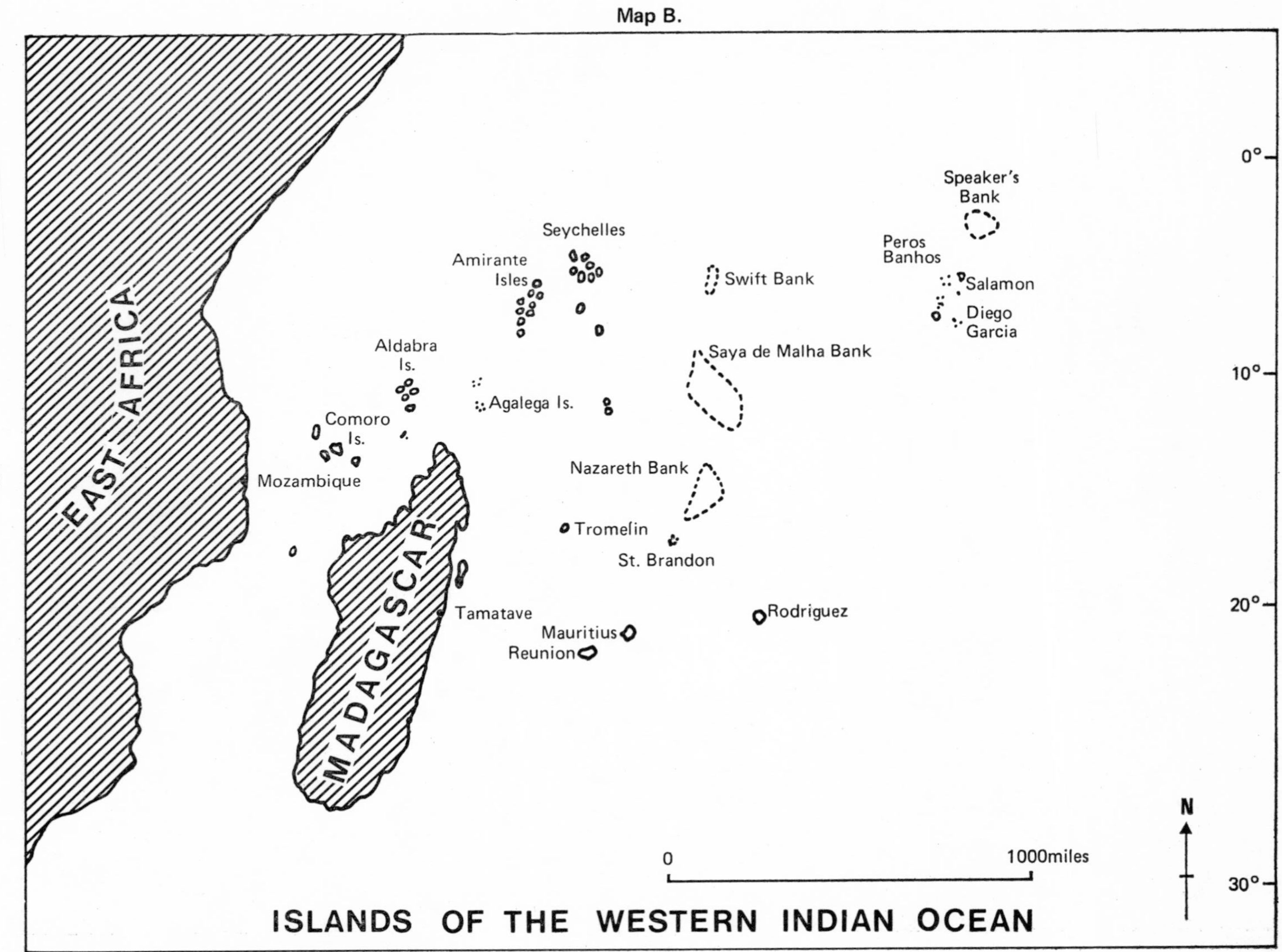
EAST AFRICA
MADAGASCAR
Mozambique
Comoro Is.
Aldabra Is.
Amirante Isles
Seychelles
Agalega Is.
Swift Bank
Saya de Malha Bank
Nazareth Bank
Tromelin
St. Brandon
Tamatave
Mauritius
Reunion
Rodriguez
Peros Banhos
Speaker's Bank
Salamon
Diego Garcia
0°
10°
20°
30°
0
1000miles
N
ISLANDS OF THE WESTERN INDIAN OCEAN

Map C

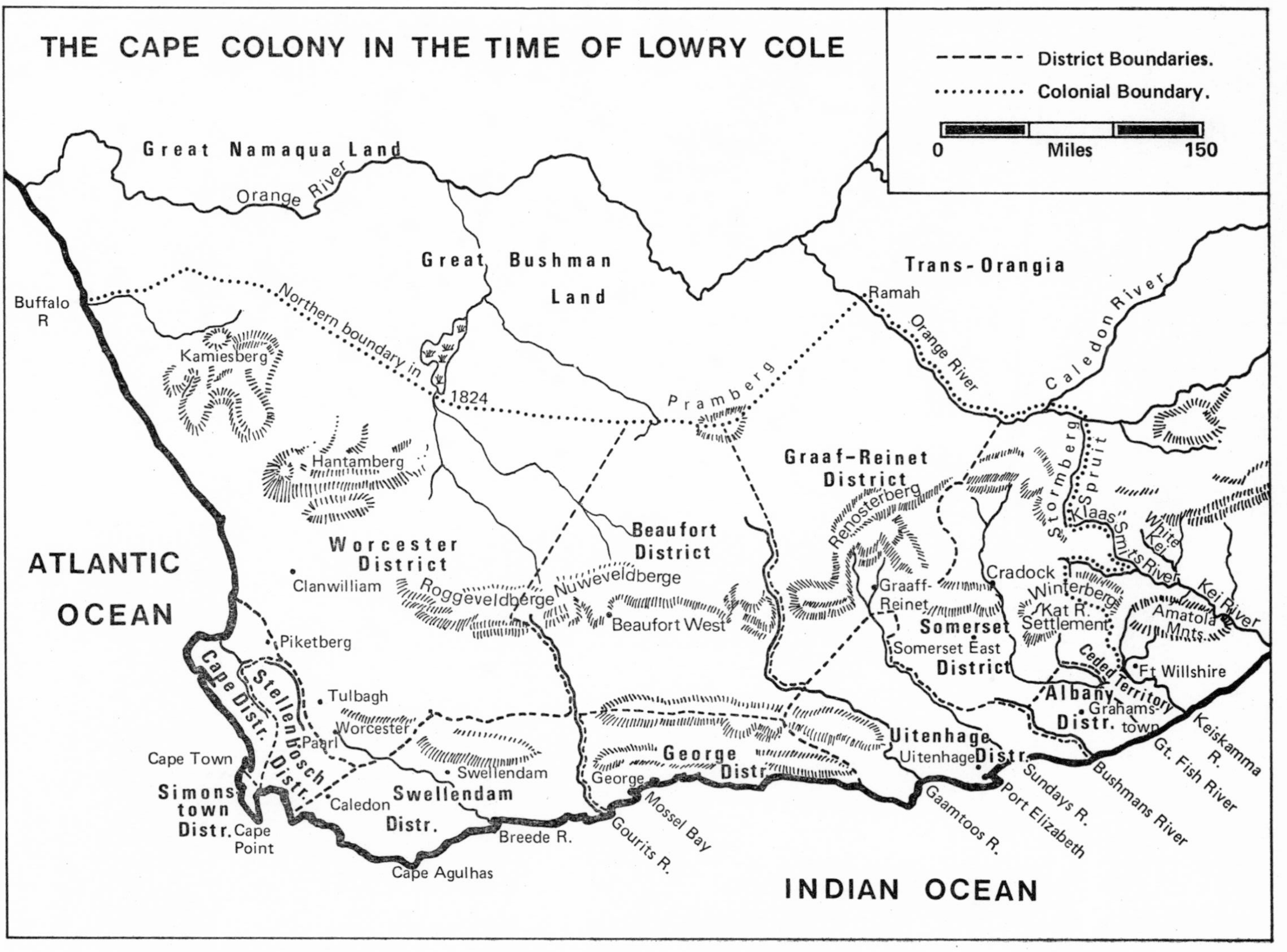

THE CAPE COLONY IN THE TIME OF LOWRY COLE
District Boundaries.
Colonial Boundary.
0
Miles
150
Great Namaqua Land
Orange River
Great Bushman Land
Trans-Orangia
Ramah
Orange River
Caledon River
Buffalo R
Northern boundary in 1824
Kamiesberg
Pramberg
Hantamberg
Graaf-Reinet District
Renosterberg
Stormberg
Spruit
Klaas' Smits River
White Kei
Beaufort District
Worcester District
Clanwilliam
Roggeveldberge
Nuweveldberge
Beaufort West
Graaff-Reinet
Cradock
Winterberg
Kat R.
Settlement
Kei River
Amatola Mnts.
Somerset
Somerset East
District
Ceded Territory
Ft Willshire
ATLANTIC OCEAN
Piketberg
Cape Distr.
Stellenbosch Distr.
Tulbagh
Worcester
Paarl
Cape Town
Simonstown Distr.
Cape Point
Caledon
Swellendam
Swellendam Distr.
Breede R.
Cape Agulhas
George
George Distr.
Mossel Bay
Gourits R.
Uitenhage Distr.
Uitenhage
Albany Distr.
Grahams-town
Gaamtoos R.
Port Elizabeth
Sundays R.
Bushmans River
Gt. Fish River
Keiskamma R.
INDIAN OCEAN